Too often the benefit of biblical schola<!-- -->M000158159
ested laypersons. Hafemann demonstrates in *The God of Promise* that biblical theology is immensely practical and foundational for all of life. Faith, hope, and love may strike us as abstract virtues removed from the nitty-gritty of everyday life. Hafemann puts hands and feet on what faith, hope, and love mean, and at the same time shows how they relate to the theology of the whole Bible. Here is a book where theology and practice are wedded together, a book that challenges the mind and the heart, a book that will transform the way you think about God and will fill you with hope for the future. This hope, as Hafemann so powerfully explains, will free us to love others as ourselves.

> —THOMAS R. SCHREINER
> Professor of New Testament Interpretation
> Southern Baptist Theological Seminary

Scott Hafemann, a master teacher who possesses an unusually tender heart for God and his people, understands the redemptive scope and structure of the Bible as clearly as any writer in our time. In *The God of Promise* he gives the thoughtful Christian a serious work of biblical theology that puts the truth on a level where many will be able to grasp it. How should we understand the covenantal structure of the Bible, the law of God, the Sabbath, good and evil in the world, the suffering of God's children, and the necessary relationship of faith to obedience? The answers Hafemann provides could foster the much needed reformation/revival I have prayed for. I will personally use this book to engage hungering hearts and inquiring minds wherever possible. I welcome this insightful work enthusiastically.

> —JOHN H. ARMSTRONG
> President, Reformation and Revival Ministries
> Carol Stream, Illinois

Hafemann has given us a sweeping, soaring account of the God of grace and glory who is at the center of the biblical revelation and of life. With this account comes a summons to live before him in a way that is faithful and, as it turns out, countercultural. This is a fine, invigorating, and refreshing study.

> —DAVID F. WELLS
> Andrew Mutch Distinguished Professor of
> Historical and Systematic Theology
> Gordon-Conwell Theological Seminary

Scott Hafemann slices away the cancerous sham of our culture's illusory hopes, and the pathetic nature of its feeble promises, in this provocative and compelling overview of Scripture's central theme. As a theological road map, *The God of Promise* unfolds faith, hope, and love's essential place on God's covenant-route home for his children— a route that leads us back to the garden of his fellowship, to experience the ultimate joy of his presence.

> —DORINGTON G. LITTLE
> Senior Pastor, First Congregational Church
> Hamilton, Massachusetts

For all too many Christians in North America, the Bible is a closed book. Even though we know we should be people of the Book, we have neglected Bible study either because we have more pressing or more interesting things to do or because the Scriptures simply do not make sense to us. In this day of instant gratification, we want our information in sound bites which will not overly burden our multi-tasking brains. Scott Hafemann's handbook offers an invaluable service to the greater part of the church that has not yet discovered the joys of studying Scripture for themselves. In a wonderful blend of insightful scholarship and pastoral concern, Hafemann provides us with a succinct and well-written sweep of the major theological themes in the Bible within a comprehensive understanding of the history of Israel, Jesus, and the mission of the church. Instead of taking the Bible apart and leaving it in disjointed pieces, as biblical scholarship is wont to do, Hafemann helpfully provides a basic framework which puts the pieces together in their proper places so that we can begin to appreciate how Scripture coheres as God's self-revelation. This book will encourage and empower a new generation of believers to become genuine people of the Book in the twenty-first century.

> —JAMES M. SCOTT
> Professor of Religious Studies
> Trinity Western University

Hafemann's excellent book is for the serious-minded reader, though one certainly does not have to be a scholar to understand it fully. Those who plumb its depths will find treasure. Among the strengths is the explanation of divine sovereignty and how it relates to the Christian faith and to the fulfillment of God's promises. This is a much needed emphasis in an evangelical world in which increasingly God is not only not viewed as the Absolute Sovereign but is also seen as not all knowing. Hafemann's book is not a merely theoretical work but is concerned at every point to relate "theology" to the daily life of the Christian. Readers will find the discussions about suffering especially helpful. Hafemann rightly shows that a diligent grappling with the interpretation of the Bible and its theological implications is essential to practical Christian living. Readers will also be benefited by Hafemann's skillful explanations of how major Old Testament themes relate to the New Testament.

> — G. K. BEALE
> Professor of New Testament, Graduate Biblical and
>   Theological Studies
> Wheaton College

THE GOD OF PROMISE AND THE LIFE OF FAITH

G O D
THE
OF PROMISE
AND THE LIFE OF
FAITH

UNDERSTANDING THE
HEART OF THE BIBLE

SCOTT J. HAFEMANN

CROSSWAY BOOKS • WHEATON, ILLINOIS
A DIVISION OF GOOD NEWS PUBLISHERS

Cover design: Uttley/DouPonce DesignWorks

First printing 2001

Printed in the United States of America

Library of Congress Cataloging-in-Publication Data
Hafemann, Scott J.
 The God of promise and the life of faith : understanding the heart of the Bible / Scott J. Hafemann.
  p. cm.
 Includes bibliographical references and index.
 ISBN 1-58134-261-6 (pbk. : alk. paper)
 1. Bible—Theology. 2. Bible—Criticism, interpretation, etc. I. Title.
BS543 .H33 2001
230'.041—dc21   2001003560

15	14	13	12	11	10	09	08	07	06	05	04	03	02	01
15	14	13	12	11	10	9	8	7	6	5	4	3	2	1

To My Sons,

John Daniel and Eric Scott

CONTENTS

ACKNOWLEDGMENTS

Books have stories of their own that, like our stories, testify to the grace of God. This particular book has come into being over the past fourteen years. It began with a spurt of writing back in 1986 during my second year of teaching at Taylor University, Upland, Ind., when the book's basic profile and main lines of argument were established. My goal from the beginning was to summarize for others what I had come to understand as the heart of the Bible's life-transforming message. My first word of thanks thus goes to my three most formative professors, Drs. John Piper, Daniel Fuller, and Peter Stuhlmacher, for the manifold ways in which they shaped my view of the Scriptures. One never grows tired of acknowledging how much we owe our teachers.

I am also indebted to the secretaries who worked at that time in the second floor typing pool of Reade Hall, whose names are unfortunately lost to history. I can still remember carrying my scribbled pages up the stairs and thankfully picking up in return typewritten prose. In those days before PCs, I could never have gotten this project off the ground without them. Moreover, Paul House, my new friend at the time, was also busy writing his own ideas about the unity of the Bible (in his case, working on the unity of the so-called minor prophets). His excitement about the Word and commitment to a scholarship that honors it encouraged me daily, as they have ever since. Heartfelt thanks are in order to him as well.

In hindsight, the contours of the book at that time were still too undefined for it to be published, though in my youthful exuberance I certainly tried! After a few rejections, however, I put the manuscript in my file cabinet, affectionately labeled it the "dead dog," and took it with me to Gordon-Conwell Theological Seminary, South Hamilton, Mass., where I taught for the next eight years. During those days, I began to refine my thinking about the Bible and its message through countless lectures and discussions with colleagues and students, all the while thinking that some day, if God willed it, I would put my thoughts together again. Special thanks to Professors Greg Beale, Richard Lints, T. David Gordon, and David Wells for the many conversations and friendship. As time went on, I filled file folders with notes expanded around the original typewritten manuscript, which eventually developed into a course on biblical theology entitled, "Faith, Love, and Hope."

Then, in God's kind providence, four things came together in the past eighteen months to make it possible for the manuscript to find the light of day. First, the Institute of Theological Studies (ITS), Grand Rapids, Mich., asked me to tape the core of my lectures on biblical theology for what has become the course, "The Christian and New Testament Theology." The challenge of doing so got me thinking intensively once again about the central message of the Scriptures. I am thankful to George Coons, director of curriculum at ITS, for his encouragement to get the tapes done—in doing so he spurred me on to pick up this project as its natural complement.

Second, while I was working on these taped lectures, Marvin Padgett, vice president, editorial, at Crossway Books, called to ask if I knew of any current work being done on a biblical theology for the serious reader in the church. I told him about my old manuscript and current interest, and without hesitation he was kind enough to look at what I had in hand. After reading my old "dead dog" on a plane ride home one night, Marvin gave me the green light to bring it to finished form. Without his interest in this work, I would never have begun the demanding task of rewriting and expanding what I had written years ago. I thank him too for his patience as I labored much longer over these pages than I ever thought I would.

Under God, then, I owe this book to Marvin and his editorial team at Crossway Books, above all Bill Deckard (and his outside editor), whose editorial skill and dedication to this project improved it greatly. I would also like to thank Crossway's guiding force, Dr. Lane Dennis, whose Christian character and commitment I have come to respect greatly. They are rare in our day. Lane, thank you for your late-night and early-morning acts of Christian devotion. Though we may end up agreeing to disagree here and there, your willingness to stand behind me in this attempt to go where the biblical text seems to lead means more than you can imagine. Your desire to be faithful to the Scriptures and the Lord, above all, is a model to me.

I am aware that the publication of a book on the message of the Bible is indeed an act of courage. Crossway has decided to publish this book of biblical theology in a day when what sells are "human interest" stories, Christian novels, and self-help books sprinkled with verses from the Bible and applied to "real life" (as if the Bible itself were somehow about something else). "Theology" has become a bad word, dry and divisive, since knowing God has become a matter of the heart, not the mind. Though Christians have traditionally been people of "the Book," today the path to personal happiness is increasingly thought to be dependent primarily on the counselor's advice concerning self-esteem, not the pastor's sermon concerning the biblical contours of faith, hope, and love. In turn, the primary role of the church, under the pastor's "professional management" and carefully honed "people skills," is no longer taken to be teaching and living out the message of the Bible but meeting the "felt needs" of the community, whatever they might be. Personal and small-group therapy, not biblical theology, drives most churches today. In the midst of all of this, I want to thank Crossway for continuing to take on projects like this.

Third, I now find myself at Wheaton College, where the honor of occupying the Gerald F. Hawthorne Chair of New Testament Greek and Exegesis allows me the time, in the midst of my teaching, to work on such projects. Not a day goes by that I do not thank God for the generosity of those who have made this position possible, and for the continuing personal and institutional support of my department and the senior administration. I pray that I will be faithful to the trust they have given me.

Fourth, Brian Vickers, a former student of mine and a current doctoral candidate in New Testament at The Southern Baptist Theological Seminary, Louisville, Ky., offered to read the manuscript chapter by chapter. His keen eye for detail, editorial experience, understanding of the Bible, and willingness to help me in the midst of his own rigorous studies and church commitments have been great gifts from God. Brian kept me from many misstatements and poorly phrased assertions. Any flaws remaining in the text are my own responsibility and witness to the fact that God calls us to progress over a lifetime, not perfection overnight! Brian's life and studies are a living witness to the reality of God's life-changing presence among his people. I look forward to the day when he will take his own studies into the pulpit or classroom full time. The future of the church is in the hands of scholar-pastors and missionaries like Brian.

Now that the project is finished, it is my long-awaited pleasure to dedicate this book to my two sons, John and Eric, who are currently twenty-one and eighteen years old respectively. It is impossible for me to summarize all that they mean to me. Though my parenting has been far from perfect, and my witness to the joy found in knowing God far too weak, I am thankful that as they move into their adult years we are still knit together as a family. My prayer is that we will all be knit together in faith. To that end, this book is for them.

In thinking about being a father, I would also like to acknowledge my debt of gratitude to my own father, Jack L. Hafemann, whose strong life of consistent integrity and constant support amazes me the older I get. Whenever I need him, he never lets me down. He practices what so many only preach.

Finally, thanks, Debara. May you ever know how happy I am for our quiet, solid life together. Your deep faith in God, expressed through your "redemption art," "biblical boxes," and teaching has convinced me that you are right: "Art is part of being smART!"

INTRODUCTION

Back to the Bible

"For I the LORD do not change . . ."
MALACHI 3:6

So faith, hope, love abide, these three;
but the greatest of these is love.
1 CORINTHIANS 13:13

These pages were written out of a real need, though one that is not always felt. In the midst of the suffocating self-love of our modern and postmodern culture, the Bible is clear that our real hunger is to know the one true God revealed in its pages. Only in doing so will we satisfy our cravings for security (faith), find the purpose for which we exist (hope), and be able to live free from slavery to self (love).

To meet these needs, we must return to the Bible. It really is that straightforward. Nothing fancy here. No eye-popping insight. God's people have always been a people of "the Book." Israel and the church have always lived from and with the Scriptures. This confidence came from the consistent conviction that of all the religious books in the world, the Scriptures, though the product of human authors, were at the same time divinely inspired and hence were the authoritative self-revelation of God's word. If we want to know anything else, there are countless sources of information and insight. If we want to know God, there is no place else to go. It's that simple.

This present attempt to return to God's Word comes from my own efforts over the past fourteen years to feed seminarians and college students the same message of the Bible that has so nourished me. The struggle to put it into writing comes from the encouragement that they too have found it to be essential food for their souls. As Jesus himself put it, "It is *written,* 'Man shall not live by bread alone, but by every *word* that proceeds from the mouth of God" (Matt. 4:4, quoting Deut. 8:3, emphasis added).

This is a simple book about a serious subject: the biblical understanding of the triune God and the implications of his never-changing character for our lives. The reader must be warned, however, that I have no religious genius to share. These pages contain no new visions or words from God "hot off the press." In fact, although we are all impacted by our presuppositions, culture, and the view of the Bible we have inherited from others, my goal, as much as possible, is to submit my own ideas and experiences to the worldview of the Bible.

Thus, the work before you is an exercise in "biblical theology." This means that its goal is not to present creative insights from my own personal perspective but to set forth the message of the Bible itself. Moreover, its purpose in doing so is to examine why the Bible declares that knowing God inevitably produces a life of faith, hope, and love, so that knowing God is itself the center and source of life. In other words, our subject matter and ultimate concern is the *theo*logy of the Bible, that is, the Bible's message about God. Everything we know about God's character and purposes (apart from creation's witness to his bare existence and brute power—see Rom. 1:20), all that can be said authoritatively about Jesus, and everything we hope to be as God's people is expressed in the Bible. There is no other Word from God.

In our day of cultural and religious pluralism, with its mushy acceptance of all claims to truth no matter how much they collide, such exclusive allegiance to the Bible seems outrageous. Indeed, if God had not revealed himself to us from outside of our own experience, and if this divine self-revelation were not accessible, then all we *would* have left would be our own culturally determined and personally limited religious "insights." But given the real needs of our world, and the real longings of our hearts, the real outrage would be for God to leave us to the relativism of our own finite understandings, groping in the dark of our own conflicting experiences.

Studying the Bible, however, is a serious and demanding task. The Bible stretches forth from the creation of the world to the creation of the new heavens and new earth, from the first coming of the Christ to his return. Its history runs from the Garden of Eden to the Garden of Gethsemane, from the exodus from Egypt to the "second exodus" at the Cross, from the covenant meal at Mount Sinai to the Lord's Supper, from the circumcision of Abraham to the baptism of converted pagans in Corinth, from the building of Solomon's temple to the temple of the Holy Spirit. Its message unfolds from the "letter" that kills to the Spirit who makes alive, from the golden calf to the new covenant, from the prophets to the apostles, from Mount Zion to the New Jerusalem, from David's son to the Son of God, from Israel's exile to her promised restoration, and from the history of Israel's divided kingdom to the mission of the church united as the kingdom of God.

At one level, the very attempt to write a book like this is thus an act of naïve hubris. I am painfully aware of my own limitations and weaknesses, intellectually and spiritually. Comfort may be taken, however, in the fact that no reader is alone. In interpreting the Bible, we stand on the shoulders of those intellectual and spiritual giants who have studied the Bible before us. So my hope is that the present effort may encourage others to continue the process by taking up the sacred pages for themselves. For this reason, there are many references to biblical passages throughout the pages that follow. These are not literary "window dressing," but some of the texts that I have thought hard about in writing this book, and this book is only as good as I am faithful to them.

Hence, the purpose of the present work is to provide a basic framework for understanding the Scriptures in a way that will stimulate us to take up the Bible for ourselves. The church at the beginning of the twenty-first century faces an identity crisis. Most Christians no longer understand even the most basic teachings of the Scriptures. The Bible, though the foundation of the faith, remains for many believers a closed book. Indeed, apart from reading isolated verses out of context, as if the Bible were a Christian "Ouija board," believers today are characterized by their biblical illiteracy. And what we do know about the Bible is so elementary that it pales in comparison to the sophistication of our technological age.

This is not entirely our fault. The lack of emphasis on the Bible in our churches and the death of biblical preaching in our pulpits (or now on our "stages") have brought about a death of understanding in our pews (or folding chairs). This should not be surprising. Given the therapeutic culture in which we live, the vast majority of seminaries no longer demand that future church leaders master even the most fundamental biblical content or interpretive skills. And with the rise of "postmodernism," we are not sure if the meaning of the biblical text can be recovered anyway, so why bother? After all, the "secret" to building a "successful" church is now thought to be getting to know the new trinity of technology, psychology, and marketing, not the Trinity of the Bible.

This book, on the other hand, is motivated by the conviction that the message of the Bible provides the only answer to humanity's most pressing need: to know God himself. Having been created by God for God, the "self" can never be "self-satisfied." Yet, having lost sight of the God revealed in the Bible, all we can see is our self, with its futile drive to meet its own ever-changing but never satisfied cravings for the second-rate pleasures of this world.

As a result, we have shrunk God to fit into our own understanding of who we are, rather than understanding ourselves in the light of who God has revealed himself to be. Our false sense of power and independence has led to downsizing God's sovereignty. In turn, instead of dependence on God for our lives ("faith"), we have substituted a mental assent to historical data that leads to making "decisions" about God. Rather than trusting in God's promises for our future ("hope"), we have fallen back on a wishful thinking that is informed by our desires for heath and wealth. Hence, although called to consider the needs of others more important than our own needs ("love"), we seek money, sex, and emotional gratification at any cost.

Losing sight of the God of the Bible has therefore produced a watered-down nominalism that makes a mockery of redemption. The reason is clear. Without a relationship with the God revealed in the Bible, we are doomed to rely upon ourselves. Without hope in God's promises as set forth in the Scriptures, all our earthly aspirations are mocked by death. And without being able to love others because God first loved us, we are left seeking "self-esteem" by trying to love ourselves more. But the "self" was never intended to carry the burden of procuring faith, hope, and love. We were never intended to meet our own needs by making an idol of the created order or its creatures. We were not designed for the disappointment that comes from chasing second-class dreams. The primary object of our affection was never intended to be anyone or anything other than God himself. The Bible is God's antidote to the poison that comes from seeking our satisfaction in anything other than knowing and enjoying God forever.

In what follows, then, we begin where the Bible begins, with what we can learn from the creation of the world (chapter 1). After looking at what life was like before sin entered the world (chapter 2), we examine what went wrong, why it went wrong, and what God has done about it (chapter 3). What it means to trust and hope in God as a result of his saving activity is the subject of chapters 4 and 5, illustrated by the life of Abraham and the history of Israel. Trust and hope, however, take place in the midst of adversity and affliction. In chapters 6 and 7 we therefore take up the reality of evil from the perspective of God's sovereignty and ask the crucial question of why God's people suffer and sin. In view of the history of sin and salvation, in chapters 8 and 9 we look at what difference Jesus makes as history's center point. Finally, we conclude with a review of what knowing God in Christ means for us as his people.

My goal in all of this is to be faithful to the message of the Bible, in order that we might be faithful to the one true God revealed in its pages. For as the apostle Paul reminded the young pastor Timothy, "All scripture is inspired by God and profitable for teaching, for reproof, for correction, and for training in righteousness, that the man of God may be complete, equipped for every good work" (2 Tim. 3:16). What was true for Timothy is true for us all.

1

WHY DO WE EXIST?

Lessons from the Creation of the World

*"Worthy art thou, our Lord and God,
to receive glory and honor and power,
for thou didst create all things,
and by thy will they existed and were created."*

REVELATION 4:11

In Genesis 1:1, the Bible's first verse, we find the most fundamental assertion in all of Scripture about who God is: "In the beginning God created the heavens and the earth." Notice that this assertion is a concrete description of what God has done (God has created) rather than an abstract statement concerning one of his attributes (God is the all-powerful Creator). God has revealed himself primarily through his activities in time and space, not through a philosophical discussion of his nature. The Bible is the record and interpretation of God's self-revelation. The Bible begins, therefore, by asserting that God is the sole and sovereign Creator of the universe. Genesis 1:3-25 then recounts "how" God made our world, including its plant and animal life, emphasizing that every aspect of it was good. Finally, God crowns his creation by fashioning mankind in his own image and giving them the mandate to be fruitful and multiply, to fill the earth, and to bring it under their supervision and authority (Gen. 1:26-28).

THE IMAGE AND KINGDOM OF GOD

Thus, the Bible also begins by presenting the most fundamental statement we have concerning the nature and purpose of mankind. The other living creatures are created merely according to their "own [various] kinds," which is to say that they are brought into existence in accordance with their different natures as merely physical creatures. In a shocking turn of events, however, humanity is not created simply as yet another "kind" of living creature but in accordance with God's own character: "Let us make man in *our* image" (Gen. 1:26, emphasis added). Though mankind is part of the created order, the point of comparison has suddenly changed: rather than being created merely like one another ("according to its kind"), mankind was also created like God!

Not surprisingly, given its obvious importance, students of the Bible have suggested many different interpretations of what it means to be created in the "image of God." But whatever else it might entail, Genesis 1:26-27 indicates that mankind "reflects" or "images forth" God in the fundamental sense that men and women are given responsibility and authority over the earth just as God takes responsibility and exercises authority over them.

> Then God said, "Let us make man in our image, after our likeness; *and let them have dominion* over the fish of the sea, and over the birds of the air, and over the cattle, and over all the earth, and over every creeping thing that creeps upon the earth." So God created man in his own image, in the image of God he created him; male and female he created them. And God blessed them, and God said to them, "Be fruitful and multiply, and fill the earth *and subdue it; and have dominion. . . .*" (Gen. 1:26-28, emphasis added).

To be created in God's image is therefore to have a particular point of comparison (not to oneself but to God) and a distinct command (not simply to reproduce but to exercise dominion). As Anthony Hoekema explains, "In exercising this dominion man is like God, since God has supreme and ultimate dominion over the earth."[1] The image of God is a description not primarily of our nature but of our function. We were created in the "image of God" not primarily to possess certain capabilities but to fulfill a certain calling *in relationship to God*. "If, as the Bible teaches, the most important thing about man is that he is inescapably related to God, we must judge as deficient any anthropology which denies that relatedness."[2]

That being created in God's image means being related to God as those who are like him becomes clear when we compare Genesis 1:26-28 with Genesis 5:3, the Bible's next reference to being in someone's image. There we read, "When Adam had lived a hundred and thirty years, he became the father of a son in his own *likeness,* after his *image,* and named him Seth" (emphasis added).[3] In this passage, being in someone's "image" describes the family relationship between father and son. We are the children of God in the same way that Seth is the son of Adam: we derive our life from God and represent him as his own. Mankind does not *possess* the image of God. Mankind *is* the image of God. Hence, the term *image of God* describes the essence of who we have been created to be. It is not something added to us which might then be lost, as if we could remain human without bearing God's image. We may not fulfill our function as God's image, but we are in his image nonetheless.

Thus, the "image of God" is primarily a *functional* designation; mankind is the one creature who is to relate directly to God in conscious dependence (God speaks commands directly to humanity) and to reflect this relationship by exercising a godlike rule over the world (Adam names the animals). To be in the image of God thus means that "mankind represents God so that what man does is what God himself would do"[4] if he ruled the world directly. By representing the rule and reign of God, Adam and Eve proclaim God's sovereign character in and through their own dominion over the created order.

The creation of Adam and Eve in God's image therefore introduces what the Bible will later call the "kingdom of God." The kingdom of God is the rule and reign of God over his people as their Lord, by which he expresses his own glory as the one and only Creator and Sustainer and Provider and Ruler of all things. Being in God's kingdom is not primarily a matter of being in a certain *realm* of his authority but of being in a certain *relationship to* his authority. Thus, the kingdom of God is expressed in and through the faith of God's people as they exercise *dominion* from the standpoint of their own *dependence* on God. God, as King, rules over mankind. Mankind, created to reflect God's character, rules over creation. The creation itself, together with mankind, therefore becomes the way in which God reveals his glory as the "God of gods," "King of kings," and "Lord of lords," that is, as the one who is sovereign over all things (Deut. 10:17; 1 Tim. 6:15). In short, creation exhibits the kingship of God.

This becomes clear in Genesis 9:6, the only other mention of the "image of God" in the Old Testament, where the death penalty for murder is based on the fact that "God made man in his own image." That murder is prohibited and that mankind should execute God's justice against it express clearly that to be in the image of God is both a relationship of *dependence* on God and a calling to *rule* in God's place over the world. Our nature as creatures dependent on God for all things is why murder is prohibited. As the Giver and Sustainer of our lives, only God himself has the right to take our lives; to commit murder is to usurp God's sovereign authority over his creation.

On the other hand, we are created to express God's sovereignty as his representatives. This is why man himself is called in Genesis 9:6 to execute capital punishment for murder ("whoever sheds the blood of man, by man shall his blood be shed"). Because God made man in *his* own image (Gen. 9:6b), those who have been given the mandate to express God's authority on earth must judge those who usurp God's authority. Moreover, the fact that God institutes this prohibition and penalty means that even a rebellious humanity has not lost their identity and role as God's image. For, as Meredith Kline summarizes the point of Genesis 9:6, "As image of God, man is a royal son with the judicial function appertaining to kingly office."[5]

The great problem arises when we who are created to act *on behalf of* God begin to think that we can also *be* God in his independence and self-determination. God, as Creator, is sovereignly self-sufficient and the supplier of all things. His will rules supreme. Humanity, created by God, is dependent on him for all things. Our rightful place, therefore, as *creatures* in the image of *God,* is between God and the world. Mankind is the pinnacle of creation but remains subordinate to God. There is a hierarchy in creation: God rules over the world through humanity as his vice-regents, while humanity rules over the world as God's representatives. To declare that men and women are created in the image of God is to declare their function in relationship to the function of the one who made them. Hence, the French scholar Jean Danielou rightly concludes that the opening chapters of the Bible show us

> what man's nature is, by teaching us that he is created in the image of God, which is to say that he is neither a god, as the myths made him

out to be, nor a product of nature, as the evolutionists saw him, but that he transcends nature and at the same time is transcended by God.[6]

Only mankind exists in the image of God, because only we are created to exercise authority over our environment and its other living creatures. Moreover, our dominion over the world as its "responsible ruler" is to be the means by which the reality and nature of God's reign are made known. To live as the image of God is to exercise dominion over the world in his place and by his command. By exercising this authority, we thus fill the earth with the glory of God's sovereignty and sufficiency.

The parent-child relationship is a good analogy. To be a child, by definition, is to be dependent on those in authority over you. On the other hand, the child "rules" over his own world. He decorates his room (and even sometimes cleans it!), cares for the cat, and decides how to arrange his toys. Still, everything he has, including his authority, is a gift from his parents. The child "rules" on behalf of his parents, but only in the spheres of responsibility which they have given to him. His authority is therefore delegated and not his own. Yet, since he has been created in the "image" of his parents, he alone can receive this responsibility. The child's place is between his parents and his pets! It is not the cat's fault if the litter box is not clean. In the same way, we alone, as God's vice-regents, have been given the responsibility to rule over all that he has created for us. In this way, we are the "children of God."

THE CREATOR/CREATURE DISTINCTION

In addition to mankind's role in creation, Genesis 1 makes two other points of importance for our study. First, its account of creation emphasizes in no uncertain terms that the Creator cannot be identified in any way with anything that he has created. In stark contrast, the various creation myths of antiquity considered the world to be an extension of the gods. The gods who created the world could thus be located *within* the world as some part of it, just as the creation could be viewed as an embodiment of the divine. There is nothing "new" in the "New Age" movement's attempts, following the impulse of Eastern religions and early Gnosticism, to identify the world with God (now viewed as some impersonal life-force).[7] Over against such attempts, God reveals himself in the Bible as the all-powerful but *separate* Creator of the world who exists *outside* of his creation. The God of the Bible simply speaks the world into existence as an expression of his power, so that the world remains forever distinct from its Creator. If we learn anything from the Bible's account of creation, in contrast to other ancient and modern creation accounts, it is that the one true God is a "self-existent, solitary, self-sufficient creator."[8]

Contrary to both ancient and Eastern ways of thinking, even mankind, though made in *God's* image, is in no way an extension of their Creator. There is no "divine spark" within us. We cannot get in touch with God by getting in touch with ourselves. God is outside of us, not within us. We are his *creatures*, not downsized versions of his deity. Nor is mankind on the way to *becoming* divine. Adam and Eve do not receive immortal souls to ensure their continuing existence; they remain creatures dependent upon God for their life.

THE FUNCTION OF CREATION

This brings us to the second important point made in Genesis 1. The order of creation, beginning with the creation of light (Gen. 1:3) and culminating in the creation of the living creatures (Gen. 1:24-25), indicates that the function of creation is to provide an environment suitable for sustaining the life of the man and woman created in God's image. As the climax of creation, everything is created for us! Hence, just as Adam and Eve cannot be equated with God, they cannot be identified simply with the rest of creation either. Though part of the created order, humanity, being in the image of *God*, is not of one kind with a caterpillar or a chimpanzee. We are not of equal status with the rest of creation. Nor should we be viewed as servants of the world, as if the environment were of more value than we are.

A concern for ecology is right, but often for the wrong reasons. Mankind is not created to provide for the world; the world is created to provide for mankind. We ought to care for the environment as its stewards, not because we are of one essence with it. We must be careful not to turn the world into an idol either by lowering ourselves to the level of the rest of creation or by raising creation to our own level. We do not take care of an oak tree because we are on the same ontological level as an oak tree. Instead, we care for creation because we are submitted to the sovereign ruler of the universe who commanded us by royal fiat to rule in his place over all that he has made. That is why "stewardship" is an appropriate concept to designate our relationship to the rest of creation—for in the ancient world a "steward" was a slave authorized to carry out his master's business in his name. Created in the King's image as his vassals or servants, we thus reflect his character and manifest his glory when we exercise dominion over all he has provided for us with the God-given wisdom and care that characterize God himself.

This means that we are to care for the world as an expression of our dependence on God's provision. Not to take care of our world is to despise God's good gifts. Abdicating our responsibility over the world is an act of ungrateful rebellion against our Provider. For, having told Adam and Eve to exercise dominion (Gen. 1:28), God then describes the provision he has made to enable them to do so (v. 29):

> And God said, "Behold, I have given you every plant yielding seed which is upon the face of all the earth, and every tree with seed in its fruit; you shall have them for food."

This text makes clear that the function of creation is to provide a home and food for mankind as a manifestation of the perfection of our Provider. The movement from the commands of Genesis 1:28 to the gift of 1:29 makes clear that humanity's dominion displays *God's* glory, since mankind's mandate is both brought about and enabled by God's provision. Keeping the commands of Genesis 1:28 does not earn the provision of 1:29; rather, the provision of 1:29 supports the commands of 1:28. Mankind was not called to exercise dominion in order to gain the food God gives, but because God had *already* granted them the food they needed. Mankind's dominion would therefore express their dependence, and their dependence would honor the One upon whom mankind depended, since the Giver gets the glory. For this reason, "God saw everything that he had made, and behold, it was very good" (Gen. 1:31).

What was so "very good" about creation? Creation was "very good" not only because it fulfilled the immediate function for which it was designed (to provide for humanity) but also because it so clearly accomplished its ultimate purpose (to reveal God's character). Since all of creation owes its existence solely to God's decision to make it, the creation is a revelation of God's sovereignty (God is the powerful Creator) and grace (God creates freely as an expression of his own sufficiency). Because of who God is in himself, God created a world that is both vast and perfectly suited to mankind. The fact that he did so is an expression of his own sovereign power to do as he pleases (Ps. 115:3; 135:5-7), but it also reveals his great love. Note the logic of Isaiah 45:18:

> For thus says the LORD,
> who created the heavens
>   (he is God!),
> who formed the earth and made it
>   (he established it;
> he did not create it a chaos,
>   he formed it to be inhabited!):
> "I am the LORD, and there is no other."

The creation itself reveals God's sovereign deity. The fact that he made creation a home for humanity reveals God's sovereign love. Mankind, in their position between heaven and earth, is the one creature who can recognize and experience this reality in a way that renders to God the glory due his name as Creator and Provider. The creation, though made for us, is therefore not about us but about God. As the psalmist put it,

> When I look at thy heavens, the work of thy fingers,
>   the moon and the stars which thou hast established;
> what is man that thou art mindful of him,
>   and the son of man that thou dost care for him?
>
> Yet thou has made him little less than God,
>   and dost crown him with glory and honor.
> Thou has given him dominion over the works of thy hands;
>   thou has put all things under his feet,
> all sheep and oxen,
>   and also the beasts of the field,
> the birds of the air, and the fish of the sea,
>   whatever passes along the paths of the sea.
>
> O LORD, our Lord,
>   *how majestic is thy name in all the earth!* (Ps. 8:3-9, emphasis added).

Furthermore, creation is not self-sustaining; it *continues* to exist only by God's power and grace, thereby expressing God's glory by its dependent nature. Since creation is not in any way independent of its Creator or free of humanity's dominion over it as those made in God's image, it can never exist by its own strength or inertia, nor can it reach its goal unless mankind rules it according to God's command. When we cut the grass, we reveal the glory of God as Creator and Sustainer of the universe! For according to the Bible, grass does not grow simply as the result of "natural" laws, nor can it become a lawn without our supervising it!

Moreover, given mankind's eventual fall into sin, the changing of the seasons and the harvest it brings come to speak not only of God's power and love but also of his *mercy*. Summers come to a sinful world because God freely promised that he would continue to sustain his creation even though mankind deserved to be destroyed (Gen. 8:20-22). As Jesus put it, God "causes His sun to rise on the evil and the good, and sends rain on the righteous and the unrighteous," which in its context provides the reason why we too, as followers of Christ, must love our enemies (Matt. 5:44-45).

From the beginning, however, God declared his original creation to be very good (Gen. 1:31) because even before sin entered the world it provided the "textbook" needed for teaching humanity *faith*, the fundamental human response to God's presence and provision. Against the backdrop of creation, Adam and Eve recognized that they owed their existence, authority, and sustenance to their maker (Gen. 2:16).

Mankind exists only because their Creator gave them breath; they continue to exist only because their Creator gives them food. This is "very good" because it demonstrates that our life is a gift from God and that no matter how strong or established we may become, we *always* live as dependent creatures. "Know that the LORD is God! It is he that made us, and we are his . . ." (Ps. 100:3). The ability to make it through the day, not to mention the day itself, is a gift.

Yet, in our current state of rebellion against God, I know of no other single idea that is more offensive to Western men and women than this one. To realize that we are created by God and hence are both owned by and dependent upon him for everything, strikes at the very core of our illusions of independence and self-importance.

This illusion often finds expression in a denial of our creation—the universe just "happened," and we evolved on the planet as a result of time and chance. On the other hand, those who believe God exists often insist that God somehow needed to create us. But the Scriptures give absolutely no indication of this divine "need." God does not "need" either the world or us to be self-fulfilled and happy:

> The God who made the world and everything in it, being Lord of heaven and earth, does not live in shrines made by man, nor is he served by human hands, as though he needed anything (Acts 17:24-25).

Indeed, the existence of fellowship within the Trinity (John 17:23-24) makes it evident that the creation of mankind was not intended to meet some deficiency in God. God was not lonely, bored, or incomplete before he created humanity. God is perfect in himself, happy in the fellowship and love that exist from all eternity between the Father, Son, and Spirit. Thus, rather than being an attempt to make up for a *lack* within the Trinity, God created mankind simply because he delights in sharing himself as an expression of his overflowing self-*sufficiency*:

> In creation God "went public" with the glory that reverberates joyfully between the Father and the Son! There is something about the fullness of God's joy that inclines it to overflow. There is an expansive quality to his joy. It wants to share itself. The impulse to create the world was not from weakness, as though God were lacking in some perfection which creation could supply. "It is no argument of the emptiness or deficiency of a fountain, that it is inclined to overflow."[9]

The creation, being brought into existence by God's command, is itself an expression of the glory of God's magnificent sovereignty, self-determination, wisdom, beauty, completeness, and love. God declared his work of creation to be "very good" not only because it reflects his own intrinsic character but also because it shows his innate glory through our creaturely dependence on him for all things. God the Creator is God the Provider. Our dependence on God for all things magnifies God's glory as the Giver of all things. For, in short, God owns us and the world in which we live. In the words of Psalm 24:1-2:

The Earth is the LORD'S and the fulness thereof,
   the world and those who dwell therein;
for he has founded it . . .
   and established it . . .

As those owned by God, we find our happiness in *God,* while God finds his happiness in *himself* and in his creation as it reflects *his* glory.[10] Only in this sense does the creation extend God's happiness: God experiences greater and greater joy because of the ongoing nature of his creation. As Daniel Fuller put it, "Jesus himself said, 'It is more blessed to give than to receive' (Acts 20:35). God's ultimate purpose is to increase his joy by sharing the blessing of the Trinity in creation. . . . Simply to do his people good gives him complete satisfaction."[11] Conversely, we bring God happiness by reflecting back to him the perfections of his provisions. In John Piper's words,

> The climax of [God's] happiness is the delight he takes in the echoes of his excellence in the praises of [his people].[12]

GOD THE CREATOR AND SUSTAINER

We have seen that the creation account in Genesis makes one essential point about the God revealed in the Bible: he is the sovereign and gracious Creator of the world. In view of this fundamental fact, to assume that the world "just is" is to conclude that the atheist is right. Furthermore, the refusal on the part of modern men and women to consider seriously the question of God as the originator of our world is not blissful ignorance but a tacit assent to the atheist's worldview. As Joy Davidman observed,

> The old pagans had to choose between a brilliant, jangling, irresponsible, chaotic universe, alive with lawless powers, and the serene and ordered universe of God and law. We modern pagans have to choose between that divine order, and the gray, dead, irresponsible, chaotic universe of atheism. And the tragedy is that we may make that choice without knowing it—not by clear conviction, but by vague drifting, not by denying God, but by losing interest in him.[13]

Thus, far from being irrelevant, the divine creation of the world is the starting point for our own self-image as well as for our understanding of others, not to mention our view of God. Why am I here? To whom do I belong? What responsibilities do I possess by virtue of the fact that I exist? Being an atheist, even by default, casts an entirely different light on these questions.

In addition, since God not only created but also sustains the world, we should never lose sight of the fact that we *continue* to owe our lives to him. God is not an absentee landlord. Unfortunately, even those who affirm that God created us often fall prey to the notion that, once created, we are on our own in our fight for survival. We seem prone to a sort of religious "survival of the fittest" or "self-development" program—"God may have put us here, but it's up to us to make the best of it." For example, I remember a religious poster (I cannot bring myself to say it was "Christian"), hung by some well-meaning Christian in the hallway of a school where I used to teach, that declared, "What we are is God's gift to us, what we become is our gift to God." The landscape on the poster was beautiful, but the message was not. Indeed, God *has* put us here. But God *keeps* us here as well, and that includes enabling us to "become" an engineer or a mother or a plumber or a clerk or a professor or a stockbroker or a politician or anything else. Even our hard work is a gift from God, not to mention the motivation and ability and opportunity to do it. We are not God's "junior executives," whose job it is to develop God's raw materials into finished products by adding our efforts to his. Instead, as the creatures made in God's image, we reflect his character and manifest his glory by exercising the dominion that he gave to us over all that he has provided and continues to provide for us. As our response to God's self-sufficiency and supply, our dependence and dominion are flip sides of the same coin. Sadly, most of humanity has not learned this lesson; most would flunk the Bible's most basic test questions: "What have you that you did not receive? If then you received it, why do you boast as if it were not a gift?" (1 Cor. 4:7). "Or who has given a gift to [God] that he might be repaid? For from him and through him and to him are all things" (Rom. 11:35-36a).

THE NATURE OF IDOLATRY

If God is our Creator, Provider, and Sustainer, how should we respond as we exercise the authority and use the gifts he has given us? Paul's own answer in the doxology just referred to from Romans 11:33-36 is clear: "To him be glory for ever" (v. 36b). Earlier in his letter to the Romans, Paul answered this question indirectly by outlining the negative way in which mankind has in fact responded to its Creator, a response diametrically opposed to what it should have been. Indeed, the Bible traces all human evil, and even the twisted nature of the natural world, back to this improper response (see Gen. 3:17-19; Rom. 1:18, 24-32; 8:20-21). In Paul's words, this root sin which underlies all other acts of disobedience is the fact that "although they knew God they did not honor him as God or give thanks to him" (Rom. 1:21a). Due to this fundamental failure, "they became futile in their thinking and their senseless minds were darkened" (Rom. 1:21b). Verses 22-23 then explain the content of this futility:

> Claiming to be wise, they became fools, and exchanged the glory of the immortal God for images resembling mortal man or birds or animals or reptiles.

In other words, *idolatry* is the futile way of thinking that results from mankind's failure to honor the One who has revealed himself through creation "as God." To honor something "as God" is to recognize it as sovereign over our lives and to depend upon it to provide for our needs, whether that be a need for food, fulfillment, security, or solace. "Idolatry" is the practice of seeking the source and provision of what we need either physically or emotionally in someone or something other than the one true God. It is the tragically pathetic attempt to squeeze life out of lifeless forms that cannot help us meet our real needs. In the words of the psalmist,

> Our God is in the heavens; he does whatever he pleases. Their idols are silver and gold, the work of men's hands. They have mouths, but do not speak; eyes, but do not see. They have ears, but do not hear; they have hands, but do not feel; feet, but do not walk; and they do not make a sound in their throat (Ps. 115:3-8).

More concretely, idolatry is the desire to meet our needs in some-thing or someone—whether that be money, science, education, loved ones, sex, power, or ourselves—other than in knowing God and relying on what he, in his wisdom, has provided for us. Among Christians, this idolatry takes the more subtle form of a syncretism in which we join our allegiance to Christ with some other perceived source of happiness. As a result, we become double-minded adherents to a hybrid "Jesus and" religion. It's prayer goes something like this: "I would be happy if only I had Jesus and _____ (fill in the blank with whatever you think will make you happy)."

But as Jesus warned, and as we have all experienced, this attempt to "moonlight" on God's claims as Creator and Provider actually makes us more miserable than if we had simply abandoned Jesus altogether. A soul divided between the Creator and the created becomes so frustrated that, if this tension is not resolved, the person will self-destruct. For, according to Jesus, it is simply impossible to serve God and money with-out hating the one and loving the other (Matt. 6:24).

HONORING GOD AS GOD

Rather than falling prey to idolatry, the proper response to the power and deity evident from creation is to honor God *alone* as the one who makes and provides all we need. According to Romans 1:21, the way in which those created in God's image honor him as their Creator and Provider is as simple as it is profound: we must thank him for what he has done. Thanking God and honoring him as God are not two sepa-rate things: to thank God is the *way* "to honor him as God," because it gives the credit for our lives to the one who deserves it (Rom. 1:21).

Thus, the essence of sin is *misguided* gratitude, not ingratitude. As dependent creatures we all, by nature, thank somebody or something (usually ourselves!) for what we experience and achieve. And the ulti-mate object of our gratitude becomes the object of our worship. In turn, the object of our worship will be the object of our service, since we inevitably serve whatever or whomever we think will meet our needs (see again Matt. 6:24).[14] This is why, in Romans 1:25, worship and service are linked together: the object of our worship always becomes the mas-ter of our behavior. This is a law of human nature, inasmuch as God made us to worship and live for him. The sin of idolatry, whether in the age-old worship of nature or in the modern worship of ourselves, is consequently the same: "worship[ing] and serv[ing] the creature rather than the Creator, who is blessed for ever!" (see Rom. 1:25).

Idolatry, whether ancient or modern, is thus the futile attempt to look for our lives to anyone or anything other than the one true Creator and Provider. Whom do I thank when things go well? To whom do I look when things go badly? What do I think will make me ultimately happy? What is my source of security? Where do I gain my sense of worth in the world? What am I striving to achieve in life, and why? The answers to questions like these will help determine whether we are honoring God as God or whether we are idolaters—whether that means we are praying to a stone image as in the prophet Isaiah's day, drooling with envy over the car in our neighbor's driveway, or latching onto the latest self-help strategy.

This is why Paul identifies covetousness with the worship of a false god (Col. 3:5) and equates idolatry with covetousness (Eph. 5:5); coveting is seeking our happiness in something or someone other than God, which is idolatry. The first and the last of the Ten Commandments are the same commandment! The command not to covet is a command not to become an idolater, since whatever we think will make us happy is inevitably the god we worship.

THE IMPLICATIONS OF IDOLATRY

Idolatry is no innocent matter. God *commands* us to have no other gods. He *demands* that we seek our ultimate happiness and security in him alone. The Creator and Provider is a jealous God who will not tolerate our giving thanks to others for what he alone does (Ex. 20:5; 34:14; Deut. 4:24; 5:9; 6:15). Nor can he condone our acting as if we or our technology can take his place as sovereign ruler of the world (Ex. 14:4, 17-18; 15:18; Deut. 4:39; 1 Kings 8:60; Ps. 10:16; 1 Tim. 6:14-16). As God declared through Isaiah the prophet,

> "I am the LORD, that is my name;
>   my glory I give to no other,
>   nor my praise to graven images" (Isa. 42:8).

In Ephesians 5:5 we therefore read that no one "who is covetous (that is, an idolater) has any inheritance in the kingdom of Christ and of God." Idolatry is an affront to God. It declares God to be second-rate by denying his sovereign power and wisdom and by considering God's gifts more important than God himself. It presupposes that we know better than God what we need and when we need it. Idolatry declares God to be insufficient. God cannot look the other way in the face of such disregard, as if honoring him were merely the best option among many. For God to do so would be to deny himself. There is, after all, only one God, and this one God cannot pretend otherwise.

Thus, for those created in God's image, the consequences of idolatry are disastrous. When God allows the desires of those who deny him to run their course, that is, when he gives them over to "the lusts of their hearts," the evil catalogued in Romans 1:24-32 is the inescapable result. Idolatry leads to a never ending quest for a second-rate happiness that is doomed from the start and can only degenerate into the kinds of self-destruction Paul describes. Those who seek their happiness and security in other gods are condemned to a life of fleeting fulfillment and to an eternity of lasting regret. The reason is clear. Nothing and no one can satisfy the deepest longings of our heart except the One who made us for himself. As Pascal put it,

> There once was in man a true happiness of which now remain to him only the mark and empty trace, which he in vain tries to fill from all his surroundings. . . . But these are all inadequate, because the infinite abyss can only be filled by an infinite and immutable object, that is to say, only by God Himself.[15]

The real terror and consequence of judgment is not falling *into* the hands of an angry God but falling out of his presence, to be left alone with our own half-filled hearts. For this reason, the psalmist reminds us that the practical atheism of idolatry is the act of a fool:

> The fool says in his heart, "There is no God."
> They are corrupt, they do abominable deeds,
>   there is none that does good (Ps. 14:1).

Moreover, the psalmist makes clear that what the "fool" believes is not a harmless matter of personal religious preference but the source of corruption and evil. As Jesus told his disciples,

> "What comes out of a man is what defiles a man. For from within, out of the heart of man, come evil thoughts, fornication, theft, murder, adultery, coveting, wickedness, deceit, licentiousness, envy, slander, pride, foolishness. All these evil things come from within, and they defile a man" (Mark 7:20-23).

Jesus' teaching is unmistakable. The condition of our "heart" determines the character of our lives. Whether or not we honor God as the Creator and Provider of all we need determines what we become.

THE LESSON FROM CREATION

The life of faith begins where the Bible begins, with a declaration that God is the Creator of the world. Moreover, the only proper response to this fundamental truth is an attitude of thankfulness arising from a continuing awareness that we are indebted to him for everything we are. There is nothing in life more basic or more crucial than this. This awareness and thankfulness are the bedrock upon which faith is built and apart from which it cannot exist. In order to trust in God we must be convinced that he alone is the sovereign and gracious Provider of all things. We must therefore be freed from the idolatry of misplaced gratitude. For no one can exercise faith in God who does not honor God "as God" by giving him alone the thanks due him as Creator of the world and Provider of our needs (Rom. 1:21). Thus, creation itself, when seen with the eyes of faith, teaches us to put away our idols by recognizing God alone as our Creator and Provider.

2

WHAT DOES IT MEAN TO KNOW GOD?

The Covenant God of the Sabbath

"You shall keep my sabbaths
and reverence my sanctuary:
I am the LORD."

LEVITICUS 26:2

God is the only true and satisfying source of life. Nothing visible can be identified with the invisible God, who made the world as an expression of his power and deity (Rom. 1:20). Indeed the creation itself drives this point home by its own inadequacy. Every attempt to squeeze a reason for living out of this world in isolation from its Creator ultimately runs dry, leaving the idolater unfulfilled, frustrated, and bitter. The insufficiency of creation is a billboard for the sufficiency of God. He alone can meet our deepest needs.

God's insistence that he alone be worshiped, so that our exercise of dominion is done in dependence on him, is therefore not an expression of evil egotism but an overture of love. God has created us in such a way that our fulfillment is wrapped up in displaying his glory. When God insists that he alone be our God, he is insisting on our happiness, since nothing compares with God when it comes to satisfying our longings. God is glorified by our dependence on him alone, and we are satisfied by trusting in his sovereignty and provision.

In fact, if God did *not* insist that we worship him alone, we would have to conclude that he is evil, or a least two-faced, since he would not be directing us to the one thing we desperately need. On the other hand, if he insisted that we worship him alone but due to his own limitations could not meet our needs, then we would accuse him of "false advertising." But because in his demand that we worship him alone God is both able and willing to meet our needs, the Bible declares that God is not only all-powerful but also all-loving. Indeed, though the Bible reveals that God's primary characteristic is his almighty, sovereign power as God the Creator and Provider (Gen. 1:1; Acts 14:15; 17:24-25; Rom. 1:20), it also makes clear that God's almighty nature is "the perfection through which perfections like his lordship over history and his love operate."[1]

This same operation of God's power expressed in his love is found in all of God's commands. God's commands are expressions of his continuing commitment and ability to meet his people's needs. As the relationship between Genesis 1:28 and 29 makes clear (see chapter 1), God commands what he commands because he has *already* provided what is necessary in order to keep the commands. In other words, God's commandments make explicit that he knows and gives what we need in the specific circumstances of our lives. In response, our obedience to his commands, as the expression of our trust in his continuing love and power, becomes the very means by which he meets our needs! In short, God's commandments are all given "for your good" (Deut. 10:12-13).

Down through the centuries, therefore, God's message remained both simple and all-encompassing: the God who revealed his power and deity through creation, and made himself known to his people as their "Lord" through the history of redemption, would continue to accompany, lead, protect, and provide for his people if they looked to him alone to do so. As Israel's words of worship and wisdom put it,

> Take delight in the LORD,
>   and he will give you the desires of your heart (Ps. 37:4).
>
> In all your ways acknowledge him,
>   and he will make straight your paths (Prov. 3:6).

THE PROBLEM WITH PEOPLE

Nevertheless, when it comes to God, people are fickle. In the battle between the seen and the unseen, tangible delights usually win. The wicked road leading to destruction is paved with instant gratification (Matt. 6:19-20; 7:13; James 5:1-6). My son John at six years old was hard pressed when faced with the choice of saving his birthday money for the toy he had "always wanted" or immediately spending it on cheaper trinkets (usually wrapped in fancy packaging) that were doomed to perish sooner than later (often before we got home!). One would think that the better toy would surely win out. But it seldom did.

Unfortunately, we adults do not fare any better, often trading the promise of enjoying God forever for transitory worldly pleasures. After all, "the love of money is the root of all evils" (1 Tim. 6:10) because it seeks its security and self-worth in material things as substitutes for God's presence. That is why the letter to the Hebrews warns us,

> Keep your life free from love of money, and be content with what you have; for [God] has said, "I will never fail you nor forsake you." Hence we can confidently say,
>
> "The Lord is my helper,
> I will not be afraid;
> what can man do to me?" (Heb. 13:5-6; see Ps. 118:6).

Nevertheless, we are blinded by wrong loves. As C. S. Lewis observed,

> We are half-hearted creatures, fooling about with drink and sex and ambition when infinite joy is offered us, like an ignorant child who wants to go on making mud pies in a slum because he cannot imagine what is meant by the offer of a holiday at the sea. We are far too easily pleased.[2]

The Sabbath as a Signpost

God, of course, knows this about us. So, as yet another expression of his powerful love and mercy, God has left us signposts that point the way back to the only real and reliable source of life whenever we lose our way among the glitter and gold of this world. Nature itself is one such witness to God's glory (Ps. 19:1-2). But without an explanation from God as to its meaning, nature remains silent concerning its significance (Ps. 19:3-4) and, in its fallen state, even misleading. For every sunset and waterfall there is a sun-baked desert and tidal wave. While it is true that

God's "eternal power and deity" are "clearly perceived in the things that have been made" (Rom. 1:20), nature by itself can communicate neither God's grace nor his commitment to provide for his people.

In order to make such realities clear, God, having created the world and humanity (Gen. 1:1-28), declared that he had created the world *for* humanity (Gen. 1:29). In doing so, he left his people with an unmistakable message of his desire and ability to provide for them. Thus in Psalm 19 the silent testimony of creation is distinguished from "the law of the LORD" (the written Word), which as God's perfect and sure testimony is the pathway to life (Ps. 19:7-8; compare Ps. 1:1-3; 119:33-40, 105).

The history of sin and redemption recorded in the Old Testament is God's strategy to teach his people in every generation this basic truth. In particular, God's plan for Israel, from the call of Abraham through the judgment of the Exile, is carefully orchestrated to illustrate the depth of God's love, the trustworthiness of his commitments, the necessity of his commands, the disastrous consequences of idolatry, and the contours of the salvation to come in Christ (Luke 24:25-27; 1 Cor. 10:1-13).[3]

The central pillar of this plan was the Sabbath. The Sabbath was Israel's constant reminder of the truths first declared in the creation.[4] Its purpose was to "jog Israel's memory" week after week concerning God's sufficiency and supply, since their memory, *even of God's greatest miracles,* was so short-lived. This is painfully illustrated by the fact that when faced with adversity just two and a half months after the splitting of the Red Sea, "the people of Israel murmured against Moses and Aaron in the wilderness" (Ex. 16:2). Thus, arising out of the creation itself (see Gen. 2:1-3), the sabbath decree was like a piece of string tied around Israel's finger, never letting her forget that the sovereign Lord was the only one who could be depended upon to meet her needs.

THE GOOD NEWS OF GOD'S REST

The importance of the Sabbath in the relationship between God and his people is further underscored by its inclusion in the Ten Commandments. Here, too, the keeping of the Sabbath is linked directly to the creation account as the basis for the command itself:

"Remember the sabbath day, to keep it holy. Six days you shall labor, and do all your work; but the seventh day is a sabbath to the LORD your God; in it you shall not do any work, you, or your son, or your daughter, your manservant, or your maidservant, or your cattle, or the sojourner who is within your gates; for in six days the LORD made heaven and earth, the sea, and all that is in them, and rested the seventh day; therefore the LORD blessed the sabbath day and hallowed it" (Ex. 20:8-11).

The Ten Commandments, like the Torah (Genesis through Deuteronomy) as a whole, look both backward and forward from the perspective of Israel's deliverance from slavery in Egypt. As the Pentateuch presents it, the Exodus, the Sinai experience, and the covenant that flows from them are the lens through which Israel's prehistory, from creation to the enslavement of Abraham's descendants, and subsequent history, from the golden calf to the Exile, are to be understood. It is not surprising, then, that the *reason* for not working on the seventh day of the week, the "Sabbath" (the name itself comes from the Hebrew for "cease" or "rest"), is that God himself took a "rest" after creating the world (Gen. 2:2b).

But why did God rest? Certainly God was not tired. God's Sabbath was not a rest of exhaustion. Rather, God ceased from his labors because his work was "finished"; there was nothing more for him to do (Gen. 2:1-2a). God's rest after his week of "hard work" thus indicated by his *actions* what he had declared earlier in his *word*, namely, that his creation was "very good" (Gen. 1:31). God's job was done. His Sabbath was like the rest a metalsmith takes after the final polishing has been applied and the pendant is complete. God rested because the world was now perfectly suited to meet the needs of mankind and, in doing so, to display the glories of its Creator. The Sabbath signified that the world God created was just the way he wanted it.

God's "rest" was the rest of satisfaction and a stamp of his approval on his work. As such, God "hallowed" the Sabbath, or set it apart, which is the same as saying he made it "holy" (Gen. 2:3; Ex. 20:11). The Sabbath was God's unique declaration of the good news that his provision for his people was perfect (Gen. 1:29-30).

KEEPING THE SABBATH

Not only did God's "rest" make a divine statement about the nature of creation, it also set a pattern for his people. Just as God's Sabbath declared his creation to be the perfect provision, so too God's people were to "keep the Sabbath" as their expression of gratitude for God's provisions in the past and of their ongoing dependence on him for the future. For Israel, each week was to be a reenactment of the week of creation. God's people were to work for six days (running the world and being nourished from it) just as God worked for six days to provide it. By doing so they take dominion over God's creation, as he commanded them. Then, after six days of enjoying God's provision, a day of rest was to be enjoyed as an echo of God's declaration that his creation is good and his provisions perfect.

Thus, by keeping the Sabbath, God's people were to proclaim about creation what God himself said about it when he "rested": God's provision is all they need to fulfill his calling in their lives. Like God, his people were not to rest on the Sabbath because they were exhausted or needed a break, but because they were content in God and his will. God's own pleasure in his provisions, signified by his "rest," was to be marked by and embodied in his people's pleasure in what he had provided—likewise signified by their rest. In this way, keeping the Sabbath expresses what it means to be created in the "image of God" (Gen. 1:27). Conversely, to break the third commandment is really to complain about what God has already provided and to distrust him for the future, thereby failing to reflect the glory of God's benevolent sovereignty. Why else would Israel work seven days a week, unless she feared that what God had given her during the week was not enough?

In Israel's history, this kind of complaint and lack of faith took many other forms as well, the most common being idolatry (breaking the first commandment) and covetousness (breaking the last commandment). But whatever its content, all disobedience to God's commands is merely a public display of discontent and disbelief. And at their core all such complaints are the same. Working on the Sabbath even though God rested on it, like all other acts of disobedience, is to throw disdain on God's gifts, like the toy-crazed child who throws a tantrum when the last Christmas present has been opened because he still wants more, or the man who neglects his family by working two jobs because he "needs" a cabin on a lake or a new car in his driveway in order to be happy. To crave more than God has given, so that we do what he prohibits in order to get it, is an idolatrous rejection of his sovereign love. For Israel to work on the Sabbath was to call God's Sabbath a lie.

THE SABBATH AS A STATEMENT OF FAITH

The centrality of the command to keep the Sabbath can also be seen in the three additional things said about it in Exodus 31:12-17:

> And the LORD said to Moses, "Say to the people of Israel, 'You shall keep my sabbaths, for this is a sign between me and you throughout your generations, that you may know that I, the LORD, sanctify you. You shall keep the sabbath, because it is holy for you; every one who profanes it shall be put to death; whoever does any work on it, that soul shall be cut off from among his people. Six days shall work be done, but the seventh day is a sabbath of solemn rest, holy to the LORD; whoever does any work on the sabbath day shall be put to death. Therefore the people of Israel shall keep the sabbath, observing the sabbath throughout their generations, as a perpetual covenant. It is a sign for ever between me and the people of Israel that in six days the LORD made heaven and earth, and on the seventh day he rested, and was refreshed.'"

First, the position of this commandment within the giving of the Law signifies its preeminence. The Sabbath is the *first* commandment given to Israel, being issued even *before* she gets to Mount Sinai (Ex. 16:22-30); and, as just quoted, it is the *last* commandment given for the people before Moses returns to them from atop the mountain (Ex. 31:12-17). Like bookends, the command to keep the Sabbath secures the content of God's relationship with Israel as established at the Exodus and implemented with the Sinai covenant. As such, the command to keep the Sabbath, established in response to God's "new creation" of his people at the Exodus (compare Isa. 43:1-2, where God's redeeming Israel from slavery in Egypt is portrayed as an act of creation), establishes the framework for understanding the Sinai covenant.

At the Exodus, as in the first creation, God "creates" Israel by acting to meet her needs and by committing himself to sustain her as she follows him through the wilderness into the Promised Land. The Promised Land, like the garden in Eden, was a microcosm of the world from which Israel, as a kingdom of priests (Ex. 19:6), was to mediate God's glory to the ends of the earth. As God prepared the empty world to meet the needs of Adam and Eve (Gen. 1:2–2:3), God's deliverance of Israel from Egypt and his bringing her through the wilderness to Canaan demonstrated his power and promise to provide for his people in order that they might fulfill their mandate (Deut. 32:10).[5]

It is not surprising, then, that the sign of this divine provision was once again the Sabbath. The Sabbath is the sign of the Sinai covenant because the Exodus marks out Israel as the people with whom God had once again, as he had done before with Adam, entered into a sabbath relationship (Ex. 31:13). For this reason, Israel's new life as God's people *began* with the Sabbath as God's reassurance to her that he was indeed committed to fight on her behalf to save her (compare Ex. 14:13-14; 16:22-30). In turn, God's instructions concerning Israel's worship in the tabernacle *climaxed* with the Sabbath as Israel's response of praise for God's provision (Ex. 25:1–31:11). And when the tabernacle was actually built, after the renewing of the covenant following Israel's sin with the golden calf, the very first order of business was to reaffirm the Sabbath (Ex. 35:1-3). The work on the tabernacle could be done only within the context of Israel's rest.

The significance of the Sabbath in Israel's history cannot be over-emphasized. It is God's statement to Israel that she is his chosen, covenant people, to whom alone he is committed to lead, guide, provide for, and deliver from evil as the unique recipients of his love. At the same time, the Sabbath is Israel's statement to God that he is her covenant God—that to him alone she will grant her worship in word and deed by resting in his will, trusting in his sustenance, praising and obeying him in every circumstance, and turning to him in time of need. And Exodus 34:21 makes clear that this applies even to the most urgent times of year, plowing and harvest, when life itself is at stake:

> "Six days you shall work, but on the seventh day you shall rest; in plowing time and in harvest you shall rest."

Second, Exodus 31:16-17 declares that the practice of keeping the

Sabbath is a *perpetual* one, an ongoing demonstration that the God who rested has chosen and separated out Israel to be his people. Thus, God's people are commanded to keep the Sabbath *continually* in response to God's election of them and as an expression of their faith in his *ongoing* commitment to them. To do otherwise would be to deny that the Creator is also the Sustainer. For as the Lord declared through Ezekiel,

> "I gave them my statutes and showed them my ordinances by whose observance man shall live. Moreover I gave them my sabbaths as a sign between me and them, that they might know that I the LORD sanctify them" (Ezek. 20:11-12; see Ex. 31:13).

Israel's sabbath-keeping thus reflects her continuing identity and irrevocable calling as God's own people, those uniquely privileged to know the Creator of the world and enjoy his sovereign provision:

> "For what great nation is there that has a god so near to it as the LORD our God is to us, whenever we call upon him?" (Deut. 4:7).

This is why God commanded that the Sabbath be kept as a "sign for ever between me and the people of Israel" (Ex. 31:17). The Sabbath signifies something fundamental about God's relationship to his people: it is a weekly bulletin that God, as Creator of the world, not only *can* but also *will* meet Israel's needs, because she is his chosen people. God called Israel to keep the Sabbath because, of all the peoples of the world, God created Israel to be his people. The Sabbath thus stood firm as a divinely established memorial to the covenant commitment God had made to his people. For her part, Israel was to "rest on the Sabbath" as a reminder of what she should do *every* day in relationship to the Creator who is committed to be her Provider: "call upon him" to meet her needs. God "keeps the Sabbath" by working for his people; his people "keep the Sabbath" by trusting him to do so.[6] Not working on the seventh day was to be the sign that Israel was continuing to rest in God's care all week long.

Finally, Exodus 31:14-15 warns Israel that "everyone who profanes [the Sabbath] shall be put to death." Just as the command to Israel to keep the Sabbath parallels God's Sabbath at creation, so too the death penalty for breaking the Sabbath parallels the death penalty instituted in the Garden of Eden (compare Gen. 2:17). The same relationship based on God's creation, commitment, and command that existed between God and Adam and Eve in the garden is now established between God and Israel at Mount Sinai.

Hence, as in the garden, so too under the Sinai covenant, the significance of the Sabbath is reflected in the severity of the punishment for breaking it. Thus, we read in Numbers 15:32-36 that,

> While the people of Israel were in the wilderness, they found a man gathering sticks on the Sabbath day. And those who found him gathering sticks brought him to Moses and Aaron, and to all the congregation. They put him in custody, because it had not been made plain what should be done to him. And the LORD said to Moses, "The man shall be put to death; all the congregation shall stone him with stones outside the camp." And all the congregation brought him outside the camp, and stoned him to death with stones, as the LORD commanded Moses.

Working on the Sabbath is a manifestation of not trusting God to meet one's needs. And to distrust God is to dishonor his glory as Creator, Provider, and Sustainer. And the consequence of not honoring God is judgment.

THE COVENANT RELATIONSHIP AT CREATION

The parallels between the reestablishment of the Sabbath under the Sinai covenant and its original significance in the Garden of Eden demonstrate that from the very beginning of creation a covenant relationship existed between God and his people. Like a treaty or a marriage, a "covenant" is a particular kind of political or legal arrangement that confirms or formalizes a relationship that already exists between two parties. Thus, the covenant ceremony in Genesis 15:12-19 ratifies the relationship between God and Abraham that was inaugurated back in Ur, when God revealed himself to Abraham in order to deliver him from idolatry (Gen. 15:7; Josh. 24:2-3; Acts 7:2). In the same way, the covenant at Sinai formalizes the sabbath relationship inaugurated in the wilderness (Ex. 16:22-30), which itself goes back to the covenant promises to the patriarchs (Ex. 2:24). And to confirm its relationship, a covenant declares its foundation in the past, outlines its stipulations for the present, and announces its expectations for the future.

There are, of course, different kinds of relationships and hence different kinds of arrangements. Because they ratify different kinds of relationships, we do not establish a political treaty the way we do a marriage—at least not anymore. Nor do we have the same kinds of stipulations and expectations in a business deal that we have in church membership. So too, the covenant between God and his people has its own particular character. In order to understand the precise contours of this "covenant" we must therefore return to what it means to be created *in* the "image of God" as the foundation for our relationship *with* God.

In addition to Genesis 1:26-27; 5:3; and 9:6 (see chapter 1), there is a fourth text that reflects on what it means to be created in God's image. Though Psalm 8:3-6 does not mention the "image of God" explicitly, it expresses by way of summary the significance of being created in God's image:

> When I look at thy heavens, the work of thy fingers,
>   the moon and the stars which thou hast established;
> what is man that thou art mindful of him,
>   and the son of man that thou dost care for him?
>
> Yet thou has made him little less than God,
>   and dost crown him with glory and honor.
> Thou hast given him dominion over the works of thy hands;
>   thou has put all things under his feet . . .

As the psalm makes clear, mankind, as a created being, has no self-sufficiency. We are not innately immortal or self-sustaining. We owe our very existence to another. Men and women are creatures made by God, and within the cosmos we are seemingly very small and insignificant creatures at that. It is barely possible even to see the planet earth on a star map, let alone find my street address. We are dwarfed by the heavens.

Yet the psalmist marvels that God has made men and women "little less than God and crowned [them] with glory and honor" in a way that is not true of any other aspect of God's creation. Unlike the rest of creation, we alone are created and called to manifest *God's* glory and honor to the ends of the earth by ruling and reigning over the world that

God has given us. We are "more" than *the rest of creation* in that the
Lord has granted to us "dominion over the works of his hands" (Ps.
8:6). We are "less" than *God* because this dominion was given to us (not
earned) by the Lord (not by ourselves). Dominion is not an inherent
right, or something we have earned by our wisdom and willpower; it is
a gift of creation. Being in God's image is not something we have *merited,* but the way we were *made.*

So we do not deserve the world we rule. Our "crown of glory and
honor" is the crown of dominion over "the works of *his* hands." Our
dominion over the world is to be carried out in dependence on God, so
that God gets all the glory for our lives. Our "crown" (Ps. 8:5) reflects
the glory of *God,* who is the ultimate and only "King." As his vice-
regents, God has put us under his feet and put all things under our feet.
This is why we emphasize that "the image of God" is a *functional* term,
expressing our relationship with God and with the rest of his created
order. As Paul House writes, "Simply put, humans are God's representatives on earth. . . . Humans exercise their 'imaging' of God by relating
to their Creator and by ruling the animals and the earth according to
the Lord's command."[7] It is striking and necessary, therefore, that Psalm
8, a psalm about the glory and honor of humanity, begins and ends with
a declaration of praise to God's majesty (Ps. 8:1, 9). Bernhard Anderson
writes:

> Though an ephemeral creature in comparison to the stars, *adam* is the
> one elevated to be God's representative on earth, the one with whom
> God enters into personal relationship, and the one in whom the praise
> of the whole creation can become vocal. "There is only one legitimate
> image through whom God is manifest in the world and that is
> humankind. . . ." This is what prompts the hymnic praise of the
> psalmist. It is not just that the Creator pays attention to this transient
> human creature. Far more than that: the Creator's grace is displayed by
> elevating human beings to a supreme place in the creation, crowning
> them as kings and queens and putting the whole earth at their disposal.[8]

In line with this truth, when Adam and Eve "wake up" and look
around, they see that everything they need has *already* been given to
them (Gen. 1:27-31). Note carefully the order of creation: God does not
first create Adam and Eve, wake them up, and then say, "If you keep my

commandment to be fruitful and multiply and have dominion, then I will give you everything you need for sustenance." The order of creation here is all-important. God does not give them an unformed wilderness to tame into a garden, but a paradise in which to live. God does not say in Genesis 1:27-31, "Be fruitful and multiply and *then* I will give you every plant for food." Instead he declares, "Be fruitful and multiply, and fill the earth and subdue it, and have dominion" (Gen. 1:28), because I have *already* given you everything you need (Gen. 1:1-25, 29-31). The commands to Adam and Eve in Genesis 1:28 are enabled by God's prior provisions. Having been created in the image of God as the crown of creation (Gen. 1:26), the command to have dominion is not a call for Adam and Eve to secure for themselves something they have not already been given. Instead, the commands of Genesis 1:28 are a call to express their *continuing* dependence on God for his provision as they extend God's rule and reign to the ends of the earth. For, given the nature of God's command (to go out and subdue the world in the days to come), God's provision in the *past* must bring with it a continuing commitment to provide for Adam and Eve in the *future,* signified by God's sabbath rest in the *present.* The keeping of God's command (Gen. 1:28) is nothing more than an expression of depending upon God's *provision* (Gen. 1:1-25), as restated in Genesis 1:28b, 1:29, and 1:30. God gives Adam and Eve dominion *before* he calls them to exercise it. Being in the image of God precedes acting like God. The commands of God always come *in response* to a relationship with God.

It is important to see, therefore, that the command for Adam and Eve to multiply and fill the earth and subdue it (Gen. 1:28) is not a summons to earn a *potential* blessing that is not yet theirs but a call to live out the blessing of life that God has already granted them. According to Genesis 2:9, 16-17, Adam and Eve may eat of *every* tree in the midst of the garden, *including* the "tree of life," except one: *only* the tree of the knowledge of good and evil is off limits. This means that before Adam and Eve sinned they were *already* enjoying eternal life as made possible by God's magnificent gifts of grace; they were not trying to prove themselves during a probation period in order to earn the right to eat of the tree of life and thereby gain a higher state of holiness or spiritual existence. Only *after* they sin does God bar the way to the tree of life, lest they continue to eat of it and live forever in their sinful state (Gen. 3:22-23).

In other words, the Sabbath signifies a *promise* from God that he has provided and will provide everything Adam and Eve need; there is nothing he will have to do that he has not already committed himself to do. Without such a promise, humanity's exercise of dominion would redound to their *own* glory and honor as they push on beyond God's original provisions to subdue the world in their own strength and wisdom. God's sabbath rest at creation brings with it, however, the implied promise that we will never outstrip God's grace. We will never go further than God has gone. We will never find ourselves in a place God has not provided. God's provision is sufficient for all our endeavors of exercising dominion in his name. God therefore declares everything to be "very good" in Genesis 1:31 in part because it will reveal his glory in the obedience of his people; their obedience is what dependence on God's provision looks like when it "goes public."

This is why it is so important to emphasize that God's sabbath rest in Genesis 2:1-3 is the conclusion to the creation narrative, not the beginning of a new series of events (the chapter division in our Bibles at Gen. 2:1 is misleading). The seventh day of creation is not the creation of Adam and Eve but God's rest from his work after he has finished providing Adam and Eve with everything they need to keep his commands. What does it mean, then, for Adam and Eve to keep the Sabbath in the Garden of Eden, or for Israel to do so in the wilderness? It means to *trust God's promises for the future, as secured in his provision from the past, so that they are willing and able to obey his commandments in the present.* In other words, "keeping the Sabbath" in the present is based on God's "sabbath rest" in the past, since it is God's "Sabbath," as the conclusion of creation, that declares the sufficiency of his provisions for the future.

Hence, although an explicit "covenant" is not established in Genesis 1–3 (but compare Hosea 6:7, where Israel's disobedience to the covenant is compared to Adam's disobedience in the garden), the same covenant *relationship* that will exist between God and his people throughout redemptive history is already in place from the beginning of creation: *First,* God acts to provide for his people as an expression of his ongoing commitment to meet their needs; *then,* and *only* then, he calls them to *respond* by keeping the commands that flow from and are made possible by this provision and promise. So, from the beginning of creation, God demands what he demands because of what he has given. God establishes a covenant relationship with his people as their God, which entails his continuing commitment to exercise his power to provide life and sustenance for his people. In turn, they become his people, which entails their commitment to trust in God's promises and provisions alone. As a result, "I will be their God and they shall be my people" becomes the basic covenant formula in the Bible.[9]

From the very beginning, the covenant relationship is therefore based on God as Provider. The establishment of the Sabbath at creation makes it clear that God reveals the magnificence of his sovereignty, expressed in love, by providing for his people. Conversely, God's people glorify his sovereign self-sufficiency, integrity, and overflowing love by trusting him in response. As Genesis 1:26-28 demonstrates, this trust shows itself in obedience to God's commands, the keeping of which is at the heart of what it means to be in a covenant relationship with God. The recipients of God's gifts honor him by obeying his commands as the outward display of their trust in the sufficiency of his grace. It follows, then, as John Piper has put it so well, that "God is most glorified in us when we are most satisfied in him."[10] This principle, embodied in the Sabbath, stands at the center of the covenant relationship established by God at the creation of the world.

THE COVENANT STRUCTURE OF THE BIBLE

The covenant relationship established in the Garden of Eden provides the basis and contours of the relationship that exists between God and his people throughout history. All the covenants in the Bible carry out the fundamental provision, promise, and purpose established at creation. As I read the Bible, this one, unified covenant relationship thus runs from the beginning of time into eternity.

The crucial thing to keep in mind about this relationship is that it does not originate with humanity, nor is it sustained by our strength or willpower. God's *first* word to Adam and Eve is not a word of command but a word of blessing (Gen. 1:28a, 29). God's acts of provision are sovereign, free acts of grace. Nobody forces God to create, provide for, rescue, or deliver his people. God's *second* word is the *command* that flows from this gift of grace (Gen. 1:28b). And, as Genesis 2:17 makes clear, God's *third* word is a *promise of blessing or curse* based on the keeping or breaking of his commands. Moreover, these "three words" are not isolated but inextricably interwoven.

This threefold covenant relationship may be outlined as follows:

GOD'S UNCONDITIONAL ACTS OF PROVISION
by which he establishes the covenant relationship
(the blessings of the covenant, given as an act of grace in the *past*)

which leads to

THE COVENANT STIPULATIONS OR "CONDITIONS"
upon which the covenant relationship is maintained
(the commands of the covenant, to be kept in the *present*)

which leads to

THE COVENANT PROMISES OR CURSES
based on keeping or not keeping the covenant
(the consequences of the covenant, to be fulfilled in the *future*)

The unbreakable link between these three covenantal elements indicates that obedience to God's will (keeping the covenant stipulations) is the direct and outward expression of trusting in God's promises as granted in his prior acts of provision. On the one hand, God initiates and provides; on the other hand, we respond by keeping his commandments, all of which express in different ways the fundamental call to trust in God alone for our future. Indeed, there is no place in the Bible where God ever comes to any of his people and says, "I have provided you with an opportunity to secure the blessing of knowing me and the grace of my provisions. But it is up to you to make the first move. Merit my blessings by keeping my commands; earn my blessings by doing my will." Instead, God always makes the first and decisive move by approaching us with his great acts of provision as acts of unconditional grace. Moreover, as we will see, part of God's provision is granting us the very ability to respond to his subsequent calls for obedience.

These great acts of divine provision—from the creation of the world to the exodus from Egypt, and from Christ's death and resurrection to his return to judge the world in righteousness, together with

God's constant work in the hearts and wills of his people—are the means by which God brings us into a relationship with him as "his people." But God's provisions never stand alone. Every act of God's past provision brings with it a commitment for the present and promises for the future. In turn, these provisions and promises inevitably lead to commands that stipulate what our response to God should be. These commands thus depend on and express the reality of what God has done, is doing, and will do on our behalf. God's demands correspond to his gifts—past, present, and future.

As we will see in the chapters ahead, this inextricable link between God's gifts, promises, and commands means that every act of disobedience expresses a failure to depend on God's provisions in the past and promises for the future. Conversely, confidence in God's promises (hope) because of a trust in his provisions (faith) expresses itself in obedience to his commands (love). God's commands thus map out the way in which we are to magnify his surpassing value, power, and love in our everyday lives.

Our lives of obedience, summarized in the command to love others, thus fulfill God's purpose of revealing his glorious character in the world. As Jesus taught his disciples, we are to let our "light so shine before men, that they may see [our] good works [of love, even loving our enemies!] and give glory to [our] Father who is in heaven" (Matt. 5:16). Moreover, inasmuch as God created us to reveal his glory through our "dependent dominion" of doing "good works," only those who honor God with lives of faith, hope, and love will find the glad satisfaction and security we all seek. For the glory of God is the good of his people.[11]

We must be careful here, since God's glory and hence our happiness as his people are at stake. Given the structure and logic of our covenant relationship with God, our keeping God's covenant stipulations can never be considered earning or meriting God's blessing or promises. The call to trust-obey God in the *present*, in order to inherit his promises for the *future*, is based solely on what he has done for us in the *past*—which includes his ongoing commitment to us here and now. Our lives of faith, hope, and love showcase God's sovereign grace, complete trustworthiness, and unending benevolence.

For this reason, the Bible's descriptions of our covenant relationship with God always begin with a "historical prologue." This prologue codifies God's *past* acts of provision, with their implication of God's *ongoing* faithfulness and love. Hence, after the Exodus, God initiates the covenant of Sinai by declaring, "You have seen what I did to the Egyptians, and how I bore you on eagles' wings and brought you to myself. . . . I am the LORD your God, who brought you out of the land of Egypt, out of the house of bondage" (Ex. 19:4; 20:2; see also Josh. 24:1-13; Jer. 31:31-34; Rom. 4:25–5:2; 1 Cor. 11:23-26; 2 Cor. 6:16-18; 2 Pet. 1:3-11). For in the words of Old Testament scholar Jon D. Levenson, "the function of the prologue is to ground the obligations of Israel to YHWH in the history of his gracious acts on her behalf."[12] Yet, as Levenson points out,

> The revelation of God in history is not, according to covenant theology, a goal in and of itself, but rather, the prologue to a new kind of relationship, one in which the vassal will show fidelity in the future by acknowledgment of the suzerain's grace towards him in the past. . . . The historical prologue is only the prologue. It ceases to be at point when the covenant takes effect. From that moment on, what is critical is not the past, but the observance of the stipulations in the present and the sort of life that such observance brings about.[13]

In this sense, all the promises of God concerning our salvation are conditional (Eph. 2:8b: we are saved *through faith*). There is no such thing as an "unconditional promise" in the Bible, except for the promise attached to the Noahic covenant, which pledges God's providential provision to "every living creature" that came out of the ark, animal and human alike (compare Gen. 9:8-17; Matt. 5:45). Even though mankind is just as evil after the Flood as before it (compare Gen. 8:21 with 6:5!), God promises not to destroy the world again until the day of final judgment—in order to provide the platform for the history of salvation to unfold (Gen. 8:22). Every covenant blessing or curse having to do with salvation or judgment, however, is wholly dependent on keeping or not keeping its stipulations, which can be summarized as a call to faith.

Nevertheless, we must remember that, although conditional, there is no such thing as a *merited* promise in the Bible; no biblical promise involves anything we deserve or earn by virtue of our own abilities, self-generated efforts, ethnic or personal distinctives, accomplishments, feelings, or beliefs. In the words of Ephesians 2:8a, we are saved "by grace."

Though all the promises of God are conditional upon our trust-obedience, the provisions of God that make it possible for us to trust God and inherit his promises are given to us unconditionally. In the words of Ephesians 2:8c-10, "this [entire process of salvation by grace through faith] is a *gift of God.* . . . For we are *his* workmanship, created in Christ Jesus for good works, which *God* prepared beforehand, that we should walk in them" (emphasis added). Our lives of obedience are therefore the "fruit of the Spirit," not exercises of our own self-generated willpower (Gal. 5:22-23—note the condition in verse 21). Although we cannot inherit God's promises without obeying his commands, our obedience to God's commands never comes from our own strength. Every act of obedience is a response in the present to what God has made possible in the past, through his own acts of provision and his promises of future deliverance.

This relationship between the past, present, and future, which is at the very center of biblical theology, is first laid out in the Garden of Eden. There God's provisions at creation, certified by the Sabbath, were the foundation upon which Adam and Eve were to obey him in the *present,* the result of which would be receiving his blessings in the *future.* As long as Adam and Eve trusted God for their future, because of what he had already provided for them in the past, they could exercise dominion as they moved out from the Garden of Eden to the ends of the earth. Their obedience to God's command was what dependence on God would look like in everyday life.

THE UNITY OF THE BIBLE

The insight that there is *one uniform* covenant relationship that runs throughout the various covenants of the Bible means that we no longer divide the Bible into two conflicting messages, "the Law" versus "the Gospel,"[14] or a "covenant of works" versus a "covenant of grace." Though there are numerous covenants throughout the history of redemption (such as the covenants with Abraham, Israel at Mount Sinai, Aaron, Phineas, David, and the church, that is, the "new covenant"), they all embody the same threefold relationship between God and his people first established at creation: 1) God's provision; 2) its corresponding covenant stipulations; 3) its consequent covenant blessings or curses. As a result, the commands of the Bible are always embedded within a larger, preexisting relationship with God, in which we keep his stipulations in the present because of his own provisions and commitments in the past that secure his promises for the future. The covenant relationship is therefore established, maintained, and fulfilled as an act of unconditional election in accordance with God's grace. Those whom God calls, he also enables to fulfill their calling, giving what he demands and demanding what he gives (see Rom. 8:28-30).

This means, as I have said, that I reject the common approach that divides the Bible into two messages, a "Law message" in which God demands something *from* us and a "Gospel message" in which he gives something *to* us.[15] Nor do I distinguish between "conditional" and "unconditional" promises in the Bible. Our relationship with God never *begins* with the commands of God as the precursor to receiving his blessings. The Bible makes it clear that our relationship with God always begins with the blessings of God *before* we move to what God requires from us in *response*. In describing our relationship with God, the Bible always starts with the great acts of God in the past that embody and lead to his promises for the future. In this sense, all of God's promises are given to us *unconditionally*. Only then, sandwiched between what God has done for us in the past and what he promises to do for us in the future, do we find the commands of God for the present as the necessary link between the two. Thus, though they are given unconditionally, inheriting the promises of God is at the same time *conditional*, being granted only to those who, by God's grace, keep the covenant stipulations of faith, hope, and love.

This is true whether we are talking about God's relationship with Adam in the garden, with Israel in the wilderness, with Jesus in the Promised Land, or with the church throughout the world.

3

WHAT WENT WRONG AND WHAT HAS GOD DONE ABOUT IT?

Self-Reliance and the Call to Rest

"Blessed be the LORD who has given rest to his people Israel,
according to all that he promised;
not one word has failed of all his good promise,
which he uttered by Moses his servant."

1 KINGS 8:56

From the very beginning, the fact that God alone could meet their needs was the foundation of the covenant relationship between God and his people. The sign of this simple but all-encompassing reality was God's sabbath rest at creation. Seen in this light, working on the Sabbath becomes another expression of the root sin underlying all sins: the failure to honor God as God (Rom. 1:21). Such "suppression of the truth" is always met with divine wrath, since it perverts the divine intention for creation and for mankind as the image of God (see Rom. 1:18, 24-25).

THE FALL FROM THE SABBATH

Given the covenant structure established at creation, it is clear why Adam and Eve's act of disobedience in the garden ruptured their relationship with God. In a word, it "broke the Sabbath." When Adam was told that he may "freely eat of every tree of the garden" (Gen. 2:16), he experienced, quite literally, the fruit of God's finished labors. As the Sabbath demonstrated, the reason Adam and Eve were not to work in the garden was because God had already worked for them to provide all that they needed.

However we understand Adam and Eve's activity in the garden in Genesis 2:5 and 2:15, they were not supporting themselves by meeting their own needs as a result of their own strength.[1] As God's people, Adam and Eve enjoyed the rest God initiated on the seventh day of creation. "Work" came into the picture only as part of the curse *after* the Fall, when Adam and Eve were given what they took for themselves in their sin: the burden of having to provide for themselves. Prior to their fall into sin, they were trusting in the blessing and promise of God's provision, on the basis of which they were exercising dominion over God's creation as those made in his image. God had given them everything they needed to carry out his will, including the "tree of life" (Gen. 2:9). There was nothing they needed that God had not already supplied.

There was, however, one condition that had to be met in order to *stay* in this "sabbath" rest. Adam and Eve must look to God *alone* to meet their needs, thereby rendering to God the honor due him as Creator and Provider. Hence, the way to honor God as God in the garden was by obeying a command concerning his *provision*. Moreover, given who God is and what he had done for his people, the consequence for not doing so could not be more severe:

> "You may freely eat of every tree of the garden; but of the tree of the knowledge of good and evil you shall not eat, for in the day that you eat of it you shall die" (Gen. 2:16b-17).

God warned his people that their disobedience to this command would bring death, since all that is "good" (Gen. 1:31) was at stake in this one stipulation. A failure to heed this instruction could only mean a dissatisfaction with God's provision and a disbelief in his word. Eating what God had forbidden would be a denial of the Sabbath God had instituted, a complaint concerning the sufficiency of God's gifts, a rejection of his wishes concerning the world, and a disdain for his warning. Disobeying God's command would be tantamount to calling God a liar, since disobedience is nothing more than distrust "gone public." As Paul House writes:

> It becomes clear, then, that God's favor is not unconditional in the sense that Adam may do as he pleases and still enjoy God's blessing. Rather he must abide by this simple law code to continue as he has

begun. To do so he must trust God's word and believe God's warning. Faith is required.[2]

Thus, the "Fall" in Genesis 3:1-7 is built on the temptation to call God a liar. In verse 4, the serpent tempts Eve by challenging God's warning concerning the consequences of disobedience. "You will not die," says the liar and "father of lies" (John 8:44) as he begins to ply his trade. But who *is* to be trusted? Has God provided only second best in giving them all the trees *except* one? Has God kept from them the one thing they really needed? Is Satan right that God is covering up the "real" reason for his command because, if the truth were told, God cannot stand the competition ("your eyes will be opened and you will be like God"— Gen. 3:5)? Is God trying to keep his people hungry, unfulfilled, and foolish in order to keep them dependent upon him (notice how Eve perceived the tree in Gen. 3:6)?

Eve and Adam had to decide whom they would believe: the God who declared his provision to be perfect by resting on the Sabbath; or the Tempter, who offered "more" and challenged them to decide for themselves what they needed. They went for "more" and for the "freedom" to determine on their own what was right and wrong. The fall into sin was therefore a fall into the disobedience of disbelief. No longer thankful for God's provision (they concluded that it was not enough), they no longer trusted in his promise (they decided that God had lied to them). As a result, Adam and Eve's relationship with God was destroyed.

God had promised to provide, giving Adam to Eve as her authority under God, but Eve decided that what God had provided was inadequate (Gen. 3:6a). God had declared his provision to be "very good" (Gen. 1:31), including giving Eve to Adam as his helper (Gen. 2:18), but Adam listened to his wife rather than to God (Gen. 3:6b). So they both grabbed what God, in his sovereign grace and love, had not granted. The "tree of the knowledge of good and evil" (Gen. 2:17) represented deciding for oneself what is best rather than relying on God's wisdom to lead and guide and provide as he sees fit. "The fear of the LORD is the beginning of knowledge; fools despise wisdom and instruction" (Prov. 1:7). No longer fearing God's warning, Adam and Eve no longer heeded God's wisdom. Desiring to become wise for themselves, they became fools.

The roles God had created Adam and Eve to fulfill were now perverted as a consequence of their independence. As the curse for her discontentment with God's gifts and distrust of his authority, Eve's role of "helper" to Adam was now to be filled with pain and the strife of competition (Gen. 3:16). Because of his choosing Eve over God, Adam, as "provider" under God, would be forced to work a land cursed with the same kind of rebellion he had exhibited toward the Lord. The land, left to itself, would now bear thorns and thistles. In order to eat, Adam would now have to *work,* and to do so *against* the very creation that had originally been made to meet his needs. Just as Adam had rebelled against God, so too the world was in rebellion against Adam. Moreover, as God had warned, because Adam and Eve would now have to be expelled from the garden of God's presence, so that they would no longer be able to partake of the tree of life, they would die (Gen. 3:17-24).

Thus, God's punishment for mankind's rebellious lust for independence was to give them exactly what they wanted (see again Rom. 1:24-32). Adam and Eve were now on their own, self-reliant and responsible for meeting their own needs. As a result, Adam and Eve were now competing with each other and against creation in a world that was no longer hospitable. Mankind's enjoyment of God's "rest" was over.

This independence was not the "American dream." Nor was it a sign of maturity. Adam and Eve were like rebellious teenagers venturing into life without their parents' blessing, having spurned their Father's care because they believed that he had deceived them. As a result, they ended up banished from the presence of the only One who could satisfy their souls and supply what they needed to fulfill their mandate to exercise dominion over the world. Instead of going forth with God's blessing (Gen. 1:26-28), God forced them out under his curse (Gen. 3:15-19).

Only dependence on God makes dominion possible (Gen. 1:26-28). Independence from God does not result in freedom but in slavery to the world (Gen. 3:17-19). God granted Adam and Eve life; Adam and Eve gave themselves corruption and death. Separation from God is not the means to self-fulfillment; it is the self-inflicted, divinely ordained punishment for calling God a liar, since God cannot dwell with those who spurn his glory and goodness without dishonoring himself. Hence, to be banished from God's presence and to be given over to one's own sinful desires in this life is "hell on earth."

FROM THE FALL TO THE FLOOD

Separated from their sovereign Lord and left alone to seek happiness in themselves, mankind's rebellion inevitably turns toward one another. As mankind becomes separated from God, death breeds death. As a result of his lack of contentment in God's provision and lack of trust in God's promises, Cain, because of his jealousy, murders Abel (Gen. 4:5-7; Heb. 11:4). In turn, God's punishment becomes increasingly severe. Whereas Adam and Eve were separated from God's work on their behalf but could still live off the land (albeit only by their own painful labor), Cain is separated even from the land itself. As God declares in Genesis 4:11-12,

> "Now you are cursed from the ground, which has opened its mouth to receive your brother's blood from your hand. When you till the ground, it shall no longer yield to you its strength; you shall be a fugitive and a wanderer on the earth."

Note carefully what this means, as reflected in Genesis 4:16:

> Then Cain went away from the presence of the LORD and dwelt in the land of Nod, east of Eden.

No longer being able to till the ground entails being driven further away from the very *presence of the Lord* (although God continues to exercise mercy by preserving Cain from the hostility of others—see Gen. 4:13-15). The glory of God's presence is experienced in his provision; to be separated from one is to be separated from the other. As Cain declares, "Behold, thou hast driven me this day *away from the ground;* and *from thy face* I shall be hidden" (Gen. 4:14, emphasis added).

This link between God's presence and his provision explains why, when mankind's rebellion reaches such drastic proportions that God decides to destroy them, he does so by destroying with a flood the very habitat he has provided (Gen. 6:5-7). Humanity's ever-increasing failure to honor their Creator is thus judged by a progressive reversal of the purpose of creation itself, which was to manifest God's glory through the dependent dominion of his people made possible by his provision. An increasing alienation from God brings with it an increasing alienation from God's other provisions. Mankind's evil finally reaches such a pitch that God causes the world over which humanity was to exercise dominion as his image to rise up in an act of ultimate rebellion against them. As a result, the mist that watered the garden from below (Gen. 2:6) is replaced by a flood of waters that drown the earth from above (Gen. 7:10-12; 2 Pet. 3:5-6). In a world perverted by sin, the means of life now become the instrument of death.

The Flood demonstrates that the penalty for dishonoring God by despising his provisions and distrusting his word is alienation from both the Source and sources of life. For the Scriptures associate the river that flowed out from the Garden of Eden with the life that comes from God himself. Hence, the "river of life" can be said to flow from the throne of God in the temple, just as the river flowed out of Eden, the first "temple" of God's presence with his people (Gen. 2:10; Rev. 22:1; see Ezek. 47:1-2; Ps. 36:8-9; Zech. 14:8; Joel 3:18). Against this backdrop, God's judgment in the Flood was not only an expression of his justice but also an object lesson concerning the consequences of sin. As such, the Flood in the midst of history foreshadows the future judgment at the end of history, when unbelieving humanity will suffer separation from God's presence as the source of life.

BACK TO THE SABBATH: STEP ONE—MERCY AFTER JUDGMENT

Amazingly, however, God also shows mercy in the midst of his judgment. After the Fall, when Adam and Eve deserved only his wrath, God clothed them before he banished them from the garden. In so doing, God provided for them what they had tried in vain to provide for themselves (compare Gen. 3:21 with 3:7). God's act of covering their shame signified protection from his wrath, the forgiveness of their sin, and their reinstatement as his people.[3] Furthermore, in showing mercy God does not forget justice. God's saving mercy toward Adam and Eve is matched by his curse on the serpent, whom God promises to defeat all the days of its life (Gen. 3:14; to curse one's enemy "to eat dust" is a sign of his utter defeat) and one day to destroy through the offspring of Eve herself (Gen. 3:15). The one who was deceived first will be the one through whom the serpent will be destroyed. For this reason, Genesis 3:15 is often referred to as the first declaration of the Gospel, the *protoevangelium,* which the New Testament tells us is fulfilled in Christ and his people (Rom. 16:20; Gal. 3:16; Heb. 2:14; 1 John 3:8). In response to this promise, Adam names the woman, by whom the curse of death entered the world, "the mother of all living" (Gen. 3:20)!

As an extension of this divine mercy to his people, God's kindness also includes his providential care of the wicked as that which displays his perfect love and makes the history of redemption possible (Matt. 5:43-48; Rom. 9:22-24). Thus, after Cain murdered Abel, God put a mark on him before he banished him from the land, "lest any who came upon him should kill him" (Gen. 4:15). So too, after the Flood God promised Noah that he will "never again curse the ground because of man . . . neither will [he] ever again destroy every living creature as [he had] done," even though "the imagination of man's heart is evil from his youth" (Gen. 8:21). Although nothing had changed regarding humanity's sinful condition, God promised to preserve the earth's seasons for as long as the earth remains (Gen. 8:22).

Here too God is providing a lesson book concerning his purposes for the world. Just as the Flood prefigures the judgment to come, God's acts of grace after the Flood, in which he once again brings order out of chaos in order to provide for humanity, prefigures the new creation. The blessing and command to Noah and his sons to "be fruitful and multiply, and fill the earth" (Gen. 9:1), based on the provision of food noted in Genesis 9:3, therefore recall the command and provision originally given to Adam in Genesis 1:26-31. Moreover, by delivering Noah from judgment and providing for his needs with a "new creation" for as long as this world lasts, God's judgment against sin becomes a showcase for his mercy—as he preserves his people and tempers his wrath toward the world.

BACK TO THE SABBATH: STEP TWO—THE ELECTION OF ABRAHAM

As we have seen, the salvation of God's people begins in Genesis 3:15. There, in cursing the serpent, God promised that from the woman would come *two* seeds, a "seed of the serpent" and a "seed of the woman," that is to say, two lineages or peoples. Furthermore, although there would be constant enmity between the two, the seed of the woman would one day destroy Satan himself. As the biblical narrative unfolds, the seed of the serpent is seen in the genealogies of unbelief, beginning with Cain and continuing on through Ham, Japheth, and Joktan (Gen. 4:5, 17-24; 10:2-20). On the other hand, the seed of the woman is the genealogy of God's people, beginning with Abel and continuing on through Seth, Noah, Shem, Terah, and his son Abram (later called Abraham) (Gen. 4:4; 5:1-32; 10:21-31; 11:10-26).

It is important to see that these two peoples derive from the same parentage (for example, Cain, Abel, and Seth all come from Adam and Eve, while Shem, Ham, and Japheth all have Noah as their father; and besides Abram, Terah has two other sons, Nahor and Haran). Thus, what distinguishes the seed of the woman from the seed of Satan is not their human abilities or attributes or accomplishments but solely that they have received God's mercy, granted according to his own sovereign choice. Membership in God's people is wholly a matter of God's grace. For this reason, the history of redemption can aptly be called the history of election (see Rom. 9:6-13).

Therefore, in Genesis 12:1, when God speaks again, calling Abram to leave Haran and go to Canaan (Gen. 11:31-32; Acts 7:2), it is yet another act of undeserved mercy as a result of God's sovereign election. For although God had appeared earlier to Abram while he was still in Ur of the Chaldeans in Mesopotamia and called him to go to Canaan, Abram had stopped in Haran, halfway to the Promised Land (Gen. 11:31-32; 15:7; Acts 7:2). In his mercy, God therefore steps in once again to bring Abram all the way to the Promised Land. As Paul would later put it, God's people can be sure that "he who began a good work in you will bring it to completion," all the way to the day when Christ comes to take his people home (Phil. 1:6; see Deut. 31:6; Heb. 13:5).

Why this mercy to Abraham? The Bible gives no indication of any reason whatsoever, in Abraham's own life, why God chose him over someone else. And that is precisely the point! All we learn about Abraham while he was still in Mesopotamia is that he was a pagan who worshiped other gods (Josh. 24:2). In that context, and *before* he left for Haran, "the God of glory" appeared to him (Acts 7:2). God did not reveal himself to Abraham *because of* who Abraham was, but *in spite of* who Abraham was! In revealing himself to Abraham, God was not responding to some special spiritual or intellectual qualities in Abraham; Abraham did not first reach out to God, God first reached down to Abraham. God did not meet Abraham halfway, after Abraham began a spiritual journey in search of truth; God is the one who thrust Abraham out of Mesopotamia by invading his life and then appeared to him again to keep him going.

In short, God's call and continuing commitment to Abraham was a result of God's free and sovereign choice. God elected Abraham only because *God* wanted to do so for his *own* purposes. Abraham did not deserve or merit or stimulate God's choice. It was an act of undeserved mercy as an expression of God's grace. This is why God is said to be sovereign: he does whatever he wants, without being forced or enticed or bribed to do so by his creatures or their actions. "Our God is in the heavens; he does whatever he pleases" (Ps. 115:3).

Abraham's move to Haran, and then from Haran to the Promised Land, was therefore a pursuit of the God who pursued him. In entering into and maintaining our covenant relationship with God (see chapter 2), we are always responding to God. The One who revealed himself in creating the world is the One who also creates faith in our lives by revealing himself to us. Abraham was no religious hero. Apart from God invading his life, Abraham would have remained an idol worshiper in Mesopotamia. In the words of Paul, Abraham's life thus illustrates the fact that God saves the "ungodly" (Rom. 4:5).

Moreover, as a continuing display of his mercy, motivated by his love, God never gives up on his people. Most likely it was out of responsibility to his father that Abram stopped halfway to the Promised Land (compare Gen. 11:32), but God remained true to his prior act of having invaded Abram's life by calling Abram a second time to go into Canaan. Abram reaches the Promised Land not because of his great commitment to God but because of God's great commitment to him. Indeed, not even four hundred years of slavery would be able to thwart God's promises, since they are guaranteed by the provision of his presence (Gen. 15:13-16).

It is therefore crucial to see that although God's covenant with Abram is not formalized until much later (Gen. 15:7-21), their covenant *relationship* began when God first appeared to Abram in Mesopotamia (see again Acts 7:2). The command to Abram in Haran in Genesis 12:1 to leave his country and kindred for the Promised Land (the covenant stipulation at that point) is consequently based on God's prior, unconditional provision of his presence (the historical prologue, as stated clearly in Gen. 15:7). In turn, the covenant promises of a land, a great nation, and the blessing of the nations, stated in Genesis 12:2-3, which are repeated throughout Abram's life (see, for example, Gen. 13:14-17; 15:5-21; 17:5-8; 22:15-18), are conditional upon his faith, expressed in continuing obedience to God's call. But as the narrative of Abram's life makes clear, God will give what he demands by continuing to reveal his presence to Abram and by doing whatever else it takes to preserve Abram's confidence in his promises. For if God were to allow his promises to go unfulfilled, he would dishonor his own glory—something he cannot do.

Hence, God's decision to establish a covenant relationship with Abram and his descendents was not motivated by anything in Abram himself. Nevertheless, it was not without purpose, since God is glorified in the dependency of his people. God's election is free, but it is not capricious. God has a design in all that he does. Of all the nations in the world, Abram's nation will testify to God's sovereignty by being God's own people in a land given to them by God himself (Gen. 12:4-8; 13:14-18). As God's chosen people, Abram and his descendants will display God's love through their unique experience of his presence. In contrast to other nations, he will be *Israel's* God, committed to rescuing them from evil and fulfilling the promises of salvation that are theirs alone (see God's actions in Gen. 12:10–14:24).

Thus, in Genesis 15:1 God swears to Abram in a vision, "Fear not, Abram [the covenant stipulation], I am your shield [the historical prologue]; your reward shall be very great [the covenant promise]." As an embodiment of this provision and promise, God later changes Abram's name to Abraham to signify God's sovereign authority over Abraham's life and to remind him of God's commitment to remain true to his word (Gen. 17:1-8). As John Sailhamer writes concerning the covenant in Genesis 17:3-8:

> God's part of the covenant (vv. 3b-8) consists of two promises: abundant descendants (vv. 4-6) and eternal faithfulness (vv. 7-8). As the narratives have already stressed, the descendants of Abraham who belong to this covenant will owe their existence to God alone: "I will make you a father of many nations." They will be "children born not

of natural descent, nor of human decision or a husband's will, but born of God" (Jn 1:13). The promise of abundant descendants is memorialized in the change of Abram's name to Abraham, which is interpreted to mean "father of many nations" (17:4b, 5). The choice of the word *be fruitful* in verse 6 and *multiply* in verse 2 seems intended to recall the blessing of all humankind in [Gen.] 1:29: [*sic*] "Be fruitful and multiply and fill the land," and its reiteration in 9:1: "Be fruitful and multiply and fill the land." Thus the covenant with Abraham was the means through which God's original blessing would again be channeled to all humankind.[4]

This is why God is said to be not only sovereign (God chose Abraham and his descendants; they did not choose God), but also merciful and loving. Rather than leaving the world in anarchy and confusion (see the outcome of the Tower of Babel in Gen. 11), God again took the initiative to establish a pocket of dependence like that which existed in the Garden of Eden before the Fall. As Sailhamer has observed, the line of God's covenant promises and commands thus runs from Adam (Gen. 1:28-29) to Noah (Gen. 9:1-7) to Abraham (Gen. 17:3-8). As with Noah, God's election of Abraham parallels his creation of Adam and Eve and the promise of provision granted in Genesis 1.

It is not saying too much, therefore, to conclude that the establishment of the covenant with Abraham in the Promised Land is an act of sovereign creation that recalls the creation of mankind in the world (see Mal. 2:10). The "Promised Land" is the beginning of the reconstitution of the Garden of Eden, since the goal of redemption is a new creation in which God once again dwells in the midst of his people (Rev. 21:1-4). In this sense, the end is like the beginning. The Creator is the Redeemer.

The call of Abraham is the second step in this divine plan of redemption. Through this one man, now "recreated" in the midst of this evil world, God will eventually reach out to all the peoples of the world with the reality of his presence (see again Gen. 12:2-3). To this end, God's purpose in picking Abraham, granting him the provisions of his presence, and promising that his descendants would become a great nation was to display the magnificence of his sovereign power and love by creating a people who, like Adam and Eve before the Fall, would look to him alone to meet their needs. For within this covenant relationship, Abraham's response to God's promises for the future, based on his provisions in the past (see again Gen. 15:1), is to trust that the Lord will do whatever it takes to bring those promises about, including giving Abraham an heir in his old age. Thus, in the famous summary of Genesis 15:6, "Abraham believed the LORD; and he reckoned it to him as righteousness."

Abraham's faith, as that which honors God as God, makes Abraham righteous (i.e., a loyal covenant keeper), since dependence on God is the reversal of the self-reliance at the heart of sin. To signify this response of faith, circumcision is decreed for Abraham's descendants as the representative expression of covenant obedience (Gen. 17:9-14; Rom. 4:11). To quote John Sailhamer again:

> Abraham's part in the covenant consisted in his obedience to the covenant: "You must keep my covenant" (v. 9). What this meant was immediately explained: "This is my covenant which you must keep . . . every male among you shall be circumcised" (v. 10). To keep the covenant was to practice circumcision faithfully; to break (v. 14b) the covenant was to be uncircumcised (v. 14a). Lest the reader conclude that the whole of the covenant was simply the rite of circumcision, the author included the words "and it will be the sign of the covenant" (v. 11).[5]

The act of circumcision becomes the sign representing God's covenant with his people, since it will be their initial response of faith-filled obedience to his provisions and promises. Circumcision, as an initiation rite into the covenant community, declares openly that God is "their God" (the one sovereignly committed to work for them), and that they will be "his people" (the ones committed to trust in him to do so— Gen. 17:8). Though its precise meaning is a matter of debate, for Israel the act of circumcision itself most likely signified a life that was purified before God, being open to do his will (see Lev. 26:41; Deut. 10:16; 30:6; Isa. 52:1; Jer. 4:4; 9:25-26; Rom. 2:28-29).

Abraham's faith, expressed in the obedience of circumcision (Gen. 15–17), was consequently of one piece with his overall life of obedience, which was born of a faith that began back in Mesopotamia and climaxed with his offering of Isaac on the mountain in Genesis 22. From its very beginning, Abraham's faith, that is, his growing confidence in God's promises for the future because of the sufficiency of God's provisions in the past, thus "justified" him before God as one of God's own

(Rom. 4:3, 9-12; Heb. 11:8-9; James 2:21). For as the result of God's election and grace, Abraham entered into and kept the covenant in the hope of receiving God's promises, thereby rendering God the glory due him. Hence, when the covenant promises are passed on to Isaac, Abraham's son, God declares:

> "I will multiply your descendants as the stars of heaven, and will give to your descendants all these lands; and by your descendants all the nations of the earth shall bless themselves: *because Abraham obeyed my voice and kept my charge, my commandments, my statutes, and my laws*" (Gen. 26:4-5, emphasis added).

This final summary of Abraham's life, like the earlier statement of his obedience regarding circumcision itself (Gen. 17:23), makes explicit that Abraham will inherit the covenant promises because, enabled by the provision of God's presence, Abraham kept the covenant stipulations. In short, Abraham fulfilled the covenant commands as summarized in Genesis 17:1-2 (emphasis added):

> "I am God Almighty [covenant prologue],
> *walk before me, and be blameless* [covenant stipulations].
> And I will make my covenant between me and you,
> and will multiply you exceedingly [covenant promises]."

Once again we are reminded of Noah, who also "walked with God" and was "blameless" (Gen. 6:9). Here too the link is established between the redemption being brought about through Noah and the redemption being brought about through Abraham—both of whom, as part of the redeemed people of God, kept God's covenant. For as John Sailhamer's again observes:

> In the light of the sparsity of these terms ["walked with God" and being "blameless"] in Genesis it seems likely that the author expects the reader to make an association between these two great men based on the close recurrence of both terms. "Blameless" occurs in Genesis only in these two texts [Gen. 6:9 and 17:1]; "walk before God" occurs more frequently, but in carefully chosen contexts (Enoch, 5:22; Noah, 6:9; Abraham, 17:1; 24:40; 48:15 [with Isaac]). Thus Abraham and Noah are presented as examples of those who have lived in obedience

to the covenant and are thus "blameless" before God, because both obeyed God "as he commanded them" (17:23; cf. 6:22; 7:5, 9, 16).[6]

LEARNING THE LESSON OF GOD'S CHARACTER

Anyone who knows the story of Abraham's life knows, however, that his faith did not just "happen"; he had to *learn* to trust God more and more in more and more difficult circumstances. For in his wisdom God taught Abraham to keep the covenant by placing his promises in constant jeopardy on the one hand, only to rescue them repeatedly on the other. Initially, between the jeopardy and the rescue there was panic and disobedience as Abraham sought to secure God's promises through his own strength and ingenuity. But eventually Abraham learned from God's track record of faithfulness to resist distrusting God when his word was called into question. In the end, Abraham even expected God to keep his commitment in the face of death. This is the lesson book of Abraham's life.

The first lesson in this book of faith takes place shortly after Abraham arrives in Canaan. After he expresses his faith in God's promises by marking out its boundaries with thanksgiving to God, even though the land is already inhabited by Canaanites, Abraham encounters a *famine* in the land (Gen. 12:10). Can the God who led Abraham to Canaan preserve him in Canaan, even in the midst of such severe adversity? The Canaanites are one thing, being without food is a different story altogether. One can almost hear Abraham saying, "What kind of Promised Land is this, anyway? And what kind of God has led me here? God has duped me, promising something he cannot perform." Faced with a situation in which God's promise has been called into question, and not yet having learned to take God at his word, Abraham is easy prey for the temptation to look elsewhere to meet his needs. So he goes to Egypt (Gen. 12:10b), the land of plenty due to the Nile's regular provision (the ancient world used to mark time by the Nile's falling and rising!) and Israel's perennial substitute for trusting God (Gen. 26:2; Isa. 30:1-2; Jer. 43:7; etc.). However, in order to meet his needs in Egypt, Abraham must give up both his integrity and his wife in return for material security (Gen. 12:11-16). The consequence of sin unchecked is always more sin.

There is no telling where Abraham's unbelief would have led had

God not intervened. God is patient with his people during their "school of faith," using even their failures to teach them that he can be trusted no matter what. Thus, after Abraham has experienced the consequences of not taking God at his word, God has mercy on him and rescues him from his unbelief. In doing so, God redeems Abraham's sin by transforming it into an agent of blessing. He afflicts Pharaoh for taking Abraham's wife, so that Pharaoh is more than anxious to rectify the situation. Indeed, instead of punishing Abraham for his deception, Pharaoh sends him back to the Promised Land with all his possessions intact (Gen. 12:17–13:2).

Because of God's mercy and sovereign power, his promises have not been found wanting. By delivering Abraham from Egypt, God demonstrates that he will do whatever it takes to keep his word in order to preserve his glory. Abraham should have stayed in the Promised Land in the first place, but he learned a valuable lesson in leaving. As a result of his being rescued, Abraham's dependence on God is strengthened to such a degree that soon after this he can overturn custom and offer Lot the *first* choice of land for grazing his flocks, considering Lot's need more important than his own (Gen. 13). Abraham's restored *faith* in God has led to a renewed *hope* in his promises, which in turn expresses itself in *love* for others.

This pattern—faith in God's promise, then jeopardy, distrust, and rescue, all leading to a greater dependence on God's promise—is repeated again and again throughout Abraham's life (Gen. 14–21), until he becomes so convinced that God will keep his word that even if God *himself* should call his own promises into question, Abraham will trust him. Thus, when God ordered Abraham to sacrifice Isaac (the miraculously born promised heir) as the supreme test of Abraham's growing dependence on God's promises (Gen. 22:2), Abraham's answer to Isaac's question about the missing lamb shows that he passed the test:

> Abraham said, "God will provide himself the Lamb for a burnt offering, my son" (Gen. 22:8).

How could Abraham say such a thing when he knew that his own son was to be killed? Did Abraham expect a miraculous substitution? How could he resolve the conflict between God's promise and God's command? Aware of God's promise that he would make Abraham's descendants great through Isaac (Gen. 17:16-19; 21:12), yet confronted with God's command to offer up Isaac as a sacrifice, Abraham drew the only conclusion possible in view of the trustworthiness of God's word: if God called Abraham to kill Isaac, God would also raise him from the dead (see Heb. 11:19)! So Abraham tells his servants that he and his son will go up the mountain to make the sacrifice and then they will *both* come back again (Gen. 22:5)!

Through the "roller coaster" of his life, Abraham had come to trust God no matter what. Abraham's willingness to offer up his son was therefore not an irrational leap into the dark but the only sensible response to the God Abraham had come to know. Abraham's act of faith was not absurd. "Faith" is not believing the unbelievable but trusting in God's word because of what one has come to know of God's character. And faith always "goes public" in acts of obedience, since a "faith" that does not obey is not a true, justifying faith at all (James 2:21-26; see also Rom. 1:5; Gal. 5:6; 1 Thess. 1:3; 2 Thess. 1:11; Heb. 11:17). Abraham's faith is therefore expressed in his going off with wood and knife in hand. His subsequent act of binding Isaac and laying him on the altar indicates that no matter what happened to Isaac, God is to be taken at his word and obeyed. The knife is raised. Isaac is about to be slain by his own father. But the Lord intervenes:

> "Abraham, Abraham! . . . Do not lay your hand on the lad or do any-thing to him; for now I know that you fear God, seeing you have not withheld your son, your only son, from me" (Gen. 22:11-12).

Abraham's pilgrimage of faith has led him to the position of depen-dence that Adam and Eve enjoyed prior to the Fall. Because Abraham has offered Isaac, God now "knows" (in the sense of experiencing its reality in time and space) that Abraham has learned his lesson: Abraham fears losing his relationship with God more than he fears anything else—even losing his son—so that he trusts God more than he trusts anyone or anything else—even himself. Fear is the flip side of faith. God has worked in Abraham's life to bring him to a point where looking else-where for his security (fearing the world) has been overcome by a depen-dence on God's promise (fearing God). The same man who would pawn off his wife (twice!) to save his own skin is now willing to offer up his most precious "possession" because he fears losing God. By God's grace, Abraham's idolatry has given way to the worship of God alone.

This is what it means to be saved or delivered from sin in order that we might enter into and maintain our covenant relationship with God. For his part, God forgives our sins, reveals his glory, rescues us from our heart of disbelief with its life of disobedience, and brings us back to himself again and again so that we might learn to live by faith in his promises. For our part, Abraham, as the "father" of the faithful (Rom. 4:16-17), is the beginning of a people who respond by learning over a lifetime to look to God alone to meet their needs. When Abraham names the place where he tried to sacrifice Isaac "The LORD will provide" (Gen. 22:14), he declares what all of God's people come to know is true.

BACK TO THE SABBATH: STEP THREE—THE EXODUS AS A FULFILLMENT OF CREATION

The next four hundred years of Israel's history underscore the lesson Abraham learned about God, as the pattern of his life is repeated on both an individual and a corporate scale. Even what appears to be the haphazard and sinful schemes of unpredictable people are all part of God's masterful plan of instruction. In every circumstance, God displays his ability to transform evil into good in order to keep his promises (see, for example, the intrigue between Rebekah and Jacob in Gen. 27, and the entire story of Joseph in Gen. 37–50). Nothing can stand in the way of God's accomplishing his purposes. In Joseph's words, as he reflected over his brothers' past attempts to get rid of him,

> "As for you, you meant evil against me; but God meant it for good, to bring it about that many people should be kept alive, as they are today" (Gen. 50:20).

The events of the Exodus illustrate this same lesson. God is in control of history, using even evil to preserve his people and thus reveal his own power and glory. For example, Pharaoh's purge of Israel's newborn male children served to prosper and train Moses, just as the hardness of Pharaoh's heart served to prosper Israel on the eve of her departure (Ex. 2:10; 11:2-3; 12:33-36).

Nevertheless, it often appeared as if God's plans were backfiring. Rather than letting Israel go, Pharaoh's initial response to Moses was to increase the severity of her slavery. Rather than deliverance, Moses' efforts brought only a more severe bondage (Ex. 5:1-21). Moses himself could not understand why God delayed in keeping his promise (see Ex. 5:22-23).

As the narrative unfolds, however, God's purpose becomes clear. Over four hundred years earlier God had predicted the coming slavery and deliverance of Abraham's descendants as another step in the battle between the seed of the serpent and the seed of the woman (Gen. 15:13). Israel's captivity in Egypt was therefore no mistake but a divinely orchestrated means of bringing judgment on both the Egyptians (through Israel's enslavement and deliverance) and the Amorites (through Israel's return to the land) (Gen. 15:14-16). Nor was the seesaw battle between Moses and Pharaoh a trial-and-error attempt to free God's people. Just the opposite! God designed Israel's deliverance in such a way that it became obvious to all, including the Egyptians (Ex. 14:25), that he is Lord, that the Israelites are his people, and that he alone is responsible for their freedom. Each plague, as well as the Exodus itself, hammered this point home with increasing force (Ex. 6:2-8; 7:2-6, 17; 8:10, 22-23; 9:14-16, 29-30; 10:1-2; 11:7, 9; 12:12; 14:17-18). Like a master teacher, God had a well-thought-out lesson plan, which he explained to Pharaoh through Moses:

> "Thus says the LORD, the God of the Hebrews, 'Let my people go, that they may serve me. For this time I will send all my plagues upon your heart, and upon your servants and your people, that you may know that there is none like me in all the earth. For by now I could have put forth my hand and struck you and your people with pestilence, and you would have been cut off from the earth; but for this purpose have I let you live, to show you my power, so that my name may be declared throughout all the earth'" (Ex. 9:13-16).

This passage makes clear that the events of the Exodus are intended to be a showcase for God's sovereign power and love, revealing both the election of God's people and his unmatched ability as Lord of lords and King of kings to work on their behalf. The plagues and Passover function to distinguish Israel from the Egyptians and to mock their gods and their sources of security and pride (Ex. 7:3-5; 8:23; 9:3-4; 10:1-2; 11:4-7). As a result, God is glorified through Israel's salvation from slavery. The slavery is the way in which the salvation is accomplished. Pharaoh's heart is hardened, the Egyptians are punished, and Israel is delivered in order to display God's glory to the ends of the earth by proclaiming his "name," that is to say, by making clear the nature of his character (Ex. 9:16; Rom. 9:17).

The Gospel of the Exodus is the good news that God is at work in history to reveal his glory in order to reestablish a people who will depend on him. He did so not because this particular nation was any better than the others, and not even because they were suffering—many nations were enslaved in the ancient world—but because, in his sovereignty, he had earlier chosen Abraham and his descendants as an act of grace (Ex. 2:24-25; Deut. 7:6-11; Rom. 9:14-18). In other words, the Exodus, like the call of Abraham itself, demonstrates that being rescued ("saved") is a result of God's mercy rather than our merits (see Titus 3:5-7 for its New Testament equivalent). "For [God] says to Moses, 'I will have mercy on whom I have mercy, and I will have compassion on whom I have compassion.' So it depends not upon man's will or exertion, but upon God's mercy" (Rom. 9:15-16, quoting Ex. 33:19).

As we have seen, the proper response to this sovereign grace, in which God takes the initiative to extend mercy to his people in the midst of judgment, is faith as the flip side of fear:

> And Israel saw the great work which the LORD did against the Egyptians, and the people *feared* the LORD; and they *believed* in the LORD and in his servant Moses (Ex. 14:31, emphasis added).

Moreover, the song that Moses and the people sang on the far side of the Red Sea illustrates once again that faith is fueled by the awareness that God is the One who provides. For just as Abraham named the mountain of Isaac's sacrifice "The LORD will provide" (Gen. 22:14), Moses leads the chorus in proclaiming:

> "I will sing to the LORD, for he has triumphed gloriously; the horse and his rider he has thrown into the sea. The LORD is my strength and my song, and he has become my salvation; this is my God, and I will praise him, my father's God, and I will exalt him" (Ex. 15:1-2).

As Moses' song continues, it becomes clear that God's greatest provision is not his triumph over the Egyptians as the sovereign Lord, "a man of war" who defeats his enemies (Ex. 15:3-12), but the fact that he exercises his sovereignty to lead his people back to himself:

> "Thou hast led in thy steadfast love the people whom thou hast
>   redeemed,
>   thou hast guided them by thy strength to thy holy abode. . . .
> Thou wilt bring them in, and plant them on thy own mountain,
>   the place, O LORD, which thou hast made for thy abode,
>   the sanctuary, O LORD, which thy hands have established.
> The LORD will reign for ever and ever" (Ex. 15:13, 17-18).

This is the ultimate lesson of the Exodus: the God who split the sea to save his people from slavery will "split" the inhabitants of Canaan in order to bring his people into his presence (Ex. 15:14-17). The God of Abraham and of the Exodus is the God of the Sabbath who provides for his people, and his greatest provision is himself. Moses therefore announces that the "kingdom of God" first established with Adam and Eve at creation can once again be seen in all its glory: the Exodus has made clear that the Lord is reigning over his people.

BACK TO THE SABBATH: STEP FOUR—THE REESTABLISHMENT OF REST

The way back to the Sabbath thus entailed three decisive preliminary steps. The first step back was God's covenant promise never to curse the land again (Gen. 8:21). God's covenant with Noah provides the foundation necessary for salvation to spread to the ends of the earth. God's providential care for the world is the basis of his promises to Abraham and his descendants, including the promise that the nations of the world will share in Abraham's blessing. As the launching pad for this mission to the world, God then called Abraham (step two) in order to create a people for himself who would reverse the fall into sin by depending on him as their Provider (Gen. 12–23). The third step back was to prepare this people to do so by making it obvious—through the events of more than four centuries, climaxing with the Exodus—that the Israelites owed their very existence solely to God's gracious election. For in his love, God had determined to reveal the glory of his sovereignty not only by judging the wicked but also by redeeming a people of his choice who would fulfill the mandate originally given to Adam and Eve (Gen. 24:1—Ex. 15:26).

As the fourth and final step, God therefore reinstitutes the Sabbath with Israel as a perpetual reminder that they owe their lives to his mercy. In turn, keeping the Sabbath serves as the sign of Israel's commitment to rest in God's provision as they trust in his promises (Ex. 16; 20:8-11; 31:13).

We are now back where we began. God's deliverance of Israel at the Exodus parallels his original acts of provision at creation. For this reason, in identifying himself as Israel's "Redeemer," God declares that he is "the Creator of Israel" (Isa. 43:15; see vv. 14-17). The prophet Ezekiel can even identify Mount Zion with the Garden of Eden theologically by using the descriptions of "the Garden of God" to describe the "holy mountain of God" in Jerusalem (Ezek. 28:12-14).[7] He does so because, like the Garden of Eden, Mount Zion is the place of God's presence in the land that God has provided. Against this backdrop, the reestablishment of the Sabbath after the Exodus parallels the first Sabbath after the sixth day of creation. As we have seen, this link between the reestablishment of the Sabbath with Israel and God's seventh day of creation is made explicit in the Ten Commandments (Ex. 20:8-11). The institution of the Sabbath after the Exodus is God's declaration that he has committed himself to meet Israel's needs, thereby restoring the same kind of sabbath relationship with Israel that existed between God and Adam and Eve in the garden.

Is God a merciful God who can be taken at his word? Has he recreated the conditions of the Garden of Eden for those who belong to him, albeit now within a fallen world? Is God really the sovereign "God of the Sabbath"? Can his people realistically rest in his promises? The answer to these questions, demonstrated by the three steps of provision that lead back to the Sabbath, is yes.

4

WHY CAN WE TRUST GOD, NO MATTER WHAT HAPPENS?

The Focus and Foundation of Faith

Do not be deceived, my beloved brethren.
Every good endowment and every perfect gift is from above,
coming down from the Father of lights
with whom there is no variation or shadow due to change.

JAMES 1:16-17

"Our father who art in heaven,
Hallowed be thy name."

MATTHEW 6:9

If creation itself declares God's power and deity (Rom. 1:20), the history of redemption demonstrates, without a doubt, that God is willing, able, and committed to lead, guide, and provide for his people. In Israel's case, coming to know God as Creator and Provider meant discovering, as Adam did in the garden, that the Creator is also the "God of the Sabbath" (see Ex. 20:8-11). God's sabbath rest is the advertisement he uses to publicize the significance of his first two acts of creation, the creation of the world out of nothing and the creation of Israel from among the nations (see chapter 3).

Hence, God declared through the prophet Ezekiel, "I gave them my Sabbaths, as a sign between me and them, *that they might know that I the LORD* sanctify them" (Ezek. 20:12, emphasis added). To be "sanctified" or "made holy" is to be set apart for some purpose. My grandmother used to have a set of "sanctified" dishes that were used only on Thanksgiving and Christmas. We knew they were different from all of her other dishes, that she had set them aside and kept them clean for a particular "holy" use. In the same way, God's reestablishment of the Sabbath with Israel was a sign that God had set Israel apart from all other nations as the one people to whom he would be committed in a covenant relationship. In turn, God demanded that Israel be "holy" by entering into a sabbath relationship with him. God would meet Israel's needs, but, unlike the nations around them, they must look to him alone to do so. God established the Sabbath with his provision; Israel was to keep it by her faith.

What, then, is "faith"? From the life of Abraham and the history of his descendants we learn that *faith is trusting God to do what he has promised because we are convinced by his provisions that God is both willing and able to keep his word.* Faith is therefore the only proper response to the One who is the Creator of the world (God is *able* to help) and the God of the Sabbath (God is *willing* to help). As such, it was faith in God's promises that rendered Abraham righteous before God as a covenant keeper, since it is faith that honors God as God by depending on his word no matter what:

> [Abraham] did not weaken in faith when he considered his own body, which was as good as dead because he was about a hundred years old, or when he considered the barrenness of Sarah's womb. No distrust made him waver concerning the promise of God, but he grew strong in his faith as he gave glory to God, fully convinced that God was able to do what he had promised. That is why his faith was "reckoned to him as righteousness" (Rom. 4:19-21, quoting Gen. 15:6).

To further illustrate the meaning of faith, let us rejoin Israel in the wilderness where we left her in chapter 3 in order to look at her first experience with God's sabbath commitment. As we do so, the nature, foundation, and focus of faith will become clear against the backdrop of Israel's tragic failure to continue trusting God for her life.

MANNA FROM HEAVEN AND THE CALL TO FAITH

When the account of Israel's departure from Egypt continues in Exodus 16, Israel is somewhere between Elim and Mount Sinai, two and a half months after the Exodus. By this time, the dramatic events surrounding her deliverance from Egypt have clearly demonstrated that God is able, willing, and committed to provide for her needs, even in the wilderness. But Israel is hungry, and there is no food in sight. So in a fit of forgetfulness (Ex. 14:31), Israel complains:

> And the whole congregation of the people of Israel murmured against Moses and Aaron in the wilderness and said to them, "Would that we had died by the hand of the LORD in the land of Egypt, when we sat by the fleshpots and ate bread to the full; for you have brought us out into this wilderness to kill this whole assembly with hunger" (Ex. 16:2-3).

Israel's murmuring shows that, despite their initial belief (Ex. 14:31), nothing has really changed regarding the hard-heartedness of the people. Faced with adversity, the people complain after the crossing of the Sea in the same way as they did before (compare Ex. 16:2-3 with 14:10-12). This all too "natural" response reveals that the people are blind to the point of the Exodus: since God *promised* to make of them a great nation, he *will* do so. Certainly, then, this promise must include doing whatever it takes to get them to the Promised Land. Nevertheless, the people conclude either that the Exodus was a perverse trick (i.e., God was not willing to save them after all), or that their current need has outstripped God's ability to provide. In either case, Moses has led them into the wilderness to die of starvation (Ex. 16:3).

At this point, God's great patience becomes readily apparent. Instead of destroying Israel for her lack of faith, God promises, in spite of her grumbling, to meet her need for food with manna, *one day at a time* (Ex. 16:4-5, 12).

Why only one day at a time, rather than giving the people the food they need all at once? According to Exodus 16:4, God does it this way so that he "may prove them, whether they will walk in [his] law or not." Like Abraham in Genesis 12, Israel's initial faith had given way to disbelief when faced with the prospect of starvation. And once again, as he did with Abraham, God had rescued them. Now the question becomes whether Israel, like Abraham, will respond by growing strong in her faith, giving glory to God (Rom. 4:20), or whether the nation will continue on its path of unbelief. At this point, the answer will be determined by Israel's response to God's law concerning his sabbath provision. For since the covenant with Israel at Mount Sinai has not yet been established, the "law" in view here cannot refer to the Ten Commandments or to the other statutes of the covenant. Rather, here the "law" refers to the stipulations God gives Moses concerning the manna itself: for five days a week, Israel may gather only enough manna for one day's provision (if the people gather more than that, it will spoil); but then on the sixth day they must gather twice as much in order to have enough for the Sabbath, when no work of gathering manna will be allowed (Ex. 16:5, 16-19, 21-23, 26). Having learned to rely on God's provision all week long, Israel should rest on the seventh day, knowing that the extra manna from the day before will not spoil, just as God has said.

Hence, God does not meet Israel's needs all at once in order to reveal through his commands whether or not their faith is real. The test, therefore, is simple. If the Israelites stockpile manna during the week, it is because they do not trust God to bring them more tomorrow. If they go out to gather more on the Sabbath, it is because they do not trust God's word. And this is just what happens. Although Moses commands the people during the week not to leave any of the manna until morning, "they did not listen to Moses; some left part of it till the morning, and it bred worms and became foul; and Moses was angry with them" (Ex. 16:20). Conversely, having seen the manna spoil during the week, they did not take a double portion at week's end as God had instructed them but went out to gather more on the Sabbath (Ex. 16:27).

Israel's disobedience to God's law concerning the manna showed her lack of trust in his provision and promises. By meeting Israel's needs one day at a time, God had called her to a life of faith. Israel's response made it clear, however, that unlike Abraham she would not heed God's call.

THE INEXTRICABLE UNITY OF FAITH AND OBEDIENCE

Israel's experience with the manna illustrates, by way of contrast, what it means to trust in the God who always proves trustworthy. It is apparent in reading this account that faith in God is an active dependence on his word that always expresses itself in action. The reason for this unity of faith and obedience as two aspects of our one response to God is that the promises of God are always organically linked to corresponding commands. Every *command of* God is built upon a *promise from* God. Therefore every divine call to action (obedience) is, at the same time, a divine summons to trust in God's promises (faith). The promises of God are commands in disguise, and vice versa. God commands what he commands because he promises what he promises. After the Exodus, God *promised* Israel that it would rain bread from heaven every day except the Sabbath. God therefore *commanded* Israel not to gather more than their daily ration, except on Friday. God's promise was inextricably linked with a prohibition. Conversely, trust in God's promise would mean obedience to his commands.

When the people subsequently refused to rest on the Sabbath, it was therefore a lack of *faith,* which, as we have seen, is the heart of sin. Disbelief always shows up as an act of disobedience, since every promise carries with it a command. Every time we disobey God it is because we are not trusting him. For this reason, when Israel fails to trust God's promise concerning manna on the Sabbath, God plaintively asks, "How long do you refuse to keep my commandments and laws?" (Ex. 16:28).

The Glory of God as the Assurance of Salvation

In addition to illustrating the nature of faith, Israel's disobedience makes an important point about its foundation (Ex. 16:4, 28-29). Why does God respond as if Israel should have known better? The answer provides an insight into the assurance upon which faith is built.

When the story of the manna begins, Israel had been in the wilderness only a short time. God's previous miraculous provisions were by no means a distant memory. Surely the track record of God's mighty acts in Israel's recent past provided assurance that God's commitment to her was firm. Israel's blindness to her own experience therefore angered God.

But Israel had an even greater foundation for her faith than the miracles; namely, the glory of God's character. God's commitment to Israel meant that his own reputation was on the line as she traveled into the wilderness. Given his covenant relationship with Abraham and his descendants, the fate of God's people reflects directly on his character. God's glory is at stake in the destiny of his people. Since, as he had with Adam and Eve in the garden, God had created Israel as a result of his own sovereign will, Israel's very existence and future as God's "son" (Ex. 4:22;

compare Gen. 5:3) directly reflected on God. If God called a people to himself, gave them great promises, demonstrated that he was more than able to keep them, and summoned them to trust in him for their future, but could not or would not keep his pledge, then God would dishonor himself. This, as we have seen, God cannot do (Isa. 42:5-9; 48:11). God's righteousness is revealed in his unswerving commitment to glorify himself by remaining true to his word. Once God *has* promised something, he *must* do it, for part of God's perfection is clearly his integrity.

This is why God was angered by the disobedience of Israel's disbelief in regard to the manna. Because of God's commitment to uphold the glory of his sovereignty and love, Israel should have known that God's provisions are sufficient and his promises unbreakable. "God is not man, that he should lie, or a son of man, that he should repent. Has he said, and will he not do it? Or has he spoken, and will he not fulfill it?" (Num. 23:19).

THE GLORY OF GOD AS THE BASIS OF MERCY

God's anger with Israel over breaking his law also points forward to the fact that, unlike Abraham, Israel as a nation was a "stiff-necked" people who remained hardened to God's promises and commands (see Ex. 32:9; 33:3, 5; 34:9; Deut. 29:4; Neh. 9:16-18; Ps. 78:21-22, 40-43; Ezek. 20:13, 21). Israel's disobedience in regard to the manna was therefore merely a preview of her upcoming sin with the golden calf, which would break the covenant from its very beginning (Ex. 32; Ps. 106:19-21). Israel's faith in God after the splitting of the Sea did not stand the test of time. Just as Adam and Eve broke the first Sabbath with their disbelief, so too Israel broke the Sabbath after the Exodus with their disobedience (Ezek. 20:16). Thus, just as the Exodus and its Sabbath parallels the Sabbath after creation, so too humanity's fall into sin in the garden finds its counterpart in Israel's fall into sin in the wilderness.

Yet, as with Adam and Eve in the garden, God is merciful to Israel as a people after their breaking of the covenant, not because of who they are (they deserve only God's judgment), but because of his righteous commitment to glorify himself. Indeed, down through the centuries, those who have known God best have appealed to him for mercy precisely on the basis of this understanding of why God acts.[1] Accordingly, when

Moses begged the Lord not to destroy the Israelites after their sin with the golden calf, he appealed to God's concern for his own reputation:

> But Moses besought the LORD his God, and said, "O LORD, why does thy wrath burn hot against thy people, whom thou hast brought forth out of the land of Egypt with great power and with a mighty hand? Why should the Egyptians say, 'With evil intent did he bring them forth, to slay them in the mountains, and to consume them from the face of the earth'? Turn from thy fierce wrath, and repent of this evil against thy people. Remember Abraham, Isaac, and Israel, thy servants, to whom thou didst swear by thy own self, and didst say to them, 'I will multiply your descendants as the stars of heaven, and all this land that I have promised I will give to your descendants, and they shall inherit it for ever'" (Ex. 32:11-13).

Note that in his pleading Moses reminds God not only of his prior promise to the Patriarchs but also that the Israelites are, in reality, *God's* people (compare this to God's earlier statement [v. 7] that they belonged to *Moses*). Moreover, since God's ability to save Israel has already become evident in the events of the Exodus, God cannot escape his identification with this wayward people. Moses argues, therefore, that Israel's destruction at this point would lead Egypt to conclude that God was not strong enough to keep his promise, or that his purpose in rescuing Israel had been evil from the start (see also Deut. 9:25-29). Moses knows God's heart. He knows God's concern to reveal his glory. He knows God's integrity. So Moses knows how to pray. And his prayer is answered (Ex. 32:14).

Similarly, centuries later, David, the man "after God's own heart" (see 1 Sam. 13:14; Acts 13:22), prayed for forgiveness for his adultery and murder by appealing to God's desire to glorify himself. Why else should God forgive David, except to display the wonder of his divine mercy? David, the murderer and adulterer, had nothing in himself to offer God. It is clear from David's prayer that God is his only hope:

> Restore to me the joy of *thy* salvation, and uphold me with a willing spirit. Then I will teach transgressors *thy* ways and sinners will return to *thee*. Deliver me from bloodguiltiness, O God, *thou God of my salvation*, and my tongue will sing aloud of *thy* deliverance (Ps. 51:12-14, emphasis added).

David recognizes that he is a sinner through and through. He looks to God alone for help and forgiveness, without presuming to call attention to any of his own "special" qualities or potential. Not even his identity as king counts for anything before God. David's prayer rests solely on the corresponding benefit of God's response *for God!* David argues that God's *merciful* response will cause others to return to God, while David himself will honor God with the praise appropriate for such a gracious act.

David prays in this way because he also knows God's character. He knows that God is a God of "steadfast love" and "abundant mercy" (Ps. 51:1). He also knows, however, that God demands justice and punishes the wicked, so that God would be "blameless in his judgment" if he should refuse David's prayer (v. 4). Nevertheless, David throws himself on God's mercy, trusting in God's covenant promise to forgive those who call on him for salvation. For he knows that if God were to deny such a cry for mercy, which is brought about by his own promises and character, he would be denying himself.

David's faith and prayers are built on the assurance that God, in accordance with his word, will maintain his glory by forgiving those who recognize their sin and depend on his mercy. Although he in no way *deserves* God's forgiveness, David can consequently be *confident* of it because of God's promise to be merciful to those who trust in him (see Ex. 34:6-7). God's commitment to display his glory not only in the judgment of the wicked but also in the redemption of the repentant is the refuge for sinners.

Thus, God's commitment to glorify himself in all he does is the basis of the prayer of the faithful. In Psalm 143, the psalmist therefore supports his plea for deliverance from his enemies by pointing to the fact that he is trusting in God. He does so because he knows that, in making this appeal as an expression of his dependence on God, the focus of attention is now on God himself:

> Let me hear in the morning of thy steadfast love,
>   for *in thee* I put my trust.
> Teach me the way I should go,
>   for *to thee* I lift up my soul (Ps. 143:8, emphasis added).

Notice how he supports his plea with this same idea in verses 9-10:

> Deliver me, O LORD, from my enemies!
> I have fled to thee for refuge!
> Teach me to do thy will,
> for thou art my God!

The prayer climaxes by drawing explicit attention to the fact that, because of the psalmist's decision to look to God alone for deliverance, God's reputation is now on the line:

> For thy name's sake, O LORD, preserve my life!
> In thy righteousness bring me out of trouble! (Ps. 143:11).

Since the basis of the psalmist's prayer is his faith, the ultimate purpose of his prayer is God's glory. As an expression of his faith, the psalmist therefore asks God to save him not for the psalmist's own sake (he knows that "no man living is righteous before God"—see Ps. 143:2; compare Rom. 4:4-5), but for the sake of God's *own* name. For whether in creation, providence, redemption, or judgment, God's purpose in all he does is to display and maintain his own glory.

For this reason, the psalmist's prayer for God to act for his own "name's sake" is paralleled by his prayer for God to act in his "righteousness." This parallel indicates that "the most fundamental characteristic of God's righteousness is his allegiance to his own name, that is, to his honor or glory"[2] (see, for example, Ps. 31:1-3; 79:9). A person is "righteous" when his actions are consistently "fair," that is to say, when he is guided by the same just principle in every circumstance, so that his behavior does not vary from one situation to the next. All things being equal, a judge who fines one driver $25 for going ten miles an hour over the speed limit and fines the next driver $125 for the same offense is not just or righteous.

God is righteous because he always acts in accordance with the same principle, which Psalm 143:11 makes clear is to preserve and show forth the magnificence of his own character. This explains how God can show mercy to some and condemn others and still be righteous: in both cases he is acting in accordance with his own character and maintaining his own glory (1 Sam. 12:6-8; Neh. 9:33; Ps. 33:4; 69:27; 88:11-12; 145:17; Isa. 5:16; 10:22; Lam. 1:18; Hos. 2:19; Rom. 9:14-18).[3] It follows, then, that the psalmist can conclude his prayer for help by asking

God to destroy his enemies—since both acts serve to honor God, who is both just and benevolent:

> And in thy steadfast love cut off my enemies, and destroy all my adversaries, for I am thy servant (Ps. 143:12).

Moreover, God's commitment to act for his own name's sake explains why the psalmist can support his prayer by pointing to the fact that he belongs to the Lord; for as we have seen, God's glory is on display in the lives of his servants, who are his servants *to begin with* not because of their own merits but because of God's righteousness, that is, his faithfulness to himself (Ps. 143:2). So the psalmist trusts in God to deliver him because he knows that God's love will be magnified by saving his faithful servant from his enemies.[4]

Thus, God's ways with humanity, whether it be the restoration of the rebellious, the judgment of the wicked, or the deliverance of the faithful, all flow from God's concern for his "name." In his sovereignty, God is not the "unmoved mover" of Greek philosophy but the "self-moved mover" of redemptive history. As a result, like Moses after the golden calf and David after his adultery, the Old Testament prophets realized that Israel's return from the judgment of the Exile would not be based on anything Israel could do for God but solely on God's commitment to preserve his honor. Accordingly, when Ezekiel announces the regathering of Israel from the nations, he makes it clear that, just as God had punished Israel in order to uphold his glory, he will restore his people for the same reason:

> The word of the LORD came to me: "Son of man, when the house of Israel dwelt in their own land, they defiled it by their ways and their doings; their conduct before me was like the uncleanness of a woman in her impurity. So I poured out my wrath upon them for the blood which they had shed in the land, for the idols with which they had defiled it. I scattered them among the nations, and they were dispersed through the countries; in accordance with their conduct and their deeds I judged them. But when they came to the nations, wherever they came, they profaned my holy name, in that men said of them, 'These are the people of the LORD, and yet they had to go out of his land.' But I had concern for my holy name,

which the house of Israel caused to be profaned among the nations to which they came.

"Therefore say to the house of Israel, Thus says the Lord GOD: It is not for your sake, O house of Israel, that I am about to act, but for the sake of my holy name, which you have profaned among the nations to which you came. And I will vindicate the holiness of my great name, which has been profaned among the nations, and which you have profaned among them; and the nations will know that I am the LORD, says the Lord GOD, when through you I vindicate my holiness before their eyes. . . . It is not for your sake that I will act, says the Lord GOD; let that be known to you. Be ashamed and confounded for your ways, O house of Israel" (Ezek. 36:16-23, 32).

As these passages illustrate, appeals throughout the Bible for God's mercy are directed toward the one guiding motive behind all of God's activity: his desire to portray and preserve the glory of his reputation as the God who is the sovereign Creator, gracious Provider, merciful Redeemer, and just Ruler of the world (see also Isa. 43:25; 48:9-11; 49:3; Jer. 13:11; 14:7, 9, 20-21; 33:8-9; Dan. 9:7, 13-19; John 4:34; 13:31-32; 17:4).

THE GLORY OF GOD AND HUMAN EXPECTATION

Furthermore, God's anger with Israel reflects the fact that because God is righteous—because he will always act to maintain his own reputation and glory—his people should know what to expect from him. If God makes a promise and his people trust him to keep it, he will do so; in fact he *must* do so, because of his righteousness. The psalmist looked forward to God's deliverance precisely *because* he trusted in God's sovereign love, which naturally included a promise to preserve his servants (Ps. 143:8-12).

This does not mean that we hold God hostage by our faith. God is not a prisoner of our faith, but of his own perfection. Faith obligates God to act not because it a magical incantation that can be used to control God but because faith in God's promises calls attention to God's own faithfulness. The assurance upon which faith is based is the glory of God's character, not the power of our believing. It only takes a "mustard seed" of faith to move any mountain God has promised to move (Matt. 17:20; compare Luke 17:6). Those who trust God's promises can be assured that God will act to keep them, since God will always act righteously; that is, he will not do anything to detract from his honor.

We expect no less in any relationship where a person of integrity has made a promise. By the time my son John was six years old he had figured out that if we promised to take him to the local ice cream parlor on Friday night, then no matter how tired we might be when Friday rolled around, we were going to go! If we hesitated, even for a moment, all he had to do was say, "You promised!" He had come to realize that we placed a high value on keeping our word (we were trying to imitate God to our kids—Eph. 5:1-2). We learned quickly never to make a promise we did not intend to keep.

In the same way, those who know God know that he is bound by his own promises and integrity, not by our wishes. Moreover, unlike us, God never finds himself in the uncomfortable situation of having made a promise he no longer wants to or is able to keep. God is never caught by surprise. God's promises are made in his infinite wisdom as part of his eternal plan and are backed by his matchless power. What God says, he does. God, because he is God, is a promise keeper (1 Kings 8:56). No wonder he was frustrated with Israel's lack of faith in his promise to provide the manna.

On the other hand, since God's promises are always granted as part of a covenant relationship, they are always tied to the covenant stipulations. If God makes a promise but his people do not trust him, God will eventually have to judge them in order to maintain his righteousness, as he did when he sent Israel into exile. But even then, as David and the psalmists presupposed and as the prophets pointed out, mercy triumphs in the end. Forgiveness and restoration, not judgment, are God's last words to the repentant. Ezekiel made it clear, however, that this too is an expression of God's righteousness, not of our worthiness. For this reason, and for this reason alone, both Israel and the nations will one day become Abraham's faithful descendants under a new covenant, despite their respective histories of rebellion (Isa. 2:1-4; 54:7-10; Jer. 31:1-37; 32:36-44; Rom. 11:11-16, 25-32).

This interplay between God's judgment and his mercy is clearly seen in God's response to Israel's continuing lack of faith, this time because of the "evil report" of the spies who had been sent out to investigate the "Promised Land" (Num. 13:32). In the face of Canaan's fortified cities and their towering inhabitants, all of the spies except Joshua and Caleb conclude that Israel is "not able to go up against the people; for they are stronger than we" (Num. 13:31). Believing this report instead of God's promise, Israel again plans to replace Moses with a new leader who will take them back to Egypt, concluding yet again that God had an evil intent in bringing them out of slavery (Num. 13:30-33; 14:1-4; compare Ex. 14:11; 16:3; 17:3). And when Moses, Aaron, Joshua, and Caleb attempt to persuade Israel that there is no reason to fear because God will be with them if they do not rebel, the people rise up to stone them (Num. 14:4-10). At this point, God intervenes in a way that summarizes the principles we have been highlighting:

> Then the glory of the LORD appeared at the tent of meeting to all the people of Israel. (11) And the LORD said to Moses, "How long will this people despise me? And how long will they not believe in me, in spite of all the signs which I have wrought among them? (12) I will strike them with the pestilence and disinherit them, and I will make of you a nation greater and mightier than they."
>
> (13) But Moses said to the LORD, "Then the Egyptians will hear of it, for thou didst bring up this people in thy might from among them, (14) and they will tell the inhabitants of this land. They have heard that thou, O LORD, art in the midst of this people; for thou, O LORD, art seen face to face, and thy cloud stands over them and thou goest before them, in a pillar of cloud by day and in a pillar of fire by night. (15) Now if thou dost kill this people as one man, then the nations who have heard thy fame will say, (16) 'Because the LORD was not able to bring this people into the land which he swore to give to them, therefore he has slain them in the wilderness.' (17) And now, I pray thee, let the power of the LORD be great as thou hast promised, saying, (18) 'The LORD is slow to anger, and abounding in steadfast love, forgiving iniquity and transgression, but he will by no means clear the guilty, visiting the iniquity of fathers upon children, upon the third and upon the fourth generation.' (19) Pardon the iniquity of this people, I pray thee, according to the greatness of thy steadfast love, and according as thou hast forgiven this people, from Egypt even until now."
>
> (20) Then the LORD said, "I have pardoned, according to your word; (21) but truly, as I live, and as all the earth shall be filled with the glory of the LORD, (22) none of the men who have seen my glory and my signs which I wrought in Egypt and in the wilderness, and yet have put me to the proof these ten times and have not hearkened to

my voice, (23) shall see the land which I swore to give to their fathers; and none of those who despised me shall see it. (24) But my servant Caleb, because he has a different spirit and has followed me fully, I will bring into the land into which he went, and his descendants shall possess it" (Num. 14:l0-24).

This passage makes clear that Israel's lack of confidence to enter the land was another in a long line of rebellious acts against God (Num. 14:9, 11). Just as he did after Israel sinned with the golden calf, the Lord therefore declares for a second time his intention to destroy the people and start over with Moses, thereby causing Moses to intercede for his people once more (Num. 14:12; see Ex. 32:10). Moses' response to the divine decree of judgment is the same as before: he appeals for mercy based on God's concern for his own glory (Num. 14:13-19; compare Ex. 32:11-13).

Moses' argument is airtight. If God destroys his people on the eve of their entrance into the land, the Egyptians will surely spread the word to the inhabitants of Canaan (Num. 14:13). At this point, God's reputation is spreading, since the nations now know that his presence is with Israel in the midst of the pillar of cloud and fire (Num. 14:14). Certainly, then, if God were to destroy the Israelites, the Egyptians would make a mockery of God's strength all the more, and the current inhabitants of the Promised Land would conclude that "Because the LORD was not able to bring this people into the land which he swore to give to them, therefore he has slain them in the wilderness" (Num. 14:16). Moses thus appeals for forgiveness on the same grounds as when Israel sinned with the golden calf. But now God's subsequent displays of grace can be added to the appeal (Num. 14:19), with God's corresponding promise to Moses (Ex. 34:6-7) taking the place of his promise to the Patriarchs quoted earlier in Exodus 32:13. Surely, Moses argues, God must continue to display mercy to Israel as his people.

It is not surprising, therefore, that here too the Lord grants Moses' request not to destroy the nation (Num. 14:20; see Ex. 32:14). But God's holy character must also be upheld (Num. 14:21; see Ex. 32:33-35). All those who have seen God's glory manifested through delivering Israel from slavery and preserving her in the wilderness, but who have nevertheless refused to trust him "these ten times,"[5] will not be allowed to enter the Promised Land (Num. 14:22-23).

The point is clear. There comes a time when God's patience runs out (Rom. 2:4-10; 2 Pet. 3:8-10; Jude 5). Those living in continual disobedience must not presume upon God's grace, falsely assuming that God's kindness means that he is winking at their sin. Nor should we take God's forgiveness for granted. We must not sin willfully, thinking that by doing so we are simply giving God another opportunity to glorify himself by showing forth his mercy. As Paul would put it centuries later, "Are we to continue in sin that grace may abound? By no means!" (Rom. 6:2). To do so is to reveal by one's hardened disobedience that the saving power of God (displayed at the Exodus and now manifest in Christ) is not a reality in one's life (see Rom. 6:2b-14). The writer to the Hebrews consequently draws a lesson from Israel's experience for all of God's people:

> Take care, brethren, lest there be in any of you an evil, unbelieving heart, leading you to fall away from the living God. But exhort one another every day, as long as it is called "today," that none of you may be hardened by the deceitfulness of sin. For we share in Christ, if only we hold our first confidence firm to the end, while it is said,
>
> "Today, when you hear his voice,
> do not harden your hearts as in the rebellion."
>
> Who were they that heard and yet were rebellious? Was it not all those who left Egypt under the leadership of Moses? And with whom was he provoked forty years? Was it not with those who sinned, whose bodies fell in the wilderness? And to whom did he swear that they should never enter his rest, but to those who were disobedient? So we see that they were unable to enter because of unbelief (Heb. 3:12-19).

Hence, from the wilderness generation, only Caleb, who has "a different spirit," and Joshua, since he too has God's "Spirit," will possess the land—because of their persevering faith-obedience (Num. 14:24-32; 27:18; see Deut. 34:9). The rest of Israel will wander for forty years in the wilderness as a result of her "wicked" nature as a "stiff-necked" people (Num. 14:35; see Ex. 32:9, 22; 33:3, 5; 34:9). Although the people mourned God's judgment (Num. 14:39), as they did earlier (Ex. 33:4), the narrative makes clear that their hearts remained hardened (Num. 14:40-45; 16:1-50; 25:1-5). Thus, as a sign of God's ultimate judgment on all those who refused to trust him with their lives, he immediately judges those who were directly involved in precipitating the rebellion, just as he did after Israel's idolatry with the golden calf (Num. 14:36-37; see Ex. 32:27-28).

In response to Moses' mediation, Israel as a people is kept from ultimate destruction. God remains merciful in accordance with his word. Nevertheless, as a result of their rebellion, God judges the wilderness generation for their hardened hearts. The same commitment to his glory that motivates God to have mercy also necessitates that he judge those who, by their continued disbelief, demonstrate that they "despise" him (Num. 14:11). God was merciful through Israel's "ten times" of disobedience, but there is a limit to God's patience (Matt. 24:43-44; 1 Thess. 5:1-6; 2 Pet. 3:10; Rev. 16:15). As the Lord declared through Ezekiel,

> "I led them out of the land of Egypt and brought them into the wilderness. I gave them my statutes and showed them my ordinances, by whose observance man shall live. Moreover I gave them my sabbaths, as a sign between me and them, that they might know that I the LORD sanctify them. But the house of Israel rebelled against me in the wilderness; they did not walk in my statutes but rejected my ordinances, by whose observance man shall live; and my sabbaths they greatly profaned.
>
> "Then I thought I would pour out my wrath upon them in the wilderness, to make a full end of them. But I acted for the sake of my name, that it should not be profaned in the sight of the nations, in whose sight I had brought them out. Moreover I swore to them in the wilderness that I would not bring them into the land which I had given them, a land flowing with milk and honey, the most glorious of all lands, because they rejected my ordinances and did not walk in my statutes, and profaned my sabbaths; for their heart went after their idols. Nevertheless my eye spared them, and I did not destroy them or make a full end of them in the wilderness" (Ezek. 20:10-17).

THE FOUNDATION, FOCUS, AND OBEDIENCE OF FAITH

As we have seen from the Sabbath in the garden to the Sabbath in the wilderness, God displays his glory primarily by keeping his promises to provide for his people. Moreover, *between* the promise and its fulfillment, God's people's continuing trust in him, despite the negative circumstances that seem to call his word into question, honors God's faithfulness. For this reason, it is our *faith* that keeps the covenant and is therefore reckoned to us as righteousness (Gen. 15:6). For faith is the covenant stipulation that flows from God's provisions and honors the integrity of his promises, thereby fulfilling his purpose of glorifying himself. When some of the people of Israel refrained from gathering more than one day's provision of manna, even though they were in the middle of a barren wilderness, their actions honored God as God by proclaiming his trustworthiness. Their obedience glorified God, not themselves, because it was based on his word, not their own resources or willpower. Trust in God's promises comes to light in obedience to his commands.

It is therefore crucial to see that God's commands do not stand alone. Rather, we noted earlier that God's covenant commands are "provisions and promises in disguise," since they are based on and incorporate what God has already done for us in the past (the covenant prologue) and has pledged to do for us in the future (the covenant promises). As inextricable aspects of the covenant, contentment in God's provisions, trust in God's promises, and obedience to God's commands do not and cannot exist without one another.

It is therefore a contradiction in terms to say that we acknowledge Christ's rule in our lives if we do not submit to his word. As Jesus put it, "Why do you call me 'Lord, Lord,' and not do what I tell you?" (Luke 6:46). There is no distinction in the Bible between knowing God or Jesus as our "Savior" and knowing him as our "Lord." Saving faith always expresses itself in obedience (James 2:21-24). The Bible is quite clear on this point:

> And by this we may be sure that we know him, if we keep his commandments. He who says "I know him" but disobeys his commandments is a liar, and the truth is not in him (1 John 2:3-4).

Trusting God and obeying God are not two *different* ways to relate to him, as if the former expresses a passive, emotional, or merely intellectual acceptance of what God has done for us while the latter is an active attempt to do something for God. Rather, faith and obedience are organically related aspects of our one response to God's grace. As in the "Great Commandment" (Matt. 22:34-40), faith may be oriented toward God ("love God") and obedience toward others ("love your neighbor"), but it is impossible biblically to say that we are trusting God's promises (loving God) if we are not obeying their corresponding commands (loving our neighbors).

This is why, when Jesus was asked for the one greatest commandment, he responded with two! He did so because the second, to love our neighbors as ourselves, is "like" the first, to love God with everything we are, which, given God's love for us, must entail trusting God's goodness and sovereignty in our lives (Matt. 22:39; compare Rom. 8:28). To love God *with* every aspect of our lives is to trust his love *in* every aspect of our lives. Ironically, then, we love God by relying on his love for us. Therefore, loving God cannot be separated from loving our neighbor as ourselves, since depending on God to meet our needs (loving God) sets us free to meet the needs of others (loving our neighbor).

To illustrate this important fact of biblical theology, we can take any of God's commands (all of which express what it means to love others) and ask what specific provisions and promises (all of which are expressions of God's love for us) it presupposes. For example, we have already seen how the sabbath command flows out of God's having met his people's needs in the past (the manna has come!) and anticipates his promise to meet their needs in the future (more manna is coming!). In the same way, the command "Repent and be baptized" expresses God's promise of forgiveness and the Spirit made possible by Christ's death and resurrection (Acts 2:38).

Indeed, with some reflection, every command from God can be seen to be a call to trust its corresponding promise as enabled by God's provision. Again: in view of his provisions, God commands what he commands because he promises what he promises. For example, what about the command, "You shall not kill" (Ex. 20:13)? What provision and promise does this commandment presuppose? I would put it this way: God has already shown himself to be just by his punishment of sin in the past, from the Flood to Israel's death in the wilderness to the cross of Christ. Moreover, God promises to judge all human affairs and to right every wrong when Christ returns. In the meantime, only the institutions God has ordained for this purpose as a reflection of his sovereignty have the right to take a life in judgment (Gen. 9:6). Loving God's sovereignty and his commitment to justice will therefore express itself in not taking affairs into our own hands, even to the point of not getting angry (Matt. 5:21-26). This is the argument behind Paul's words in Romans 12:19:

> Beloved, never avenge yourselves, but leave it to the wrath of God; for it is written, "Vengeance is mine, I will repay, says the Lord."

In other words, "you shall not kill" is a call to trust God's promise to vindicate our cause. As those created in the image of God, we reflect God's sovereignty and love in this regard by trusting in his promise to establish justice in the way that he, in his wisdom and timing, sees fit.

To give another example, what provision and promise stand behind the tenth commandment, "You shall not covet anything that belongs to your neighbor" (Ex. 20:17), the commandment that gets to the root of sin itself (Rom. 7:7-12)? If God *forbids* us to think that we would be happy if only we had something someone else has, must he not also be *promising* us that he will make us so satisfied and secure in him that we will no longer feel the envy that comes from discontent and worry? And in order for such a promise to be believable, must not our current relationship with God already bring with it such a satisfaction? In other words, God's command not to covet is based on the provision of his presence and the corresponding promise that he alone can satisfy the longings of our hearts. For God to say, "You shall not covet," is for him to say, "I will satisfy, trust in me." To covet is to disbelieve this truth, not loving God for who he is in himself. Moreover, as we saw in chapter 1, the "Ten Commandments" thus begin and end with essentially the same command (see again Paul's equation of idolatry with covetousness—Eph. 5:5; Col. 3:5). As with the command not to covet, the command, "You shall have no other gods before me" (Ex. 20:3), says essentially, "The God who delivered you from slavery in Egypt (Ex. 20:2) promises to be sufficient in all circumstances as your sovereign Provider, Redeemer, Lord, and Judge—so trust in him alone."

Put positively, keeping the command not to covet honors the all-sufficiency of God, since it expresses our trust that our deepest needs will be met in our relationship with God now and in his promises for our future, not in what this world has to offer. This is the example of Moses, whose pursuit of God and identification with Israel, even at the cost of great suffering, revealed that he "considered abuse suffered for the Christ greater wealth than the treasures of Egypt, for he looked to the reward" that only God can give (Heb. 11:26). And this is why the early Christians "joyfully accepted the plundering of [their] property, since [they] knew that [they themselves] had a better possession and an abiding one" (Heb. 10:34).

The life of faith is a continuous experience of "comparison shopping" in which we are "buying" with our attitudes and actions that which we think will really make us happy. The good news in obeying the commandment "Thou shall not covet" is that in doing so we will not be disappointed, since God is of more value than anything this world has to offer. This is why the fear of God, reflected in faith and manifested in obedience to his commands, is the beginning of wisdom (Gen. 22:12; Ps. 1; 2:1-22; 119; Prov. 1:7). Given who God is and the magnitude of his promises, Jesus is right: seeking God first and serving him alone is the only "smart" thing to do (Matt. 6:19-20; Mark 10:17-31; Luke 12:32-34).

In the same way, God's corresponding command that we "keep [our] lives free from love of money, and be content with what [we] have" is based squarely on the promise that "I will never fail you nor forsake you," so that we need not look to money for our security (Heb. 13:5). Instead, because of what God has said, we can say, "The Lord is my helper, I will not be afraid; what can man do to me?" (Heb. 13:6). This divine commitment is the same presupposition behind Jesus' command in the Sermon on the Mount that we "seek first his kingdom and his righteousness, and all these [materially necessary] things shall be yours as well." As a result, Jesus can command us not to worry about tomorrow (Matt. 6:33-34). For when God says, "You shall not worry," he is also saying, "I will provide." On the other hand, one cannot claim to love God and at the same time worry; the two are mutually exclusive (see Matt. 6:24).

The essential unity of faith and obedience therefore corresponds to the fact that the focus of faith is on God's *promises* for our *future*, while its foundation rests on God's *provisions* in the *past*. The provisions and promises of God bind the Creator to his creatures in such a way that they can be called to obedience in response.[6] Hence, from the standpoint of the Bible, to say that we "have faith in God" means that we are trusting in God's promises for our future because of what God has already done for us in the past. As Calvin said,

> We make the freely given promise of God the foundation of faith because upon it faith properly rests. . . . faith properly begins with the promise, rests in it, and ends in it.[7]

THE GLORY OF GOD AND THE LIFE OF DEPENDENCE

Finally, the inextricable relationship between faith and obedience means that when faced with the inadequacies of our lives as revealed in the contours of God's commands, the answer to our lack of faith is not found in ourselves. Since the flip side of obedience to God's commands is faith in his promises, the way to a transformed life of God-honoring virtue is not to work on our "willpower." The message of the Bible is not a self-help program; nor does it support the human potential movement or teach a Christianized version of the "power of positive thinking."

The good news of the Bible is that faith-obedience is simply our response to the great provisions and promises of *God,* who brings about and sustains our lives. *He* is the One who calls us to himself, supplies the power of his presence, and with his promises provides the motivation to trust-obey him, thereby granting us "all things that pertain to life and godliness," that we might become like him in his holiness (2 Pet. 1:3-4). *God* is the One who invades our lives with his *Spirit* and opens our eyes to the magnitude of his promises in *Christ,* so that we can't help but respond to his glory (see 2 Cor. 1:19-22; 3:18; 4:3-6). As a result, and only as a result, we are able to respond in faith-obedience. *Faith-obedience is brought about by God's provision of his presence and is sustained by a God-given focus on his promises.*

The Bible is clear about this. It offers us no hope apart from God. It has no illusions concerning an innate human goodness. It reveals with a shocking honesty that "the heart is deceitful above all things, and desperately corrupt" (Jer. 17:9). We are sinners not because we sin but because we are rebels by nature, imprisoned "under the power of sin"

(Rom. 3:9; see also Ps. 51:5; Eph. 2:1-3). Left to ourselves, "no one seeks for God" (Rom. 3:11; see Ps. 14:2) and "no one does good, not even one" (Rom. 3:12; see Ps. 14:3). On our own, we have neither a power, nor a potential, nor a right way of thinking adequate to produce the obedience God demands. Only a changed heart can bring forth a changed way of life (Mark 7:14-23). All attempts to "pull ourselves up by our own bootstraps" are doomed to failure. Rather than searching within our selves for the resources needed to live our lives, our only hope is to look outside of ourselves to God.

Thus, apart from the *provision* of the transforming power of God's presence, we will remain "dead" in our "trespasses and sins" (Eph. 2:1). Without God's *promise* to finish the good work he has begun in our lives we have no hope of reflecting Christ's character in our lives (Phil. 1:6). The *only* reason we can be commanded to "work out our own salvation with fear and trembling" is because "God is at work in us, both to will and to work for his good pleasure" (Phil. 2:12-13). Our hope resides in the fact that God delights in displaying the glory of his grace and power by taking sinners, just as they are, and transforming them into his own image (2 Cor. 3:18).

Though the focus of our faith-obedience is God's promises, the ultimate foundation of our faith is therefore God himself. The great provision upon which our covenant relationship is based is knowing God for who he is. For the way that God's "divine power has granted to us all things that pertain to life and godliness" is "through the *knowledge* of *him* who called us to his own glory and excellence, *by which* he has granted to us his precious and very great promises" (2 Pet. 1:3-4, emphasis added). Our knowledge of God himself is the means both to experiencing "his divine power" and to inheriting "his precious and very great promises." For the presence of God, not our own insight or willpower, evokes and sustains faith. This is why perfect faith exists in heaven, because there we will know God perfectly (1 Cor. 13:12). "Faith abides" forever (1 Cor. 13:13) because God abides forever and because, made in his image, we remain his dependent creatures forever. To be in heaven is not to cease to be human but to become perfectly human, which is to say, perfectly dependent on God himself in every circumstance as we join him in exercising dominion over his creation (Gen. 1:26; Rev. 21:22–22:5).

Faith therefore abides *forever* because nobody in God's presence would want to do anything else. It is impossible to know God and be in his presence and not trust him. Faith abides throughout eternity because it is the everlasting response of the person

> . . . who dwells in the shelter of the Most High,
>   who abides in the shadow of the Almighty,
> [who] will say to the LORD, "My refuge and my fortress;
>   my God, in whom I trust" (Ps. 91:1-2).

WHY DOES GOD WAIT SO LONG TO MAKE THINGS RIGHT?

"Saved in Hope"—Living for the Future

*If for this life only we have hoped in Christ,
we are of all men most to be pitied.*
1 CORINTHIANS 15:19

It was the game everyone looked forward to seeing, the Mets against the Rangers for the championship of the Upland, Indiana, Pee Wee "World Series." Could the Mets beat the team that had not lost a championship in three years? For my son and the other rookies nothing seemed impossible, not even this. After all, the Mets had Mike at first base, easily the best player in the league. And if his ability alone were not enough, due to some quirk in the rules Mike had magically turned nine years old while still in the league for six- through eight-year-olds. He was a towering giant. No one else had a *nine*-year-old, not even the Rangers. Mike's mere presence meant *hope*. Where Mike was, with all his ability, acquired maturity, and size (to a six-year-old, Mike was "big"!), hope for victory abounded. He was a walking promise of potential. It was inconceivable to have Mike on one's team and not have hope, even against the Rangers.

It was natural, then, that before the game began, all the Mets' six-year-olds hung around Mike, slapping each other on the back, laughing nervously, and looking to his cool disposition for comfort. After all, wasn't it Mike who had gotten the team to this game? The Rangers, fresh from some extra "late night" practices, looked very confident taking infield practice. But Mike was there in all his nine-year-old glory and strength. So there was hope.

But even a nine-year-old at first base cannot stop a fly ball to the outfield fence. The Mets lost in the last inning, their only defeat in an otherwise perfect season.

As I reflected later on the way that the boys responded to Mike's presence, I realized it was analogous to our relationship with God. Like the Mets, once we come to know that God is on our "team," that he is our Creator, Provider, and Redeemer, it becomes inconceivable for us to be in God's presence and not have hope. Of course the big difference is that, unlike Mike, nothing gets past God.

THE GOD OF HOPE

God's presence creates hope in us for essentially the same reason that my son had hope every time he saw Mike before a game. Since Mike had an ability to play baseball far greater than the other Pee Wees, and because his reliability had been proven again and again, Mike's mere presence brought with it an unspoken promise of victory. Because my son had come to *trust* Mike's ability and reliability, he had *hope* whenever Mike was in the game.

Similarly, just as it is impossible to know God and not have faith, so too it is impossible to have faith and not have hope. We trust God in the *present* because of what he has already done for us in the *past,* which leads us to depend on him for our *future.* Faith looks forward, not backward, but it looks forward precisely because of what is behind it. The foundation and focus of our faith are, respectively, the *provision* and *promises* of God.

Since the focus of faith is the promises of God, it becomes impossible to trust God and not have *hope for the future,* since a promise by definition is a pledge to do something that has not yet been fulfilled. This is true whether the promise is a boy's pledge to do his best at first base, God's promise to accompany Israel into the Promised Land, or Christ's promise never to forsake his people (Ex. 3:7-10; Matt. 28:20; Rom. 8:23; Titus 2:13; Heb. 9:28; 13:5). Thus, whenever we trust a promise, whatever it might be, doing so invariably rivets our attention on its *future* fulfillment. Moreover, when someone who can be trusted makes a promise, we begin looking forward to its fulfillment with a *certainty of expectation* that transforms hope from merely "wishful thinking" into a confidence for the future. We may hope it does not rain on the weekend, but this hope does not have the kind of assurance that accompanies hoping in our resurrection from the dead because of Christ's promise.

Hope in God's promises, therefore, is not a wishful longing but a faith-filled confidence for the future. It is simply impossible to trust one of God's promises and not anticipate its coming true. To know God is to trust him. And to trust God is to trust his promises. And to trust God's promises is to be sure of their fulfillment. This assurance concerning the future, anchored in God's promises, is what the Bible calls "hope."

Take Abraham, for example. Through Abraham's earlier experiences he came to know that God is both willing and able to do what he promised (see chapter 3). So when God promised Abraham that he would be the father of a great nation (Gen. 12:2, 7; 15:5, 7; 17:3-8), Abraham's knowledge of God led him to trust this promise in spite of the adverse circumstances that seemed to call it into question. In Paul's words,

> [Abraham] did not weaken in faith when he considered his own body, which was as good as dead because he was about a hundred years old, or when he considered the barrenness of Sarah's womb. No distrust made him waver concerning the promise of God, but he grew strong in his faith as he gave glory to God, fully convinced that God was able to do what he had promised (Rom. 4:19-21).

Because Abraham trusted God, he trusted God's promises. As a result, Abraham began to hope in their fulfillment even though his circumstances indicated that the situation was hopeless. As Paul pointed out, Abraham's own body was "as good as dead" and Sarah's barren womb was shriveled up (Rom. 4:19). His circumstances spoke *against* hope, but the promises of a trustworthy God spoke in favor of it. Consequently, to quote Paul once again,

> In hope [Abraham] believed against hope, that he should become the father of many nations; as he had been told, "So shall your descendants be" (Rom. 4:18).

Abraham's knowledge "that God was able to do what he had promised" produced faith in God's promise (Rom. 4:20-21). And Abraham's faith in God's promise provided hope in the midst of a hopeless situation. In fact, the link between faith and hope is so close that, as Paul puts it, faith is exercised *"in* hope" (Rom. 4:18). Moreover, Abraham not only believed *in* hope, he believed in hope *against hope* (Rom. 4:18)— against those circumstances that called his hope into question.

Abraham is Paul's model of what it means to have faith. Abraham's knowledge of God led to a conviction concerning the trustworthiness of his promises that in turn produced hope in the midst of the most adverse circumstances. Moreover, as Paul points out, it was this faith that gave glory to God (Rom. 4:20). As Romans 4:21 makes clear, faith glorifies God because faith is the result of being convinced of God's integrity. God is honored when his people are so convinced of the truth of his Word that they continue to hope when the situation seems hopeless.

GOD'S PURPOSE IN UNFULFILLED PROMISES

As we have seen, God's ultimate purpose in all that he does is to bring glory to his name. Faith and hope are the ways in which God glorifies himself in the lives of his people. He accomplishes the former (faith) by revealing his ability and trustworthiness. He accomplishes the latter (hope) by making the *object* of faith his *promises*.

This means that the life of faith is not primarily an experience in which our longings are immediately fulfilled. Instead, it is characterized by an expectation of what God *will* do as we continue to trust in him. "We walk by faith, not by sight" (2 Cor. 5:7). It is our confidence in the fullness of the resurrection glory still to come, not the suffering and second-rate pleasures that we see in the present, that determines how we live this side of Christ's return (see 2 Cor. 4:18–5:1).[1] But if God's promises were fulfilled immediately, then hope would no longer exist, nor would it need to exist. For "hope that is seen is not hope. For who hopes for what he sees?" (Rom. 8:24).

Given the fallen world and our own sinfulness, however, God's people have always struggled with the fact that trusting God in the present means having to hope for the fulfillment of his promises in the future. Nevertheless, God makes promises so grand that their final fulfillment cannot take place in the midst of this present evil age. Nothing this side of Christ's return can be confused with what God ultimately promises for his people. The short-term payoffs of this world pale in comparison to the "precious and very great promises" God grants his people (2 Pet. 1:4). God's promises cannot be downsized into the idols of temporary health and wealth. The promises of God are so much greater than anything this world has to offer that, when trusted, they fill a person with hope for what is *not yet* a reality but will one day certainly be true. Even our experience of God's presence is merely a down payment of the glory to be revealed to us in the age to come (Rom. 8:18; 1 Cor. 13:12; 2 Cor. 4:17; 1 John 3:2).

The magnitude of God's promises means that only God himself can bring them about, thereby saving us from the self-deception of thinking we can supply what only God can provide. The writer to the Hebrews therefore reports that, like the rest of God's people, Abraham "died in faith, not having received what was promised, but having seen it and greeted it from afar . . ." (Heb. 11:13). For "faith is the assurance of things hoped for, the conviction of things not seen" (Heb. 11:1). Indeed, hope is faith's

> inseparable companion. . . . hope is nothing else than the expectation of those things which faith has believed to have been truly promised by God. Thus, faith believes God to be true, hope awaits the time when this truth shall be manifested. Faith is the foundation upon which hope rests.[2]

LEARNING TO HOPE AFTER THE EXILE

Learning to hope in the unfulfilled promises of God is the lesson of faith that derives from the circumstances surrounding Israel's initial return from exile in Babylon, beginning in 538 B.C. This is a lesson that cannot be learned apart from God's redeeming, life-transforming grace. The history of Israel is the story of God's ongoing work to create a people who would trust in him. It is also the story of Israel's failure as a nation to maintain faith in her Creator, Provider, and Redeemer in the midst of adversity (see chapters 3 and 4). For as Israel's history unfolds, beginning even *before* the Exodus, it becomes evident that, although a remnant of the people did learn to trust God's promises, the nation as a whole remained hard-hearted (Ps. 106:6-43; Jer. 7:23-26; Ezek. 20:5-31[3]). As God warns Ezekiel, the people have always been a "nation of rebels" (Ezek. 2:3; see Deut. 31:24-29). At the Exodus, God delivered Israel from slavery circumstantially but he did not deliver the people as a whole spiritually from their slavery to sin (Deut. 29:4; Isa. 6:9-10; 29:10; Rom. 11:7-8; 2 Cor. 3:14). God eventually exiled them from the Promised Land as punishment for their faithlessness, just as he had banished Adam and Eve from the garden for their sin. As with the relationship at creation, the covenant at Sinai was broken from the beginning (Ex. 16:28; 32:1-20).

But just as God clothed Adam and Eve and promised redemption through the seed of the woman (Gen. 3:15, 20), so too the Exile is not the end of Israel's history. If Israel's experience teaches us anything, it is that "the LORD is merciful and gracious, slow to anger and abounding in steadfast love" (Ps. 103:8), a truth first declared after Israel broke the covenant in the wilderness (Ex. 34:6). Even in the Exile, God's mercy triumphed over judgment. The Exile was not designed to destroy Israel as a people. Rather, God had acted to preserve the honor of his name in view of the nation's rebellion. At the same time, he sustained the remnant of the faithful within Israel and reaffirmed his promise one day to deliver Israel as a whole from their sin of unbelief and from the self-destruction that their unbelief brought with it (Jer. 31:1-40; Ezek. 36:22-38). Isaiah 42:24-25 and 48:17-19 make clear that the Exile was "Yahweh's righteous judgment on Israel's sin . . . ; but it involved no surrender of his purpose (which would be an unimaginable dishonor to his name), for it was his intention, having purged Israel, to redeem (ch. 48:9-11)."[4]

The display of God's wrath in the Exile did in fact call out and purify a portion of the people, the "remnant," and strengthen their faith in God as their Creator and Provider (2 Kings 19:30-31; Ezra 9:8, 13). As Isaiah had prophesied,

> In that day the remnant of Israel and the survivors of the house of Jacob will no more lean upon him that smote them, but will lean upon the LORD, the Holy One of Israel, in truth. A remnant will return, the remnant of Jacob, to the mighty God. For though your people Israel be as the sand of the sea, only a remnant of them will return. Destruction is decreed, overflowing with righteousness. For the Lord, the LORD of hosts, will make a full end, as decreed, in the midst of all the earth (Isa. 10:20-23).

Clearly, restoration would follow rebellion for all those who repented in response to God's wrath (see, for example, Isa. 1:19-27; Mic. 7:18-20). God even promised to bring this remnant back to the Promised Land, in language reminiscent of his creation mandate to Adam and Eve in the garden and to Noah after the Flood (Gen. 1:28; 9:1):

> "Then I will gather the remnant of my flock out of all the countries where I have driven them, and I will bring them back to their fold, *and they shall be fruitful and multiply.* I will set shepherds over them who will care for them, and they shall fear no more, nor be dismayed, neither shall any be missing, says the LORD" (Jer. 23:3-4, emphasis added).

In the words of Jeremiah 31:7-9, recalling God's first deliverance of Israel from Egypt,

> For thus says the LORD: "Sing aloud with gladness for Jacob, and raise shouts for the chief of the nations; proclaim, give praise, and say, 'The LORD has saved his people, the remnant of Israel.' Behold, I will bring them from the north country, and gather them from the farthest parts of the earth, among them the blind and the lame, the woman with child and her who is in travail, together; a great company, they shall return here. With weeping they shall come, and with consolations I will lead them back, I will make them walk by brooks of water, in a straight path in which they shall not stumble; for I am a father to Israel, and Ephraim is my first-born."

Thus, in a "second Exodus" act of new creation, God himself would miraculously deliver his people from captivity and establish them in a restored land (Isa. 11:11-16; 43:16-21; 52:11-12). As a result, Jeremiah states,

> "Therefore, behold, the days are coming, says the LORD, when it shall no longer be said, 'As the LORD lives who brought up the people of Israel out of the land of Egypt,' but 'As the LORD lives who brought up the people of Israel out of the north country and out of all the countries where he had driven them.' For I will bring them back to their own land which I gave to their fathers" (Jer. 16:14-15).

In restoring Israel after the Exile, God's great covenant provision at the Exodus was to be replaced by an even greater act of God's redeeming grace. In fact, the restoration of Israel was to be of such grand proportions that the prophets used the most expansive imagery possible to describe it. Ezekiel likened it to a valley of dry bones suddenly brought back to life (Ezek. 37:1-14). Other prophets pictured it as a return to a paradise like that of the Garden of Eden, where peace would reign, crops would flourish without toil, ferocious beasts would be friendly, and justice would prevail as God's will was established and obeyed.[5]

Furthermore, after the Exile God would recreate Israel as a single holy nation, restore her independence under the reign of a Davidic king, revive a pure worship of God in a wondrously rebuilt temple, and raise Israel to a place of predominance in the world. Even the Gentiles would stream into Jerusalem to join Israel in the worship of God and to learn his Law as it goes forth from Mount Zion, the newly glorified center of a great kingdom of peace.[6] The promise included nothing less than God himself dwelling in the midst of his people, so that, as Ezekiel put it, the name of Jerusalem "henceforth shall be, The LORD is there" (Ezek. 48:35). In short, at the core of Israel's hope was the promise that "the central certainty of Israel's faith—'God is in the midst of us'—will one day be seen in blessed reality."[7]

The actual return from exile in Babylon, however, was a pale resemblance of what God had promised through the prophets! Rather than a miraculous intervention, in 538 B.C. God used the political policy of a pagan ruler, Cyrus, who was consequently identified as God's "messiah," to bring about the return to the Promised Land (see Ezra 1:1-4; 6:3-5; Isa. 44:28–45:1). And instead of a mighty throng triumphantly marching through a divinely prepared wilderness (see Isa. 40:3-5), the initial return under the leadership of Shesh-bazzar was so insignificant that Ezra skips right to the more substantial but by no means overwhelming number who came later with Zerubbabel (see Ezra 1:11–2:2). The expectation that God would establish Israel as a glorious, independent state that would reign over the Gentiles was replaced by the reality of a small, struggling city that lay mostly in ruins and was still dependent upon the Persian Empire for its survival (see, for example, Ezra 4:7; 5:17). "With even minimally modest expectations unfulfilled, how far short the reality was of the glowing promises. . . . As year followed disheartening year, the morale of the community sank dangerously."[8] As the prophet Zechariah put it, instead of the glories God had promised, it was a "day of small things" (Zech. 4:10).

Even the rebuilding of the temple, the focus of God's presence and center of Israel's worship, was only finished in 516 B.C. after twenty-two years of hard struggle. It was eventually completed not as a result of a direct, supernatural intervention from God but only because the Jews were able to convince the Persian superpower of its prior commitment to allow the temple's construction (see Ezra 6:1-12). Moreover, from the beginning of its construction, those who remembered Solomon's temple wept because of the new temple's paltry proportions (see Ezra 3:1–6:15 and compare Ezra 3:1-13 with 1 Kings 5:1-18).

Quite amazingly, during this same period the prophets Haggai and Zechariah continued to proclaim that God had not abandoned his people, even though the city was unstable and the temple was to be a mere shadow of its former glory. Haggai declared that God was still with them "according to the promise that [he] made you when you came out of Egypt" (Hag. 2:5). "In a little while" God would "shake" the earth and the nations, bring their treasures into the temple, and make it far more glorious than the previous one built by Solomon (Hag. 2:6-9). Though the beginnings were modest, Zechariah promised that God would once again dwell in the midst of his people, Jerusalem would prosper, and the nations would join Israel in worshiping the Lord (see Zech. 1:16-17; 2:10-12). Though still small and weak, those who had returned to Jerusalem were nevertheless God's people, the faithful remnant of Israel within the land (Hag. 1:12-14). God had not forgotten his promises, in spite of the fact that the present circumstances seemed to call them into question:

"Thus says the LORD of hosts: I am jealous for Zion with great jealousy, and I am jealous for her with great wrath. Thus says the LORD: I will return to Zion, and will dwell in the midst of Jerusalem, and Jerusalem shall be called the faithful city, and the mountain of the LORD of hosts, the holy mountain. Thus says the LORD of hosts: Old men and old women shall again sit in the streets of Jerusalem, each with staff in hand for very age. And the streets of the city shall be full of boys and girls playing in its streets. Thus says the LORD of hosts: If it is marvelous in the sight of the remnant of this people in these days, should it also be marvelous in my sight, says the LORD of hosts? Thus says the LORD of hosts: Behold, I will save my people from the east country and from the west country; and I will bring them to dwell in the midst of Jerusalem; and they shall be my people and I will be their God, in faithfulness and in righteousness" (Zech. 8:2-8).

Thus, the story of God's people after the Exile is the account of their struggle, like Abraham before them, to trust God's promises in the midst of adversity (Hag. 1:1–2:9; Zech. 1:16; 4:6-10; 6:15). On the one side stood the word of God. On the other stood the circumstances that called these promises into question. Yet God had already begun to keep his promises. The people had started to return to the land, a temple was built, and the city did make progress—evidence that God was at work on behalf of his people. Indeed, the fact that God even used Israel's enemies to bring this about was a further demonstration of his ability to keep his promises (see Ezra 4:1–6:12). Nevertheless, the history of Israel in the Old Testament ends with the promises of Israel's restoration after the Exile still largely unfulfilled.

THE OLD TESTAMENT PATTERN OF HOPE

As he did with Abraham, God made promises to Israel that he only partially fulfilled. Yet, also as with Abraham, God displayed his power in such a way that Israel could be assured of his continuing commitment to keep his word. So rather than losing their faith because of what God had not done, the faithful remnant among the people simply *redirected* their expectations into the future. The promises that were not being fulfilled completely in the present would be brought to completion at a later date. Thus, like Abraham, they "died in faith, not having received what was promised, but having seen it and greeted it from afar" (Heb. 11:13). The life of faith is a life of confident expectation concerning God's future acts of grace.

From Abraham to the initial return from the Exile, a pattern therefore emerges. God reveals his presence, displays his power to demonstrate his trustworthiness, makes a promise, and then only *partially* fulfills it. The *provision* is granted so that faith is established and sustained, but the object of faith, God's *promises*, remains unfulfilled. In short, God's promises are inaugurated but not consummated. During the history of redemption, the promise of God's presence is here but it is not yet here in all its fullness.

In his sovereignty, God purposely forestalls the fulfillment of his promises because he wants to foster not only faith but also hope. Promises are given but only partially fulfilled so that faith will flourish into an abiding confidence for the future. God instills hope in the hearts of his people by revealing enough of himself to sustain faith but not so much that faith's focus on the future is no longer necessary. God's delay in keeping his promises is therefore part of his great design to create a people who trust and hope in him. And because the promises of God are still to be fulfilled, "the believer becomes essentially one who hopes."[9] As the psalmist proclaims, "For thou, O Lord, art my hope, my trust, O LORD, from my youth" (Ps. 71:5).

The hope that results from God's unfulfilled promises must not, however, be confused with wishful thinking. Since hope in God's promises is based on faith in God's trustworthiness, the believer responds in the *present* to unfulfilled promises with a renewed conviction concerning their *future certainty*. God cannot lie. The promises *will* be kept; if not today, then tomorrow.

Hope, then, becomes the "anchor of the soul" in times of difficulty. Our confidence in what God will do in the future enables us to endure adversity in the present. The famous definition of faith in Hebrews 11:1 is therefore framed in terms of hope: "faith is the assurance of things hoped for, the conviction of things not seen." Faith is identified with an assurance and a conviction concerning what has not yet happened because faith in God's promises, based on the integrity of God's character, always gives rise to hope. The people of God have this hope not because they are naïve but because they "know whom [they] have believed" (2 Tim. 1:12). Hence, the history of Israel in the Old Testament calls us to maintain our faith in the Lord, "the hope of Israel" (Jer. 17:13), no matter what. For as we read in Psalm 78:5-7a,

> [The Lord] established a testimony in Jacob,
>   and appointed a law in Israel,
> which he commanded our fathers
>   to teach to their children;
> that the next generation might know them,
>   the children yet unborn,
> and arise and tell them to their children,
>   so that they should set their hope in God,
> and not forget the works of God.

THE RESURRECTION OF JESUS AND THE HOPE OF CHRISTIANS

Today, as Christians, we claim with the writer of Hebrews that Jesus Christ is the "initiator and perfecter of our faith" (Heb. 12:2, my translation), and that, as Paul said, "all the promises of God find their Yes in [Christ]" (2 Cor. 1:20). The foundation that makes the focus of our faith possible is therefore not only God's works on behalf of Israel but also, and more importantly, Jesus himself. We are people of the book and followers of the "Word become flesh" (John 1:14). Paul's reflections concerning Abraham once again can help us understand what this means.

In Romans 4 we read that the promise made to Abraham and his descendants—that they should inherit the world (v. 13)—is guaranteed to all those who "share the faith of Abraham, for he is the father of us all" (v. 16). But to trust God the way Abraham did we must, like Abraham, be convinced that God is both *willing* and *able* to keep his promises (Rom. 4:20-21). Faith is based on the conviction that God is powerful enough to do what he says, and that he is really committed to doing it.

In Abraham's case, this meant being convinced that God was both able and willing to remain true to his word that he had *already* made Abraham "the father of many nations" (Gen. 17:5; Rom. 4:17), even though Sarah's womb was barren. For Abraham, faith therefore entailed being convinced that God could and would bring life out of death—nothing short of a miracle! And in the words of Romans 4:17, Abraham trusted God's promise not as an act of self-generated willpower but

> in the presence of the God in whom he believed, who gives life to the dead and calls into existence the things that do not exist.

Even though the birth of a son from Sarah's shriveled womb and Abraham's tired body would be tantamount to giving "life to the dead," Abraham's knowledge of God made trusting such a promise possible: *"In the presence of . . . God"* Abraham "believed" (Rom. 4:17, emphasis added). As a result, "his faith was reckoned to him as righteousness" (Rom. 4:22; see Gen. 15:6) because it fulfilled God's righteous demand that his creation render him the glory that is rightfully his.

God's own character, expressed in his actions, is the standard of righteousness. As those made in his image, we are "righteous," therefore, when we mirror God's actions. God glorifies himself by keeping his word. We glorify God by trusting his word. Thus, in trusting God's promise, Abraham "honored him as God" (Rom. 1:21) because he was "fully convinced that God was able to do what he had promised" (Rom. 4:21).

But what about us? What must we be convinced of in order to trust in God's promises? Inasmuch as Paul says that we share the faith of Abraham, the answer must be that we too, like our "father" in the faith, must be "fully convinced" that God has the power to raise up life from the dead (Rom. 4:17). As Paul puts it, the same righteousness Abraham enjoyed "will be reckoned to us who believe in him that raised from the dead Jesus our Lord" (Rom. 4:24).

God's promises to his people are of such a magnitude that, in order to trust them, we must be sure of God's ability even to create life from the dead. As it was for Adam and Eve before the Fall, God's creative power is thus the foundation of faith, so that redemption is to be understood as an act of new creation (Isa. 43:1; 2 Cor. 4:4-6; 5:17). The good news is that the resurrection of Christ is faith-building *evidence* that God has precisely this kind of life-from-the-dead power.

But how can I be sure that, if I bank my hope on God's promises, God will be just as committed to engage his awesome power for me as he was for Jesus? Here too, Jesus himself is the answer to this crucial question: Jesus "was put to death for our trespasses and raised for our justification" (Rom. 4:25). Jesus' death establishes our relationship with God by bringing about the forgiveness of sins, while his resurrection guarantees that this forgiveness is real, sufficient, and permanent. In raising Jesus from the dead, God says yes to his promises for those who trust in him, just as he did for Jesus (2 Cor. 1:20). The resurrection of Christ from the dead is God's stamp of approval on Jesus' life and death as our messianic King, demonstrating clearly that on the cross the Christ was not being punished for his own sins but for the sins of his people (Acts 2:22-36; Gal. 3:13). The Resurrection vindicates without a doubt Jesus' claim to be God's Son and proves that his death was in fact the "ransom for many" that Jesus claimed it would be (Matt. 20:28; compare Matt. 16:21; 20:18-19; Mark 10:45; Acts 3:14-15; 10:39-43; 13:32-39; Rom. 1:4; 1 Pet. 1:18-21). With Jesus interceding for us as our "defense lawyer" before the judgment throne of God, no one can bring a charge against us (Rom. 8:33-34; 1 John 2:1).

Christ's resurrection, then, certifies that he is our Lord and Savior. It demonstrates the unmatched power of God, and, in view of the Cross, displays his willingness to engage it on behalf of those who trust in him. As such, the unleashing of God's power as Creator in the resurrection of Christ is the foundation of Christian hope. As Peter put it,

> Blessed be the God and Father of our Lord Jesus Christ! By his great mercy we have been born anew to a living hope through the resurrection of Jesus Christ from the dead, and to an inheritance which is imperishable, undefiled, and unfading, kept in heaven for you, who by God's power are guarded through faith for a salvation ready to be revealed in the last time (1 Pet. 1:3-5).

We may be assured of what God has promised to do in the future because of what he has already done in the past in raising Jesus from the dead. In turn, this hope, as the opposite of wishful thinking, is the power of the Christian life. As Dietrich Bonhoeffer observed from a Nazi prison, where he would soon die for his Christian convictions:

> The importance of illusion to one's life should certainly not be underestimated, but for a Christian there must be hope based on a firm foundation. And even if illusion has so much power in people's lives that it can keep life moving, how great a power there is in a hope that is based on certainty, and how invincible a life with such a hope is. "Christ our hope"—this Pauline formula is the strength of our lives.[10]

THE ROLE OF SUFFERING IN THE LIFE OF HOPE

The resurrection of Christ demonstrates that God can and will transform even the severest suffering into a glorious triumph. In view of Christ's resurrection, we too come to trust in the God who "gives life to the dead" (Rom. 4:17, 24). In the *present*, however, we must, like Abraham and the remnant after the Exile, maintain our faith in the midst of circumstances that seem to call God's power, willingness, and commitment to help into question, for the suffering and disappointment that color our lives, not to mention the relentless evil and pain that permeates our world, constantly speak against our hope.

It is not surprising, therefore, that after establishing the basis for Christian faith and hope in Romans chapter 4, Paul turns in chapter 5 to our suffering as Christians. Here he makes two important points. On the one hand, suffering does not cause those who are forgiven and justified to give up on God's *love,* even though at first glance suffering seems to suggest that God has given up on them. On the other hand, suffering does not force them to downsize their view of God's *power,* even though in the face of suffering it seems that, if God is good, then he must be limited in his ability to carry out his desires.

Paul asserts that the reason for this Christian confidence is that suffering itself, when experienced from the standpoint of faith, initiates a chain-reaction in which "suffering produces endurance, and endurance produces character, and character produces hope . . ." (Rom. 5:3-4). For the person of faith, suffering and disappointment do not lead to despair over God's love or discouragement over God's power, but to hope in God's glory as God (Rom. 5:2; 8:18; 2 Cor. 4:16-18). Thus, being convinced of God's sovereignty and love, even in the midst of afflictions, Paul calls God's people to *rejoice* in their suffering as an instrument for good in the hand of God (Rom. 5:3).

The Resurrection is such convincing proof that God is both willing and able to keep his promises that negative circumstances, far from causing us to despair, serve to strengthen our character and fortify our hope by providing a platform for faith (Rom. 5:1-4). As we discover that God works *all* things, no matter how severe, for the good of making us like Christ (Rom. 8:28-29), our security in him and consequent courage to face life's afflictions increases. Being called to become like Christ, we thus learn obedience in the same way Christ did, who, "although he was a Son, learned obedience through what he suffered" (Heb. 5:8).

In turn, the more Christlike character we develop, the stronger our hope becomes. When we are confident of God's sovereignty and love, the evil around us and within us causes us all the more to long for God's coming redemption, since, "according to God's promise we wait for new heavens and a new earth in which righteousness dwells" (2 Pet. 3:13). As a result, every suffering we experience in the present, when embraced in faith, produces a deeper hope for that time when, by his resurrection power, God "will wipe away every tear from their eyes, and death shall be no more, neither shall there be mourning nor crying nor pain anymore, for the former things have passed away" (Rev. 21:4). Our experience of evil and death in the present causes us to hope *even more* for righteousness and resurrection in the future. Hence, in Paul's words in Romans 5:2, having obtained access to God's grace through Christ (the covenant provision) we are confident of sharing the glory of God in the future (the covenant promise), so that, filled with hope, we rejoice in the present even in the midst of suffering (the covenant stipulation).

To many, however, such rejoicing in the midst of suffering still sounds like nothing more than pious wishful thinking. It is crucial to argue historically for the validity of the Cross by pointing to the Resurrection, but how does Paul know personally that his faith and hope are not merely unfounded optimism? And even if true, how can he be sure that God's forgiveness in the Cross and display of power in the Resurrection apply to him? What keeps his hope from simply being one more version of the power of positive thinking? In Romans 5, Paul goes on to give two persuasive answers to these questions.

THE HOLY SPIRIT AND HOPE

Paul's first answer is the Holy Spirit. Our hope as Christians

> does not disappoint us, because God's love has been poured into our hearts through the Holy Spirit which has been given to us (Rom. 5:5).

Our hope that God will transform our suffering into a platform for the display of his glory and a pathway to our happiness will not disappoint us because we have already experienced the first step in this process, namely, the granting of God's Spirit to us as a demonstration of his love. The gift of God's power and presence in our lives is his *personal* pledge that we belong to him (see also Rom. 8:9). My experience of the Spirit makes clear that God's objective display of his power to bring life from the dead, exhibited ultimately in the resurrection of Christ, is being directed toward *me*. God's love, poured into our lives, is thus a primary goal of his sending his Son. Jesus died on the Cross, was raised from the dead, and ascended to the place of authority in the presence of the Father, *in order that* he might pour out in the lives of his people the same Spirit that raised him from the dead (Acts 2:33).

But there is even more! The fact that God himself dwells in our lives by his Spirit brings with it two additional implications for our hope. First, our reception of God's Spirit means that God has "adopted" us as his "children," as a result of cleansing us from our sins, and in so doing has empowered us for a new way of life as members of his "family" (Rom. 8:14; see also Ezek. 36:25-27; Acts 2:38; 1 John 3:24). Paul can therefore say that "any one who does not have the Spirit of Christ does not belong to him" (Rom. 8:9; see also 1 Cor. 12:3). Furthermore, if we are God's adopted children (the covenant provision), manifest in our new Spirit-led obedience to our "heavenly Father" (the covenant stipulation), then we can be confident that we will inherit all that he has promised on that day when our "adoption" is complete (the covenant promise—Rom. 8:23; Gal. 5:5). This is what Paul means when he says we have been "sealed" in the Holy Spirit "for the day of redemption" (Eph. 4:30). Or, in the words of Romans 8:11-17:

> If the Spirit of him who raised Jesus from the dead dwells in you [COVENANT PROVISION], he who raised Christ Jesus from the dead will give life to your mortal bodies also [COVENANT PROMISE] through his Spirit which dwells in you. So then, brethren, we are debtors, not to the flesh, to live according to the flesh [COVENANT STIPULATION]—for if you live according to the flesh you will die [COVENANT CURSE], but if by the Spirit you put to death the deeds of the body [COVENANT STIPULATION] you will live [COVENANT PROMISE]. For all who are led by the Spirit of God are sons of God. For you did not receive the spirit of slavery to fall back into fear, but you have received the spirit of sonship [COVENANT PROVISION]. When we cry, "Abba! Father!" it is the Spirit himself bearing witness with our spirit that we are children of God [COVENANT PROVISION], and if children, then heirs, heirs of God and fellow heirs with Christ [COVENANT PROMISE], provided we suffer with him [COVENANT STIPULATION] in order that we may also be glorified with him [COVENANT PROMISE].

To possess the Spirit means that God has incorporated us into his covenant "family" as his legal heirs (Gal. 4:5-7). Thus, because we are his children, we not only experience his love for us in the present but also look forward to sharing in his glory in the future. God's children hope for their inheritance:

> See what love the Father has given us, that we should be called the children of God; and so we are. . . . Beloved, we are God's children now [COVENANT PROVISION]; it does not yet appear what we shall be, but we know that when he appears we shall be like him, for we shall see him as he is [COVENANT PROMISE] (1 John 3:1-3).

The second implication of having received God's Spirit is that God will never disown us as his children. The Spirit is God's "down payment" on his promises, thereby securing them for the future (2 Cor. 1:22; 5:5; Eph. 1:14). Just as a home buyer puts down a large sum of earnest money as a deposit to demonstrate his intent to complete the purchase, so too God grants us his Spirit as a guarantee of his commitment to buy us back from sin completely.

Conversely, once a buyer has emptied his savings to secure his mortgage with a down payment, the bank knows that he will do whatever it takes to finish the purchase, lest he lose his original investment. So too we can be sure that God, having poured out his Spirit in our lives, will do whatever it takes to ensure our redemption.

In view of the covenant relationship outlined in Romans 8:11-17, this divine commitment must include enabling us by means of his Spirit to "put to death the deeds of the body" and "to suffer with Christ" in order that we might live and be glorified with Christ as his "fellow-heirs," for no one will be able to stand righteous before God on the basis of his own abilities or accomplishments (Ps. 143:2; Gal. 2:16). The "down payment" of the Spirit is thus the basis for our assurance not only that we are his children *now,* but also that God will certainly grant us our inheritance in the *future* (Phil. 1:6, 10-11). Since all of God's commands are inextricably linked to his provisions and his promises, God gives by the presence and power of the Spirit (the covenant provision) the obedience that he requires (the covenant stipulation), in order that he might fulfill his covenant promises. The life of hope is therefore a life of faith, fueled by the Spirit, from beginning to end.

THE CROSS OF CHRIST AND THE HOPE OF CHRISTIANS

Paul's second reason for his confidence in his own resurrection and in the future restoration of all things is the *timing* of the Cross as further evidence of God's commitment to keep his word. The fact that God delivered Israel when she was still enslaved in Egypt was a signpost of his unswerving covenant commitment to lead, guide, and provide for her as a people.[11] In the same way, we too can be sure that God's promises will not disappoint us because, "while we were yet sinners Christ died for us" (Rom. 5:8). In the words of Romans 5:6, "while we were still weak, at the right time Christ died for the ungodly." If the exodus from slavery secured Israel's hope, how much more the death of God's only Son for sinners! The cross of Christ defies description as a display of God's unfailing love, since in our experience "one will hardly die for a righteous man" (Rom. 5:7), let alone for people as wretched and rebellious as we were before God rescued us.

The point is clear. God did not demand that we first demonstrate our allegiance to him *before* Christ would agree to die in our place. To demand that we somehow show ourselves deserving of forgiveness in order to regain our status as his children would have been futile. What can ungodly, rebellious sinners offer God that would move the holy Creator of the universe to sacrifice his only Son on their behalf? So God acted first, motivated solely by his own sovereign love, to grant mercy to his people as the ultimate expression of his grace (Ex. 33:19; Isa. 63:7; Rom. 9:15-18; Eph. 2:4; Titus 3:5; 1 Pet. 1:3). Christ died for us not *because* we were sinners but *in spite of* that fact (Eph. 2:4-6, 8). Christ died for us because the Father and the Son loved the unlovable.

That God loved the *ungodly,* so that Christ died for *sinners,* led Paul to draw a simple but profound conclusion:

> (9) Since, therefore, we are now justified by his blood, much more shall we be saved by him from the wrath of God. (10) For if while we were enemies we were reconciled to God by the death of his Son, much more, now that we are reconciled, shall we be saved by his life (Rom. 5:9-10).

In order to feel the force of this argument, we must realize that Paul's "much more" comparisons in this passage run from the more difficult cases to the easier ones (a so-called *a fortiori* argument—an argument "from the stronger"). The certainty of the conclusion is therefore based on the fact that the harder thing has already been accomplished. If God has already declared us *just* or *innocent* by virtue of his Son's death (the harder thing to do), then it is all the more certain that the Son will save us from God's *wrath* at the final judgment (the easier thing to do). The reason for this is stated in verse 10 (note the "for" that introduces the verse). If Christ *died* for us while we were still his *enemies* in order to bring about our *reconciliation* to God (the more difficult thing to do), then it is all the more certain, now that we are his *reconciled people,* that Christ's *life* (that is, his subsequent work as the resurrected Christ) will *deliver us* from God's judgment (the easier thing to do).

In other words, the hardest part of our salvation, Jesus' dying on the Cross for his enemies, has already been accomplished! The love and power it takes to present God's people pure on judgment day ("to save us by his life") pales in comparison to the love and power it took to die for us "while we were yet sinners." So Paul can conclude that if we have already been justified by Christ's death, we can be certain that Christ's life is sufficient to save us in the end.[12] In view of what it took for Christ to *make* us God's children, Christ will also do whatever it takes to give us our inheritance *as* God's children.

"He who did not spare his own Son but gave him up for us all, will he not also give us all things with him?" (Rom. 8:32). The answer, of course, must be yes! It is inconceivable that God would send his Son to die for people whom he did not fully intend to save from his coming judgment. For as we have seen in chapter 4, once God commits himself to a people, his own glory is wrapped up in their destiny. And since God's purpose in everything he does is to glorify himself, he cannot promise to rescue those who trust in Christ and then not do so![13]

The hope of Christians is therefore as sure and secure as the realities of the Cross and the Spirit. Together they certify that no circumstance or tragedy can thwart God's love (Rom. 8:35-39). Those who hope in God's promises cannot be disappointed. For our faith is not based on our love for God but first and foremost on God's love for us, a love demonstrated historically at the Cross (Rom. 5:8) and personally in our own lives through the Spirit (Rom. 5:5).

The Spirit convinces us that we are God's children; the Cross causes us to realize what it took for God to make us his children. Having become his people, we can be confident that God's promise to restore our lives is as sure as Christ's own resurrection (Rom. 6:4; 1 Cor. 6:14; 2 Cor. 4:14). This is so not only because the resurrection power of the Spirit enables us to put to death the sinful deeds of our body (Rom. 8:13) but also because the glory of God's grace is at stake in the destiny of those who have received his Spirit (2 Cor. 1:22). Thus, "If the Spirit of him who raised Jesus from the dead dwells in you, he who raised Christ Jesus from the dead will give life to your mortal bodies also through his Spirit which dwells in you" (Rom. 8:11). In response, we, like Paul, proclaim that "If God is for us, who is against us? . . . It is God who justifies; who is to condemn?" (Rom. 8:31, 33b-34a).

THE CERTAIN HOPE OF GOD'S PEOPLE

God's purposes have not changed. Just as he worked in Israel's history to teach his people faith and hope, God continues to work today to create a people who trust in his promises for their future. Christians after the Cross, like the remnant after the Exile, find themselves "saved in hope" (see Rom. 8:24). Rather than receiving immediately all that God promises them in Christ, God's people must still look to the future for the final fulfillment of the promise. Like all other people, Christians get sick, lose jobs, struggle in school, divorce, become perplexed, feel lonely, depressed, or disappointed, raise disabled and rebellious children, get into accidents. They also suffer the effects of natural disasters, corrupt political establishments, or ungodly economic systems. On top of all of this, they may be persecuted for their faith. Thus, from their own experience believers "know that the whole creation has been groaning in travail together until now;" and "not only the creation," but they themselves, "who have the first fruits of the Spirit, groan inwardly as [they] wait for adoption as sons, the redemption of [their] bodies" (Rom. 8:22-23).

But those who have received the "first fruits of the Spirit" experience such universal suffering differently than unbelievers. Their unfulfilled but certain hope gives them a perspective on their afflictions not shared by those who do not expect to inherit God's promises: they view their present suffering from the vantage point of the future. Instead of resignation, Christians meet their circumstances with an inward "groaning" like that of a woman giving birth, since they realize that the pain they are experiencing will one day give way to the glory of God (see also 2 Cor. 5:1-5). Sin and sickness are not the last word! Suffering is the pathway toward the believer's final redemption. Where the unbeliever sees a world filled with senseless suffering, the Christian sees suffering as part of the redemptive process that God has ordained to magnify his glory for the good of his people (see chapters 6 and 7).

Like the pain of childbirth, we know that our suffering has a purpose. Even when confronting our last enemy, death, we grieve, but not "as others do who have no hope" (1 Thess. 4:13). For with Paul, we "consider that the sufferings of this present time are not worth comparing with the glory that is to be revealed to us" (Rom. 8:18; see also 2 Cor. 4:16-18). Christians know where they are going.

Christians also know how they are going to get there. The crucified but risen Christ constantly reminds us that suffering is not a detour on the way to a glorious future. This is why James can command us to count all of our trials part of our joy, because we know that trials, by purifying our faith, produce the endurance needed to "be perfect and complete, lacking in nothing" (James 1:2-4; see also 1 Pet. 1:3-7).

Trials, when experienced in God's presence, strengthen our longing for God's coming redemption. Suffering weans us from this world and rivets our attention on the world to come. As we become increasingly convinced of what lies ahead, learning to trust God in every circumstance, suffering becomes a platform for perfecting our faith in the promise that "in everything God works for good with those who love him, who are called according to his purpose" (Rom. 8:28). In fact, as those who are "saved in hope" (see Rom. 8:24), we *must* love God by trusting in this promise if we wish to fulfill his purpose in calling us to himself. This brings us then to the subject of our next chapter.

6

WHY IS THERE SO MUCH PAIN AND EVIL IN THE WORLD?

Suffering and the Sovereignty of God

For why is all around us here
As if some lesser God had made the world
But had not force to shape it as he would?
ALFRED, LORD TENNYSON

Tennyson's question demands an answer. Even at four years old, my son Eric was aware of the problem. One day, when his older brother hit him on the forehead with a wildly thrown ball, I responded quickly with a word of comfort. "We can sure be thankful that God kept the ball from hitting you in the eye. Think of how God was watching out for you! He really loves you." To which Eric replied between sobs, "Then why didn't God stop the ball *before* it hit me?"

Another good question. It's the question raised by all of history. In the previous chapter we noted that the gap between the declaration of God's promises and their fulfillment is occupied with the suffering of those who are "saved in hope" (Rom. 8:24). Furthermore, we saw that God's people suffer not because God cannot or will not keep his promises of protection and provision, but because God has *purposefully* delayed fulfilling them.

So, Lord Tennyson and Eric were right to pose their questions. Most would agree that God *could* rescue us from all evil, but he chooses not to do so. God *could* prevent us from sinning in the first place, but he chooses not to do so. God *could* rule the world in such a way that the wicked are always immediately punished and the righteous always prosper, but he chooses not to do so. Indeed, God *could* have prevented sin and suffering from entering the world to begin with, but he chose not to do so.

But why create a world in which all living creatures must "groan in travail," yearning for redemption (see Rom. 8:22-23)? Why create a people who would end up needing to be rescued from themselves? Indeed, if God's purpose in all he does is to reveal his own glory in order that his creation might praise him (Eph. 1:3-14), why create a runaway world that defies his will, "as if some lesser God had made the world"?

SUFFERING AND GOD'S SOVEREIGNTY: THREE COMMON APPROACHES

Responding to suffering and evil, and eventually death, is *the* challenge of life. Eric was right. Faced with the horrendous evil that permeates our world, no problem is as perplexing and painful as the problem of reconciling God's absolute, sovereign power with his all-encompassing love. The existence of evil seems to force us to limit one or the other. If God is all-powerful, then he cannot be all-loving. If he is all-loving, then he must not be all-powerful. As John Hick put it, "If God is perfectly loving, he must wish to abolish evil; and if he is all-powerful, he must be able to abolish evil. But evil exists; therefore, God cannot be both omnipotent and perfectly loving."[1]

This is, as it is usually called, "the problem of evil." If God is both sovereign and loving, then evil, all evil, must somehow fit into God's ultimate, good, and perfect plan. But can we really conclude that the evil in the world around us, from genocide to child abuse, from cancer to starvation, is somehow part of God's sovereign and loving will for his creation? And can we *worship* such a God? Hence, "the problem of evil" also calls into question the character of those who worship God as loving and all-powerful. In the words of the eminent atheist Bertrand Russell,

> Apart from logical cogency, there is to me something a little odd about the ethical valuations of those who think that an omnipotent, omniscient, and benevolent Deity, after preparing the ground by many millions of years of lifeless nebulae, would consider Himself adequately rewarded by the final emergence of Hitler, Stalin and the H-bomb.[2]

Indeed, to the world outside of faith, believers do seem "a little odd." Faced with such a challenge, the most common contemporary response to the problem of evil among Christians is to reconcile God's love and power by redefining what it means for God to rule the universe. In this view, although God is sovereign, he *limited* the exercise of his power in order to create people as free and independent self-determining creatures. In our rebellion against God, we freely choose the sin that produces the suffering of our world. Our free will, not God's will, is thus responsible for the world's evil. As Greg Boyd summarizes it,

> . . . the potential for evil lies in the nature of free will. . . . Once God gave people this freedom, however, the purpose for their actions lies in *them*, not God. Since it was not settled ahead of time how people would use the freedom God gave them, God cannot be blamed for how they use it.[3]

Some of those who posit human free will as the source of evil even take the next step, like Boyd himself does, and conclude that, "The reality of sin and damnation, in other words, demonstrates that God's purposes do not always come about."[4] This limitation in God's ability to design, not to mention control, the future "allows us to say consistently in unequivocal terms that the ultimate source for all evil is found in the will of free agents rather than in God."[5] Moreover, according to the "openness of God" position (sometimes also called "free-will theism"), since people are truly self-determining, God cannot know with certainty the future choices of his free-will creatures until they make those choices. Though God may be able to predict our actions with amazing accuracy due to his wisdom, we may still surprise him at any time by doing the unexpected. God therefore responds to human choices after the fact, often changing his mind and course of action. In contrast, the classic "free-will" position (usually called "Arminian theology" after its first systematic theologian, Jacob Arminius, 1560–1609), posits that humanity is free, but that God still has foreknowledge of all things and thus responds to them "in advance" by virtue of being an "eternal being" who is outside of time.

Both views affirm, however, that God *could* stop us from making the wrong choices that lead to evil and suffering—but then we would no longer be the free persons God intended us to be. Although it leads to evil, God's *self-limitation* is therefore also *loving,* because it preserves the freedom that makes meaningful interpersonal relationships possible. As C. S. Lewis argued, God curtailed his own sovereignty in order to give mankind the gift of freedom,

> because free will, though it makes evil possible, is also the only thing that makes possible any love or goodness or joy worth having. A world of *automata*—of creatures that worked like machines—would hardly be worth creating. The happiness which God designs for His higher creatures is the happiness of being freely, voluntarily united to Him and to each other in an ecstasy of love and delight compared with which the most rapturous love between a man and a woman on this earth is mere milk and water. And for that they must be free.[6]

For most who adopt this free-will position, God is therefore still all-powerful but he has chosen not to interfere with the free will he has given men and women. In relationship to the world, God's sovereignty is an unrealized sovereignty, not an actual sovereignty. Evil exists not because God is limited in his power but because God has limited *himself* in exercising his sovereignty.

But despite this divine self-limitation in terms of his sovereignty, there has been no corresponding self-limitation when it comes to God's love (now defined in terms of empathy and emotion in relationships, rather than referring to God's superintending all things for his glory). Indeed, according to this view, God's love demands that he not exercise his power to its fullest extent. God's love trumps his sovereignty. Only in allowing men and women the freedom to choose evil does God make it possible for authentic love to exist.

The assumption here, from the free-will perspective, is that love can only exist where men and women are independent, free creatures who determine their own destinies by the choices they make. Thus, the most loving thing God can do is to limit the expression of his sovereignty in order to guarantee human freedom, even at the cost of Hitler, Stalin, the threat of nuclear war, and hell, the most horrendous evil of all. In this view, "the LORD reigns" (Ps. 99:1), but not over the destinies of men and women. And this is love.

Finally, some respond to the problem of evil by taking the free-will and "openness of God" positions one step further and denying God's sovereignty *itself*.[7] In this extreme view, God, being limited *by nature*, is in the *process* of growth and change just like his creation, so that God and his creation must cooperate and suffer *together*. In this "process theology," God is not sovereign over history but is just as influenced by history as we are, whereas in Arminian thought and in "free-will theism" God retains his ultimate sovereignty over the world, even if the creation of humanity has dramatically limited its force. In process thought, however, God "has big plans for the future of the world, but He can accomplish His plans only if the world cooperates."[8] In process thought, God is just as dependent on us for his future as we are on him for ours. In the words of Alfred North Whitehead, process theology's founding father, "It is as true to say that God creates the World, as that the World creates God."[9] How we respond to God will determine how God can respond to us and vice versa.

Hence, in process theology, human freedom and God's finite, temporal nature combine to "solve" the problem of evil. As Rabbi Harold Kushner put it almost twenty years ago in his national bestseller, *When Bad Things Happen to Good People,* "God can't do everything, but he can do some important things."[10] For Kushner, our comfort in the midst of suffering is not in God's absolute sovereignty but in knowing that, "if God is a God of justice and not of power, then He can still be on our side when bad things happen to us."[11]

In response to the problem of evil, free-will Arminianism (God does not determine our actions but nevertheless foreknows them), open theism (God does not determine our actions and therefore cannot foreknow them), and process theology (God cannot determine or foreknow our actions) all reject the idea that God is the ultimate, all-powerful cause behind all actions and events, circumstances, and decisions. God may be "on our side" and he may empathize with our pain, but is not sovereign over suffering.

For example, here is Boyd's answer to a woman who had prayed, fasted, and received confirmation from God through her circumstances that her marriage was God's answer to her desire for a partner in mission, but whose husband later abused and deserted her:

God felt as much regret over the confirmation he had given Suzanne as he did about his decision to make Saul king of Israel (1 Sam. 15:11, 35; see also Gen. 6:5-6). Not that it was a bad decision—*at the time,* her ex-husband was a good man with a godly character. The *prospects* that he and Suzanne would have a happy marriage and fruitful ministry were, *at the time,* very good. Indeed, I strongly suspect that he had influenced Suzanne and her ex-husband toward this college with their marriage in mind.

Because her ex-husband was a free agent, however, even the best decisions can have sad results. . . . Suzanne's ex-husband had become a very different person from the man God had confirmed to Suzanne to be a good candidate for marriage. This, I assured Suzanne, grieved God's heart at least as deeply as it grieved hers.[12]

Boyd's response makes clear that if the existence of free will is the key to suffering, God only deals in "prospects." God may "influence" us toward right decisions, but we can resist his grace, and even our initially right decisions often go awry. After all, who can control whether any of us will resist God's will at any time for any purpose? Even if God knows the future ahead of time, he cannot interfere with our choices without curtailing our freedom. And in the more extreme openness and process views, in which human autonomy means that God cannot know the future, God answers our prayers only in accordance with what seems good to him "at the time." If we are *truly* free, the future is *really* open.[13] Moreover, when this "open" view of God is extended to the point of including even his character, the process theologian must conclude that, "God wants the righteous to live peaceful, happy lives, but sometimes even He can't bring that about. It is too difficult even for God to keep cruelty and chaos from claiming their innocent victims."[14] Thus, according to Kushner, when the author of the book of Job is "forced to choose between a good God who is not totally powerful, or a powerful God who is not totally good, [he] chooses to believe in God's goodness."[15] From Kushner's viewpoint, like that of process theology in general, God's desires are loving, but he just does not have the power to accomplish them on his own.

The free-will, openness of God, and process theology positions feel compelled, in the face of evil, to conclude that God must be limited in the exercise of his sovereign power, as a result of either a prior self-limitation or the limited nature of his own character. Either God *will* not act to restrain evil or he *cannot* do so, even as he did not cause or allow it to take place in the beginning. In either case, evil exists because God is somehow not able, by decree, design, or nature, to ordain and providentially use it for his own glorious purposes.

It is my conviction that the Bible does not support such a conclusion. I am convinced that the Bible teaches that God is both omnipotent and omniscient regarding all events, as well as being loving in all that he performs. This can only mean, as the critics of my position realize, that

> if God is all good and always does what is best, and if God knew exactly what Hitler would do when he created him, we must conclude that God believed that allowing Hitler's massacre of the Jews (and many others) was preferable to his not allowing it. If you accept the premises that God is all good and all powerful and that he possesses exhaustively settled foreknowledge, the conclusion is difficult to avoid. . . . Though classical theologians have proposed a number of different reasons why God allows suffering, they have tended to agree that there is a specific divine purpose for every specific event, including specific evils.[16]

I do not shrink from such a deduction. I believe this is what the Scriptures teach. Moreover, I bank all my hope on it. My purpose here, however, is not to present an in-depth refutation of the free-will, open theist, or process positions (though I feel constrained to say that the latter two views are outside the bounds of orthodox Christian doctrine, since they advocate a limitation in God's character). Nor is this the place to enter into a detailed discussion of free will and predestination.[17] Rather, I have briefly presented these contemporary responses to the problem of evil in order, by way of contrast, to make my own approach to the problem of suffering as clear as possible.

SUFFERING AND GOD'S SOVEREIGNTY: A FOURTH APPROACH

From my perspective, the Bible teaches that God is *actively* sovereign over and *intimately* involved in directing the affairs of both mankind and nature. In Scripture, God's sovereign rule, and hence his foreknowledge (God knows all things in advance because he brings them about), encompass everything from the rise and fall of nations, the existence, decisions, and specific acts of rulers, the outcome of battles, and the disbelief and evil schemes of individuals (including the crucifixion of Jesus—see Acts 2:23; 3:18; 4:28), to the success and failure of crops, the movement of insects, the existence of storms on the sea, the granting of rain and drought, and even the perpetual coming of every new day and season.[18]

More importantly, the eternal destiny of all men and women is in the hand of God, who, yes, even predestines them according to his own sovereign will (Rom. 9:6-24; Eph. 1:3-6; Rev. 13:8). God foreknows his people not because he is outside of time but because he predestines those whom he subsequently calls, justifies, and glorifies (Rom. 8:29-30). Our faith, together with the grace of God that effects our salvation, is thus a gift of God, motivated by his love and sovereignly given as an act of mercy (Eph. 2:4, 8). Even our consequent obedience as Christians is brought about by the will and power of God in our lives (Ezek. 36:27; Jer. 31:33; Eph. 2:10) and is therefore best characterized as "fruit of the Spirit" (Gal. 5:22-23) or as the "fruits of righteousness which come through Jesus Christ" (Phil. 1:11). As Christians, we have been "chosen and destined *by God* the Father and sanctified *by the Spirit* for obedience to Jesus Christ" (1 Pet. 1:2; compare 4:11).

God is also sovereign over evil. In saying this, it is crucial to keep in mind that God is by no means the *direct* source of evil. Satan, evil spirits, and mankind are all held responsible for the evil in our world that comes about because of immoral intentions (James 1:13-14). Even natural evil is ultimately linked to the Fall and the curse on mankind in the Garden of Eden, which came about in response to the temptation brought about by Satan (Gen. 3:17-19; Rom. 8:19-22).

Nevertheless, evil exists in the world only because God ordained it as a necessary part of his master plan for the world. Thus, God actively controls its extent and purpose. Admittedly, this is not easy for us to comprehend. The reality of God's sovereignty over evil, however, is clear. For example, though Satan directly afflicts Job, he does so only in accordance with God's permission and limitations (Job 1:11-12; 2:5-6). And although Satan is the one who strikes Job, God responds by saying that Satan "moved me against [Job], to destroy him without cause" (Job 2:3), thereby declaring God's own sovereignty over the situation. As for Job, he responds in the same way when his wife urges him to "Curse God, and die" (Job 2:9) because of his suffering:

> "You speak as one of the foolish women would speak. Shall we receive good at the hand of God, and shall we not receive evil?" (Job 2:10a).

On the one hand, the response of Job's wife shows she knew that God was ultimately responsible for Job's suffering. On the other hand, Job's response to his wife shows his wisdom, since, as we saw earlier in regard to Abraham's offering up of Isaac (Gen. 22:12), the fear of the LORD is the beginning of wisdom (see Prov. 1:7). Thus, in recognizing and responding to God's sovereignty over evil, "in all this Job did not sin with his lips" (Job 2:10b). Like Abraham, Job depended on God's provision, even when that provision entailed evil and death.

Similarly, in 1 Kings 22:23, God is said to be responsible for sending a "lying spirit" into the mouth of the prophets." In response the prophet Isaiah, like Job, does not shrink back from proclaiming the Lord's sovereignty even over evil:

> "I am the LORD, and there is no other,
>   besides me there is no God;
>   I gird you, though you do not know me,
> that men may know, from the rising of the sun
>   and from the west, that there is none besides me;
>   I am the LORD, and there is no other.
> I form light and I create darkness,
>   I make peace and I create evil,[19]
>   I am the LORD, who do all these things" (Isa. 45:5-7).

This passage takes on even more significance once we realize that it is directed to the pagan king Cyrus, whom God is using to accomplish his divine purposes even though Cyrus himself does not know the Lord. Thus, no matter who the human authority might be, Lamentations 3:37-38 declares,

> Who has commanded and it came to pass,
>   unless the Lord has ordained it?
> Is it not from the mouth of the Most High
>   that good and evil come?

And Amos can proclaim, "Does evil befall a city unless the LORD has done it?" (Amos 3:16). Finally, this same recognition of God's ultimate sovereignty, even over evil, is reflected in Jesus' words to Peter in Luke 22:31-32:

> "Simon, Simon, behold, Satan demanded to have you, that he might sift you like wheat, but I have prayed for you that your faith may not fail; and when you have turned again, strengthen your brethren."

In answer to Jesus' prayer, Satan's desire to destroy Peter is cut short by God's sovereign power over evil—though God does permit Satan to tempt Peter to deny Christ three times. Here, as with Job, God is shown to be the One who directs the extent and path of Satan's ways. This is why Jesus instructs his disciples to ask *God* not to lead them into temptation, but to deliver them from the evil one (Matt. 6:13; Luke 11:4). God is not the *source* of evil, but he is Lord over its existence, scope, and intensity. "[God] himself tempts no one" (James 1:13), but no one is tempted apart from God's will. For this reason, because "God is faithful," Paul is certain that God "will not let [us] be tempted beyond [our] strength, but with the temptation will also provide the way of escape, that [we] may be able to endure it" (1 Cor. 10:13). God is sovereign even over Satan's schemes, and he will not allow Satan to shipwreck his people's faith.

Indeed, since God is sovereign over every event and circumstance, good and bad, "fate" does not exist. "Luck" is an illusion. "Chance" is a fiction. "In the end," as John Piper concludes, "one must finally come to see that if there is a God in heaven, there is no such thing as mere coincidence, not even in the smallest affairs of life: 'the lot is cast into the lap, but the decision is wholly from the LORD' (Proverbs 16:33). Not one sparrow 'will fall to the ground without your Father's will' (Matthew 10:29)."[20]

In listing this chain of verses from the Bible, I do not presume to remove the pain caused by evil and sickness. I know the heart-wrenching anguish that can be caused by suffering. I am aware of the persecution currently being inflicted on Christians around the world. I have seen firsthand some of our planet's worst poverty and have extended pastoral care to people in deep grief. So I do not assert God's sovereignty over evil in a frivolous fashion or without realizing how dark and demonic our world can be.

Rather, I affirm with a deep sense of awe and mystery, and with many unanswered questions, that God's sovereign hand stands behind the countless manifestations of evil in our world. It is with a deep sense of wonder that I read passages such as Exodus 4:11, where God responds to Moses' complaint that he has a speech defect with the solemn declaration, "Who has made man's mouth? Who makes him dumb, or deaf, or seeing, or blind? Is it not I, the LORD?" The most radical statement in the Bible is that there is only *one* God, which means that the "buck" must stop with him.

THE SOVEREIGN GOD AS THE GOD OF LOVE

Scripture is equally clear concerning the character of the one sovereign God. "God is love," which is why those who do not act in love toward others can be said not to know God (1 John 4:8). The God who is absolutely sovereign is also thoroughly loving. To assert that God sovereignly directs evil for his own purposes is therefore not to attribute a light and dark side to God's character. God is not sometimes good and sometimes evil, depending on his mood. God *always* acts in love, even when he was "moved . . . to destroy [Job] without cause" (Job 2:3).

God is all-loving in his sovereignty over evil because he allows, guides, transforms, and even designs it for a good and loving eternal purpose that far transcends the evil itself but could not be accomplished without it. Herein lies the mystery of creation and redemption. Since God could have prevented evil from ever taking root in the world, we must conclude that evil is an essential part of God's overall plan for creation. As Paul put it in relating God's wrath to his mercy,

> What if God, desiring to show his wrath and to make known his power, has endured with much patience the vessels of wrath made for destruction, *in order to* make known the riches of his glory for the vessels of mercy, which he has prepared beforehand for glory, even us whom he has called, not from the Jews only but also from the Gentiles? (Rom. 9:22-24, emphasis added).

These are hard, heart-stopping words. In the history of redemption it becomes clear that God hardens and softens hearts as he wills, like a potter shapes his pots for different uses (Rom. 9:17-21). And then, rather than showing forth the power of his wrath immediately, God endures throughout history the "vessels of wrath" destined for destruction (Rom. 9:22). Why? *In order to* make known the full riches of his glory through displaying mercy to both Jews and Gentiles (Rom. 9:23-24). Thus, God is all-loving precisely because everything, including his own wrath on evil, serves the purpose of his mercy.

In view of the witness of Scripture, therefore, we do not come closer to solving the problem of evil by diminishing God's active and purposeful involvement in any sphere of life. To remove God's sovereignty from the realm of evil *before* it occurs forces us to conceive of God either as playing "catch-up," by redeeming evil only after we have carried it out (after all, in this view, to intervene sooner would jeopardize our free will), or as standing on the sidelines, sympathetic in our struggles but unable to help. Apart from God's sovereignty, God's love in the midst of suffering is downsized to an emotional response of "caring."

To limit God's love to empathy is to leave the evil of our world unchecked and beyond God's control and hence without an ultimate purpose. If God enters into the affairs of history only after they take place, or merely empathizes with them from afar, then the evil itself remains meaningless. From this perspective, all we can say when evil strikes is that we happened to be in the wrong place at the wrong time under the wrong circumstances, all of which has nothing to do with God's will. Moreover, since evil is not just an occasional event but also characterizes the human heart, this means that God, for all intents and purposes, is fenced off from our entire lives.

Part of what it means to be "saved in hope," however, is to be convinced that suffering has a purpose as part of the process that God has ordained to reveal his character (see chapter 5). Therefore, "to love God" is to trust him in *every* circumstance, convinced that "in everything God works for good with those who love him, who are called according to his purpose" (Rom. 8:28).

THE CHARACTER OF GOD'S SOVEREIGNTY IN SUFFERING

In 2 Corinthians 1:3-11, Paul praised God because he was confident that God would comfort the Corinthians in the midst of their suffering (2 Cor. 1:6-7, 11).[21] The basis for Paul's confidence was his own experiences of God's comfort, which Paul received through being delivered from his suffering and through being strengthened to endure adversity when God did not remove it (2 Cor. 1:6, 8-10; 4:7-12; 6:3-10; 11:23–12:10). Hence, Paul's argument was built on his underlying conviction that God's sovereignty extends over *all* circumstances. For Paul, *God* is the One who leads him into suffering, sustains him in its midst, and delivers him from it, all to the glory of God himself, which is at the same time the eternal good of his people (2 Cor. 1:9; 2:14; 4:13-18; 12:9-10).

Clearly, then, to curtail the extent of God's power or purposes in the world is to cut off the possibility of comfort in the midst of adversity. The comfort that comes from God outlined in 2 Corinthians is not God's empathy as someone who feels our pain but is helpless in the face of tragedy. Nor is God's comfort the actions of a "fourth quarter quarter-back," brought in to save the day just before the final whistle blows. There is no comfort in suffering if God is not sovereign over it.

Against "downsizing" God in order to cope with the "problem of evil," Paul confesses that the ultimate divine purpose in suffering is the revelation of God's glory (2 Cor. 1:3, 11) *through* the sanctification of his people (2 Cor. 1:4-10). Consequently, although we cannot understand fully all of God's intents in the tragic events of life, it *is* possible to say that an essential part of God's purpose in all things is to honor himself by creating a people who, like Christ, trust him in every circumstance (2 Cor.1:9-10; compare Rom. 8:28-30 and Phil. 3:10 with Heb. 5:8). Faith in the midst of adversity thus derives from knowing that God's commitment to comfort his people is a reflex of his commitment to glorify himself.

Such a conviction, however, does not make evil less evil or sugarcoat it in any way. Evil is evil, not good in disguise. Instead, a high view of God's sovereignty allows us to affirm that the world is not running out of control (Acts 2:23-24; 3:18; 4:28). Nor is it at the mercy of human whim, ignorance, or political design (Acts 17:26). As C. H. Spurgeon observed over a century ago, this is at the heart of the good news of the Gospel (see Isa. 52:7):

There is no attribute of God more comforting to his children than the doctrine of Divine Sovereignty. Under the most adverse circumstances, in the most severe troubles, they believe that Sovereignty hath ordained their afflictions, that Sovereignty overrules them, and that Sovereignty will sanctify them all.[22]

For as John W. Wenham has rightly pointed out,

It is in fact cold comfort to say to a heart-broken person whose only child has been killed or whose husband has been fearfully injured: "This is not God's doing or God's will; we live in a disordered world in which evil has been let loose; we must expect these things where sin reigns; but keep trusting God." . . . How infinitely more comforting, more biblical and more glorifying of God it is to say with Amos in defiant faith: "If disaster falls has not the Lord been at work?" (Amos 3:6).[23]

Thus, in order to remain consistent with the Scriptures, it must be affirmed, in spite of the evil in our world, that God is both all-powerful and all-loving. Moreover, it is our highest moral duty and deepest joy to worship the God who rules our universe with wisdom (Ps. 99:1-3; 100:3-5).

SUFFERING AS A CHRISTIAN

Of course, the Bible never glorifies suffering of any kind in and of itself, since suffering is the result of sin. But Romans 8:15-17 makes it clear that we should not expect the Spirit to keep us from suffering, for in a fallen world it is part and parcel of the path to our future glory. As Paul pointed out, "through many tribulations we must enter the kingdom of God" (Acts 14:22).

What are the "tribulations" Christians face? Certainly, Christians experience suffering as a consequence of their own sins and as a result of living in a sinful world. But there are three other kinds of suffering Christians experience precisely because they have the power of the Spirit at work in their lives.

First, according to Romans 8:18-25, Christians experience the suffering that comes from expectation. Christians live in the presence of God's Spirit, who is the down payment of their glorious future (2 Cor.

1:22; Eph. 1:13). As a result, they experience a longing and an expectation not known by those outside of fellowship with God. Since they glimpse what life will be like when they see Christ face to face, in the meantime the unrighteousness of the present world weighs heavy on them. Having seen the righteousness of God revealed in Christ (Rom. 1:16-17), they are waiting "for new heavens and a new earth in which righteousness dwells" (2 Pet. 3:13).

The "normal" pettiness and pride of everyday life can be extremely painful to the person filled with God's Spirit. The believer knows there is something better. Indeed, he or she has already been experiencing it. Hence, as with a mother in labor pains, everyday life causes us to "groan inwardly as we wait for adoption as sons, the redemption of our bodies" (Rom. 8:23).

Second, because the Spirit is at work in the lives of Christians, they may suffer for doing what is right in a wicked world (1 Pet. 3:14-17). The more they become like Christ, having the "fruit of the Spirit" (Gal. 5:22-23), the less they are like the world around them. Inevitably, then, they will experience to some degree the same rejection that Jesus did for living a godly life in an ungodly world. "Indeed, all who desire to live a godly life in Christ Jesus will be persecuted" (2 Tim. 3:12). Jesus himself taught,

> "'A servant is not greater than his master.' If they persecuted me, they will persecute you. . . . But all this they will do to you on my account, because they do not know him who sent me" (John 15:20-21).

This does not mean that Christians are to be self-righteous troublemakers, who are spurned simply because they make a nuisance of themselves. Paul instructed his converts "to aspire to live quietly, to mind your own affairs . . . so that you may command the respect of outsiders" (1 Thess. 4:11-12). And he taught, "Repay no one evil for evil, but take thought for what is noble in the sight of all. If possible, so far as it depends upon you, live peaceably with all" (Rom. 12:17-18). Being obnoxious is not a fruit of the Spirit. Instead, as Jesus taught his followers, the Christian's primary purpose in the world is to "let your light so shine before [others] that they may see your good works and give glory to your Father who is in heaven" (Matt. 5:16).

As a consequence of this calling, the Spirit's work in our lives may often include suffering for doing right, inasmuch as being "the light of the world" (Matt. 5:14) will mean confronting evil in our spheres of influence. Those who seek to live in the "light" of God's presence are commanded to "take no part in the unfruitful works of darkness, *but instead expose them*" by their contrasting lifestyle and willingness to stand for the truth (Eph. 5:8-11, emphasis added; see also 1 Cor. 16:13; Gal. 2:4-5; Phil. 3:16-4:1; Jude 3-4; Rev. 2:2; etc.). We are also to defend the defenseless and those without rights (Deut. 10:19; 24:14, 17; Ps. 68:5; 146:9; Isa. 1:23; James 1:27). Conflict between light and darkness is at times necessary and unavoidable (see 2 Cor. 6:14–7:1). And in the midst of this conflict, it is usually the Christian, not the unbeliever, who will suffer.

Nevertheless, when attacked for their righteousness, Christians are to follow in the footsteps of Jesus, who by faith responded to such suffering by *not* responding. In the words of 1 Peter 2:22-23,

> He committed no sin; no guile was found on his lips. When he was reviled, he did not revile in return; when he suffered, he did not threaten; but he trusted to him who judges justly.

For this reason, Paul admonishes God's people to "never avenge yourselves, but leave it to the wrath of God; for it is written, 'Vengeance is mine, I will repay, says the Lord'" (Rom. 12:19, quoting Lev. 19:18). God's people refuse to retaliate not because they do not care about the truth but because they trust in God's promise to right all wrongs (see chapter 4). In the meantime, rather than fighting back, we are to do good to and pray for our enemies, thereby overcoming evil with good (Matt. 5:44; Rom. 12:14, 20-21). Though nothing will seem more foreign in our *self*-worshiping culture, drunk as it is with "standing up for our rights," those who follow Christ are to suffer patiently for doing the truth, all the while being concerned with the welfare of others, not their own (Lev. 19:18; Mark 12:31; Rom. 13:9; Gal. 5:14; James 2:8). For by fighting for the rights of others rather than for our own, we image forth God's character as our sovereign, loving, and just ruler!

Third, and not surprisingly in light of their call to be "the light of the world," Christians may be harassed and ostracized, or even imprisoned and killed because of their commitment to Christ in and of itself. Sometimes this suffering is very subtle. Being considered "weird" or "religious," and therefore no longer part of the "real world," is something many Christians put up with in school, at work, or in the neighborhood. But sometimes this suffering is not so subtle. From the very beginning, Christians have suffered severely for their faith, both socially and physically, often paying for it with their lives. The age-old dictum that "the blood of the martyrs is the seed of the church" is often true.[24]

Even in our time, as the Jewish human rights activist and Hudson Institute scholar Michael Horowitz has observed, "The mounting persecution of Christians eerily parallels the persecution of Jews . . . during much of Europe's history."[25] Worldwide, an average of 159,000 Christians a year are now losing their lives because they believe in Jesus, with 200 million to 250 million believers suffering physical and political persecution, and an additional 400 million not being able to practice their faith freely![26] And it is shocking how a scandal of silence has covered up this worldwide persecution of Christians.[27] Again, Horowitz reacts: "The silence and indifference of Western elites to the beatings, looting, torture, jailing, enslavement, murder, and even crucifixion of increasingly vulnerable Christian communities further engages my every bone and instinct as a Jew. My grandparents and those who lived with them in the ghettos of Poland would well understand the meaning, and the certain effects, of such patronizing hostility."[28]

At the same time, though we mourn this persecution and must resist it vigorously, it is crucial to recognize that such suffering is not the consequence of being out of God's will but is a direct result of the work of God's Spirit in the lives of his people. Thus, the apostle Peter, who was eventually martyred himself, can write,

> Beloved, do not be surprised at the fiery ordeal which comes upon you to prove you, as though something strange were happening to you. But rejoice in so far as you share Christ's sufferings, that you may also rejoice and be glad when his glory is revealed. If you are reproached for the name of Christ, you are blessed, because the spirit of glory and of God rests upon you. But let none of you suffer as a murderer, or a thief, or a wrongdoer, or a mischief-maker; yet if one suffers as a Christian, let him not be ashamed, but under that name let him glorify God (1 Pet. 4:12-16).

SUFFERING IN THE FOOTSTEPS OF JESUS

God's will for his redeemed people is that they become like Christ. To this end, the Spirit's work includes leading them into and through situations of suffering. Thus, we share not only in the effects of our own sin and of the fallen world around us but also in the suffering God sends to "[discipline] us for our good, that we may share his holiness" (Heb. 12:10). "For the Lord disciplines him whom he loves" (Heb. 12:6, quoting Prov. 3:11-12; see also Deut. 8:5; 1 Cor. 11:32; Rev. 3:19). In all of these experiences, God is at work to "conform" us "to the image of his Son" (see Rom. 8:29).

Again, this should not surprise us. If God's goal is to recreate Christ's character in us, then it is only natural that the way in which Christ "increased in wisdom and stature, and in favor with God and man" (Luke 2:52) should be our way too: "Although he was a Son, he learned obedience through what he suffered" (Heb. 5:8). Jesus experienced all of the "Spirit-led" sufferings we have outlined above. Jesus suffered the pain of expectation. He longed for the establishment of the kingdom and could even weep in sorrow over mankind's present state of rebellion and sin (Luke 19:41). Though he knew that Lazarus' death was "for the glory of God," he still wept at his tomb (John 11:35). Jesus also suffered the effects of a fallen world, from his temptation in the wilderness, to the temptation in the Garden of Gethsemane, to having to embrace death itself. And he suffered continuously for the sake of righteousness; indeed, his suffering on the Cross provides the perfect example of patiently enduring unjust persecution for doing what is right. Finally, Jesus suffered abuse, and ultimately even death, because of his identification with God. Jesus' claim to be God's messianic Son was the ultimate source of his rejection and crucifixion (see Mark 14:61-65; John 10:29-39; 19:7). Thus, precisely because Jesus was anointed with the Spirit as God's Son, he was led through a lifetime of suffering, culminating in the Cross (Matt. 4:1; 26:39-42; Mark 1:12; Acts 2:22-23; 4:27-29).

It is therefore not an overstatement when Scripture declares that Jesus learned obedience through his *suffering*. Furthermore, as Hebrews 2:10 points out, it was *"fitting* that God, for whom and by whom all things exist, in bringing many sons to glory, should make the pioneer of their salvation perfect through suffering" (emphasis added). Jesus' suffering was not experienced *in spite of* God's sovereign will but *because of* it. God, the One "by whom all things exist," made Jesus perfect through suffering. Hebrews 2:14-18 explains the divine reasoning behind Jesus' school of suffering:

> Since therefore the children share in flesh and blood, he himself likewise partook of the same nature, that through death he might destroy him who has the power of death, that is, the devil, and deliver all those who through fear of death were subject to lifelong bondage. For surely it is not with angels that he is concerned but with the descendants of Abraham. Therefore he had to be made like his brethren in every respect, so that he might become a merciful and faithful high priest in the service of God, to make expiation for the sins of the people. For because he himself has suffered and been tempted, he is able to help those who are tempted.

Clearly, Jesus did not suffer because the Father had limited himself so that Jesus could be free and independent. Nor was God empathetic but uninvolved in the course of Jesus' life and death. From the beginning of his ministry, the Spirit led Jesus into situations of temptation and weakness (Matt. 4:1). And when it came to his death, Jesus was "delivered up according to the definite plan and foreknowledge of God" (Acts 2:23), as "foretold by the mouth of all the prophets" (Acts 3:18). In crucifying Jesus, "both Herod and Pontius Pilate, with the Gentiles and the peoples of Israel" were gathered together at a specific time and place "to do whatever [God's] hand and [God's] plan had predestined to take place" (Acts 4:27-28).

Thus, Jesus' suffering did not make suffering obsolete for his followers. Instead, Jesus' example of faith in the midst of suffering becomes the fitting pattern for our experience as God's people. Jesus taught that "a disciple is not above his teacher, nor a servant above his master; it is enough for the disciple to be like his teacher, and the servant like his master" (Matt. 10:24-25). Inasmuch as Jesus learned obedience through the things that he suffered, suffering becomes the matrix in which we too learn obedience as his disciples.

But what still haunts us is why God would establish such a "school of suffering" in the first place. Why design a world in which Christ's suffering on our behalf does not bring an immediate deliverance from evil but causes us to suffer in his footsteps? What did Jesus learn through suffering that taught him obedience? What then are we to learn from our own Spirit-led suffering, in order that we too "might walk in newness of life" (Rom. 6:4)? These are the questions to be explored in the next chapter.

7

WHY DO GOD'S PEOPLE SUFFER?

The School of Affliction

For it has been granted to you
that for the sake of Christ
you should not only believe in him
but also suffer for his sake.
PHILIPPIANS 1:29

Although they may be surrounded by family, friends, and colleagues, most people live alone. That is to say, their world is empty of God. And without God in their world, there is no hope (Eph. 2:11-12). So when serious suffering strikes, driving them to despair, their cry of "Why me?" goes unanswered. Their resulting anguish creates bitterness against God and resentment of others, often unleashing a lifestyle of self-pity and self-indulgence. Without God in their lives, people see a world of senseless suffering and conclude, "What difference does it make what I do?"

SUFFERING AS A SCHOOLMASTER

But for those who have come to know God in Christ, suffering is the schoolmaster that God uses to raise them in faith and hope and to produce in them the perseverance needed to be saved (2 Tim. 2:12; Heb. 10:36; James 1:12). For Jesus predicted that as the Gospel is preached throughout the world, his disciples will face all manner of trials and tribulations, hatreds and wickedness, and death, so that "most men's love will grow cold" (Matt. 24:12). On the other hand, "he who endures to the end will be saved" (Matt. 24:9-14; see Luke 21:10-19; Rev. 2:9-11).

This is the point of Jesus' parable of the sower, the seed, and the soils

(Mark 4:1-20). The sower sows the word of God, the Gospel (Mark 4:14). But as soon as it is sown, Satan immediately snatches the seed from alongside the path, which represents those who hear the word but do not accept it. Other seed is sown on rocky ground, so that it cannot develop deep roots and soon withers away. These are the people who receive the word with joy *for a while* but fall away when tribulation comes (Mark 4:16-17). Still other seed is sown among thorns and is eventually strangled. These are the ones who hear the word, but "the cares of the world, and the delight in riches, and the desire for other things, enter in and choke the word, and it proves unfruitful" (Mark 4:18-19). In contrast, the seed sown in the good soil represents those whose reception of God's Word endures in the midst of suffering, whether it be the "negative" suffering of tribulation and worry or the "positive" suffering of materialism, both of which call God's promises into question. No matter what surrounds it, the good soil hears the word, accepts it, and produces fruit (Mark 4:20).

This is not a picture of three different levels of spiritual growth among believers, as if faith were a mere mental assent to the truth of the Gospel that may or may not endure and bear fruit in a life of faith. Rather, the parable depicts the difference between being a Christian and being an unbeliever. Though the "rocky ground" and the ground full of "thorns" both "receive the word" for a season, and even do so with "joy," the proof of being a true believer is perseverance. As the life of Abraham illustrates (see chapter 4), perseverance, not perfection, is the sign of saving faith (Heb. 6:4-8, 15; 2 Pet. 2:20-22; Rev. 2:4-5). Thus, different believers produce different amounts of fruit, some "thirtyfold," others "sixtyfold and a hundredfold," but all persevere and all produce fruit (Mark 4:8). In contrast, Israel's faith after the Exodus, though strong in the moment of the miracle (Ex. 14:31), soon withered in the midst of adversity (Ex. 32:7-10; Num. 14:20-22).

Jesus' parable makes clear that suffering serves to separate genuine faith from its counterfeits. Anyone can believe in a Santa Claus god. Suffering with Christ, however, destroys such a notion. If our allegiance to Christ's sovereignty and trust in his goodness are not deeply rooted in a heart that has encountered his all-surpassing glory, enduring suffering will become a burden too heavy to bear. On the other hand, suffering strengthens resolve and increases the value of Christ for those who, in response to the presence of the Spirit in their lives, genuinely trust God's love and power (see chapter 5). Rather than destroying faith-induced hope, suffering spurs it on. It is the fire that fortifies faith, stripping away the illusion of the world's glamour and gold and unmasking our powerlessness to solve our own problems or provide for our own security (Luke 12:16-21). Suffering therefore teaches us to esteem God's promises as our only hope.

Moreover, suffering as a Christian is a sign that God is powerfully at work in our lives. Longing for our final redemption, suffering for doing right, and being persecuted for our faith are all evidence that God has begun the good work of making us like Christ. Our suffering consequently becomes a great encouragement to our faith, since those who share in Christ's sufferings know that they will also share in his resurrection (Rom. 8:17; Phil. 3:10). In Jesus' words,

> "Blessed are you when men revile you and persecute you and utter all kinds of evil against you falsely on my account. Rejoice and be glad, for your reward is great in heaven, for so men persecuted the prophets who were before you" (Matt. 5:11-12).

And so Peter speaks of rejoicing "in so far as you share Christ's sufferings, that you may also rejoice and be glad when his glory is revealed" (1 Pet. 4:13), because it shows that "the spirit of glory and of God rests upon you" (1 Pet. 4:14).

As followers of Christ, we often suffer not because we are out of God's will but because we are in it, not because we lack faith but because we have faith. We suffer not because we need to be filled with the Spirit but because we already are. Stronger faith does not mean less suffering, but more suffering means stronger faith. Far from calling our faith into question, our afflictions result in our becoming more and more like Christ himself.[1]

SUFFERING AS A TASKMASTER

Make no mistake. Suffering in and of itself is not the revelation of God's power. Suffering itself is not glory, death itself is not life, nor is weakness power. The Bible never glorifies affliction. Rather, Paul makes it clear in 2 Corinthians 4:8-18 that deliverance from suffering, the power to endure suffering, and the renewal of our lives through suffering all take place *by God's grace and Spirit*. Paul's suffering as an apostle was *not* the glory of Christ; Christ's glory was mediated *through* Paul's suffering (2 Cor. 1:8-11; 2:14-16; 4:7-11; 6:3-10; 11:23–12:10). It is easy to get tripped up here. For instance, some of the early Fathers held to the idea that actively seeking martyrdom was the highest form of Christian witness. But this is a dangerous misapplication of the biblical view of suffering.[2] In the Bible, suffering itself is not intrinsically good nor a Christian virtue per se. It is not suffering *itself* that teaches us faith, so that seeking suffering becomes the way to holiness. Rather, suffering is a course in God's school of faith to use as *he* sees fit. How, when, where, to what degree, and for how long God's people suffer is up to God.

Furthermore, since affliction is not an end in itself, God's people can be sure of one of two things when suffering strikes: either God will deliver them from the affliction or he will comfort them in it, so that they might "patiently endure" (2 Cor. 1:6; see 2 Cor. 4:7-12; 12:7-10). In either case, God will not allow his people to suffer beyond what they can handle (see Phil. 2:27).

Again, we must be careful here. God did not rescue Paul in Asia (2 Cor. 1:8-11) or spare Epaphroditus from death (Phil. 2:27) in order to encourage others to seek a miraculous deliverance from affliction. Rather, these acts of deliverance were intended to encourage Paul and the rest of God's people to *endure suffering* in their *own* lives as a profound testimony to God's sufficiency (2 Cor. 1:6; 4:7-12; Phil. 4:6). This side of Christ's return, God does not reveal his power and love in our lives primarily by performing miracles but by enabling us to persevere in the midst of adversity because of our trust in him. God rescued Paul in the *past* to teach him to trust in God for his *future*, in order that he might endure in the *present* (2 Cor. 1:10 with 4:7-12). When Paul declared that he could "do all things in [the Lord] who strengthens me" (Phil. 4:13), he was not talking about displaying great acts of willpower or performing miracles of deliverance but about his God-granted ability to remain content and rejoice in the Lord "in any and all circumstances" (Phil. 4:11-12). In placing Paul in a situation where he despaired even of life itself (2 Cor. 1:8), the only thing God destroyed was Paul's self-confidence (2 Cor. 1:9). In return, Paul received God himself. In response, Paul praised God and called others to join him in doing so (2 Cor. 1:3, 11).[3]

But the type of endurance being spoken of here does not imply that we accept affliction or welcome death as normal parts of life.[4] Endurance is not acquiescence. Faith is not passivity. A refusal to complain does not mean embracing suffering as the way things ought to be. Suffering and death are part of the curse (Gen. 2:17; Rom. 5:12), not part of the creation. Death is an *enemy*, to be wiped out when Christ returns (1 Cor. 15:26). The Gospel is not a psychological coping mechanism but the promise of resurrection life in the future. We do not look the other way in the face of affliction. Rather, we tackle suffering head-on by trusting in God's promise of *future* redemption because of his *past* acts of provision. As a result, we are enabled to persevere in the *present*, with lives of transformed obedience (Rom. 8:1-39).

We must not be naïve, however. I am not suggesting some sort of superficial, syrupy, "Oh, Praise the Lord" response to the heartaches and tragedies of our world. The fight of faith is not easily fought nor is it quickly won. The dawning of the kingdom means that we are engaged in a spiritual warfare that demands vigilance and courage to stand with Christ in every situation (Josh. 1:9, 18; Ps. 27:14; 1 Cor. 16:13; 2 Cor. 5:6-8; Phil. 1:20; etc.). Suffering is a call to arms in which we are to match God's goodness and promises against our sin and Satan's evil (1 Pet. 5:8, 10). It is a time to test our convictions concerning God's word and to purify our faith in his power (1 Pet. 5:9). It is a call to draw closer to God than we have ever been before. "Cast all your anxieties on him, for he cares about you" (1 Pet. 5:7) is the battle cry of faith and hope in the midst of affliction. The psalmist who sighed, "My soul melts away for sorrow," also cried, "strengthen me according to thy word" (Ps. 119:28). The righteous one who suffers cries out in lament,

> . . . I am in distress,
>   my eye is wasted from grief,
>   my soul and my body also.
> For my life is spent with sorrow,
>   and my years with sighing;
> my strength fails because of my misery,
>   and my bones waste away (Ps. 31:9-10).

Yet he also confesses,

> But I trust in thee, O LORD,
>   I say, "Thou art my God" (Ps. 31:14).

In the end, then, although we must not sugarcoat suffering with pious platitudes, we must nonetheless wrestle through pain to a deep-seated praise of God's sovereignty and love. A profound joy in the midst of adversity is the mark of a true faith born of the Spirit (1 Thess. 1:5-6), since only God himself can sustain our faith and hope, and thus our happiness, in the face of distress.

SUFFERING AS A "BLIND DATE" WITH GOD: THE LESSON OF JOB

In a very real sense, then, suffering strips away our idolatry. The Cross and the Spirit lead us to faith and hope in God alone in the midst of affliction (Rom. 5:1-11; 8:31-39). In the words of the psalmist, "*God* is our refuge and strength, a very present [or well-proved] help in trouble" (Ps. 46:1, emphasis added; see also Ps. 18:30; 121:1-2). Thus, when the psalmist is in the pit of despair, acknowledging openly that "my tears have been my food day and night" (Ps. 42:3), his heart yearns for God himself:

> As a hart longs
>   for flowing streams,
> so longs my soul
>   for thee, O God.
> My soul thirsts for God,
>   for the living God.
> When shall I come and behold
>   the face of God? (Ps. 42:1-2).

Suffering drives us to seek God like no other experience this side of heaven. In the words of George MacDonald, himself no stranger to affliction and poverty, "Gladness may make a man forget his thanksgiving; misery drives him to his prayers."[5] We learn hope through what we suffer because suffering puts us in touch with God.

This is the greatest lesson of the book of Job. As its prologue indicates, Job's "very great" suffering, including the loss of his resources, servants, children, and even his own physical well-being, was not the result of his sin. Rather, Job's many afflictions resulted from God granting Satan's desire to test the genuine nature of Job's faith (Job 1:1–2:13, especially 1:8-12; 2:3-6). Satan suspects that Job trusts God only because of his circumstantial blessings, and consequently asks "the theological question of the book, 'Does Job serve God for nothing?' (Job 1:9)."[6] Job's suffering, God counters, will demonstrate that Job serves God for the worth found in serving God alone, but "only through pain and loss can this question of God's worth be answered."[7]

Job's initial responses to his afflictions prove God right. After the loss of his property and family, Job does not curse God to his face, as Satan said he would (Job 1:11), but reaffirms God's sovereignty and worships him as Lord:

> Then Job arose, and rent his robe, and shaved his head, and fell upon the ground, and worshiped. And he said, "Naked came I from my mother's womb, and naked shall I return; the LORD gave, and the LORD has taken away; blessed be the name of the LORD" (Job 1:20-21).

As we noted earlier, even after Job's suffering is intensified by his own painful sickness, so that his wife now joins Satan in advising him to "Curse God, and die" (Job 2:9), Job replies,

> "You speak as one of the foolish women would speak. Shall we receive good at the hand of God, and shall we not receive evil?" (2:10a).

Therefore, the author of Job can say, "In all this Job did not sin with his lips" (Job 2:10b).

What an amazing testimony of submission to God's sovereignty! Job does not worship God because God has prospered him but because he is convinced of God's supremacy. Job even thanks God for his sovereignty over evil. In the midst of affliction, Job "blesses" God (Job 1:21). God therefore declares to Satan in Job 2:3 that Job is a "blameless and upright man, who fears God and turns away from evil," because he "still holds fast his integrity, although you moved me against him, to destroy him without cause."

The prologue to the book of Job demonstrates that for the believer the *primary* question raised by suffering is not the problem of reconciling evil with God's goodness. Though this question is not ignored in the dialogues between Job and his friends, "the problem of suffering . . . provides the occasion for probing a much deeper question, namely, the character of man's relationship to God!"[8] Job's suffering moves us from the question of evil to see how, in *every* circumstance, God's people ought to meet their sovereign Lord. In this sense, suffering is like a "blind date" with God.

Job's "date" is going to have profound implications for Job's view of God's sovereignty. Remember, Job's friends supported the prevailing notion that suffering is a form of divine punishment. In their view, faithfulness is rewarded by prosperity while sin is punished by poverty, sickness, and hardships (see Job 4:7-11; 8:1-22; 11:1-6, 13-20; 20:29; 22:1-11; etc.). Yet as the psalmists lamented, the wicked often prosper and the righteous suffer (see, for example, Ps. 10 and 73:3-12). Job too points this out with dismay (see Job 21:1-26), and in the face of his friends' accusations that he must be suffering because of some hidden sin, he resolutely maintains his own innocence (26:1–27:23). Job is suffering *in spite of* the fact that he is righteous, not because he is wicked (see Job 9:15, 20, 21; 27:1-6; 31:5-40).

Job's integrity destroys the arguments of his friends. But eventually that same integrity becomes a platform for Job to challenge God's ways. In Job's suffering, God seems hidden and aloof, and Job cries out again and again for an answer; but there is no reply. The only replies are the misguided answers of his friends. As time passes, Job is tortured by God's silence in the face of his affliction (Job 13:22-24; 19:1-7; 23:3). "To Job, God's omniscience has become cruel, God's power an excuse for bullying tactics (Job 7:17-20)."[9]

For Job, God has become a capricious tyrant (9:18-19), a savage beast (16:7-9), a treacherous assailant (16:12-14), the source of terror (6:4), and an irresistible but unknown power that seems to delight in doing bad to humans (7:17; 9:5-13; 12:13-25). Under the pressure of unrelenting anguish, life begins to look meaningless, since Job's relationship to God no longer seems meaningful.[10] He even curses the day he was born (3:1-10).

Things now start breaking in Job. His original response of humble worship, which first *preserved* his integrity, gives way to pride and defiance precisely *because of* his integrity. Job's initial profound insight into

God's sovereignty now prompts his downfall. For under the pressure of continuing affliction, Job's conviction concerning God's sovereignty leads him to question God's goodness. After all, Job *was* righteous! Whereas Job's friends accused him of sinning, Job, knowing that his suffering did not come from his sin, accuses God of being unrighteous. Using the metaphor of a lawsuit, Job even threatens to take God, the judge, to court for his failure to keep the covenant (Job 9–10; 13:13-18, 20-24; 19:26-27; 23:2-4; 29–31; 42:5).[11] Like the psalmist, Job longs to see God face to face because of his suffering—not, however, to gain strength from God's presence but to serve God with a "covenant lawsuit." Unlike the prophets, who put Israel "on trial" for her failure to be faithful to the covenant, Job now makes God the defendant. It appears as if Job's suffering leaves him no choice: if he was faithful, then God must be unfaithful; if he was righteous, then God must not be. If God cannot answer this charge, he is not worth serving and death becomes preferable to life (9:1-13; 10:18-22).

Yet even his desire to take God to court shows that Job has nowhere else to go. Job knows that, when all is said and done, though he is distraught with God beyond despair, God alone is his only hope for redemption (19:25-27). *The option is not to stop believing in God, but to rethink what kind of God must be believed in.* Job's suffering, therefore, does not drive him away from God but relentlessly toward God in search of answers.

But when God finally answers, it is not what Job expected (Job 38:1–42:6). "Out of the whirlwind" (Job 38:1) Job does not hear an apology for his suffering, or a reason for its duration, or an explanation of its course. Job never learns about the dialogue in heaven between God and Satan. Apparently none of this was Job's business. He was simply to trust God's will. Nor does God respond to Job's harping about his innocence. Job's innocence was never in question. The issue was not, from God's standpoint, that Job suffered "without cause" (Job 2:3). The problem was that Job did not realize what it meant for God to be God. It was not Job's place to know God's purposes or to question God's ways. The real issue to be solved "in court" was not God's faithfulness to his covenant but Job's growing defiance against his sovereign Lord.[12]

Thus, when Job encounters God, he hears one of the most sustained presentations of God's sovereignty, wisdom, and power found in the

Bible (Job 38:4–41:34). In it, God censures Job's criticism with question after question:

> "Where were you when I laid the foundation of the earth?
>   Tell me, if you have understanding" (Job 38:4).

> "Have you commanded the morning since your days began,
>   and caused the dawn to know its place?" (Job 38:12).

> "Have the gates of death been revealed to you,
>   or have you seen the gates of deep darkness?" (Job 38:17).

> "Do you know the ordinances of the heavens?
>   Can you establish their rule on the earth?" (Job 38:33).

> "Is it by your wisdom that the hawk soars. . . .
>   Is it at your command that the eagle mounts up?" (Job 39:26-27).

> "Have you an arm like God?" (Job 40:9).

Of course, Job cannot answer God's questions. And after each question God declares his own might and majesty. The overall effect is to leave no doubt not only that God is supremely sovereign as Creator and Sustainer but also that he has a purpose for all that he does—though it is often beyond what his creatures can comprehend. So when finally confronted with God himself, Job is at a loss to speak (compare Job 31:35 to 38:2-3 and 40:3-5). Chastised, Job is put in his place as a creature wholly dependent on his Creator for all things. Being struck dumb by God's presence, Job drops his "lawsuit" against the Almighty.

Job's sin was not his insistence that he was innocent. He had been. Job's sin was making his innocence a basis for complaint and the ground of his hope for redemption. Even godly virtue, when viewed as entitling us to certain "rights" with God, can become an idol. God, the source of our virtue, is not subservient to it. As Bernard Anderson has insightfully pointed out,

> Job had been talking as if he knew exactly how God should run the world. His sense of integrity had been the basis of his presumptuous claim that God should have treated *him* better. Outraged that he could not square his innocence with his fate, Job had dared to challenge and

judge his Creator. . . . [therefore] Yahweh's answer came in the form
of a rebuke—an overwhelming reminder that the first religious obli-
gation of the creature is to acknowledge and glorify the Creator.[13]

Job learned his lesson (see Job 40:3-5). While Satan poses the theological question of the book (Job 1:9), Job's famous words of repentance become its answer:

> "I know that thou canst do all things, and that no purpose of thine
> can be thwarted. . . . Therefore I have uttered what I did not under-
> stand, things too wonderful for me, which I did not know. . . . I had
> heard of thee by the hearing of the ear, but now my eye sees thee, there-
> fore I despise myself, and repent in dust and ashes" (Job 42:2-6).

Humble words. Powerful words. They leave no loophole for any
part of God's universe to be outside his will. What makes them even
more amazing is that they are the words of someone who is still severely
suffering. At this point in the story, Job's grim circumstances have not
changed. In another respect, however, everything has changed, for Job
has met *God*. This is Job's ultimate "answer" to his suffering. The
"why" of his suffering is not answered. But the purpose of suffering
becomes clear: encountering God as sovereign Lord and Master, the
architect of the universe. To quote Anderson once again,

> The crux of the human problem, according to Israel's faith, is not the
> fact of suffering but the character of man's relationship to God.
> Outside the relationship for which man was created, suffering drives
> men to despair or to the easy solutions of popular religion. Within the
> relationship of faith, suffering may be faced in the confidence that
> man's times are in God's hands and that "in everything God works for
> good with those who love him, who are called according to his pur-
> pose" (Rom. 8:28).[14]

Hence, it is only *after* Job's encounter with God and only after Job's
consequent repentance that God restores Job's fortunes by prospering him
with "twice as much as he had before" (Job 42:10). In addition, he
answers Job's prayers for his friends (those who know God can love even
their former accusers!). But now these blessings take on a different qual-
ity. Having encountered God in his sovereignty, Job realizes that this bless-

ing is a matter of God's free grace and mercy, pure and simple. Readers of Job see that the real restoration of Job's "wealth" is his increased knowledge of God himself, not his material blessings. In and through Job's suffering and restoration, God has worked all things together for good (Rom. 8:28). The restoration of Job's fortunes is an Old Testament picture of the final redemption awaited by all of God's people.

Nevertheless, the focus of the book is not on the restoration of Job's circumstances but on God's sovereign character. Like Paul, Job has learned the "secret of facing plenty and hunger, abundance and want" with God-honoring contentment (Phil. 4:11-12); the secret is in relying on the sufficiency of God himself. The source of the "problem" of evil and its solution are therefore both the same; the Bible is uncompromising in its monotheism:

> What this fact means is that Yahweh is totally sovereign over ease and pain, for both divine command and divine permission leave God in charge of human events. It also means that there is no other God to whom sufferers may turn for healing or relief. Job must approach Yahweh for answers concerning his situation. His friends and family must do so as well. Monotheism thereby becomes both solution and difficulty where suffering is concerned.[15]

The fundamental lesson of the book of Job, like that of the Bible as a whole, is therefore quite simple: our sole hope and only anchor in the midst of suffering or prosperity is knowing God and God *alone* in his sovereignty and grace. Moreover, Job teaches that our suffering itself is the matrix within which we learn this all-important lesson, since suffering, like no other experience on earth, brings us "face to face" with God himself. The primary purpose of suffering is to make God known to us.

This is not an easy "answer" to the problem of evil. To say that suffering ultimately exists so that God can glorify himself by making himself known in all his majesty and mercy is of little comfort for most people. Only those who recognize that their deepest joy is knowing God will take solace from such a conclusion. But as the book of Job also illustrates, this is a hard lesson to learn.

A poignant modern-day example is C. S. Lewis's experience of meeting God through the severe suffering he encountered in the loss of his wife, Joy Gresham. More than twenty years earlier, in writing *The*

Problem of Pain, Lewis had testified that suffering serves a good purpose, since it drives us to God:

> It is not simply that God has arbitrarily made us such that He is our only good. Rather God is the only good of all creatures. . . . The kind and degree may vary with the creature's nature; but that there ever could be any other good is an atheistic dream.[16]

In his subsequent novel, *Till We Have Faces,* the Job-like figure Queen Orual therefore declares at the end of her pilgrimage,

> "I know now, Lord, why you utter no answers. You are yourself the answer. Before your face questions die away. What other answers would suffice?"[17]

However, when Lewis's wife, with whom he had fallen in love and married late in life, died, Lewis confessed that his ideas about who God is and how he acts were called into question. Nevertheless, through his suffering, Lewis eventually came to know more profoundly than ever before the God he had written about. In Lewis's own words,

> He always knew that my temple was a house of cards. His only way of making me realize the fact was to knock it down. . . . My idea of God was not a divine idea. It has to be shattered time after time. God shatters it Himself. Could we not almost say that this shattering is one of the marks of His presence? . . . And only suffering could do it.[18]

SUFFERING AS A MIDWIFE FOR GOD'S GLORY: THE EXAMPLE OF PAUL

Making himself known in the suffering of his people is therefore a primary way God reveals his glory, both to us and to others. God called Paul as an apostle to a life of suffering in order that others might see the power of God displayed in his life—which Paul saw as a great honor (see Acts 9:15-16; Phil. 2:17-18; 3:10; Col. 1:24; 2 Tim. 1:11-12). In 2 Corinthians 2:14a, Paul therefore *thanks* God for leading him into situations of suffering: "But thanks be to God, who in Christ always leads us in triumph." By employing this dramatic image, Paul makes clear both his calling to suffer as an apostle and its purpose in the world. In the ancient Roman empire, vanquished foes were taken back to Rome after great victories in battle and marched through the streets in "tri-umphal processions" as a way of displaying the strength and superior-ity of their conqueror (in Paul's case, God!). The shocking reality, however, was that these processions usually climaxed with the death of the captives at the end of the parade. To be "led in triumph" thus meant to be led to one's death as the means of displaying the glory of the vic-tor! Paul uses this metaphor to describe his life as an apostle, since for him "death" is a symbol for his life of suffering as a whole (in 1 Cor. 15:31 he refers to his suffering as dying every day).

God is to be praised for leading Paul "as a captive to death in a Roman triumphal procession,"[19] since this is the means of spreading "the fragrance of the knowledge of God everywhere" (2 Cor. 2:14b; see 2 Cor. 4:7). When Paul praises God for leading him to "death" in 2 Corinthians 2:14, he is therefore thanking God for his suffering as the vehicle through which the power and presence of God is being revealed in and through his life.

Once again, we must be careful. Paul does not praise God for his suffering because of an over-inflated ego that makes him imagine he is on a par with Christ. Nor is Paul a masochist. Paul praises God for lead-ing him "to death" because he values the Gospel of "the glory of God in the face of Christ" (2 Cor. 4:6) more than anything else in this world. To that end, Paul rejoices. He has been called to mediate through his suf-fering the significance of Christ's death (see also 1 Cor. 4:9; 2 Cor. 4:11). The message of the Gospel is embodied in the life of its messenger.

This is why Paul can say that, as the "aroma of Christ," his *own* suffering brings about the same contrasting twofold effect caused by the Cross. This becomes evident in the following parallels:

1 Corinthians 1:17-18	2 Corinthians 2:14-16a:
1. Paul is sent to preach in a mode that corresponds to the cross of Christ (1:17; compare 2:1, 4).	1. Paul is "being led to death," which is a mode of existence that reveals the cross of Christ (2:14).
2. For (18a)	2. For (15a)
3. the word of the cross	3. we are an aroma of Christ to God (15a)
4. is folly to those who are perishing (18a)	4. among those who are perishing . . . to those a fragrance from death to death (15c, 16a)
5. [but] to us who are being saved it is the power of God (18c).	5. [but] among those who are being saved saved . . . to those a fragrance from life to life (15b, 16a).

These parallels make clear that the cross of Christ determined both the manner of Paul's life and the content of his message. In turn, his manner of life displayed his message. Consequently, Paul's life and ministry functioned to further the process of salvation ("life") and judgment ("death") in the lives of others. To reject Paul and his message as "folly" merely confirmed that one was already "perishing." On the other hand, to accept Paul and his message demonstrated that the power of God was already at work to save. Paul's ministry and message were one; what he could say about the cross of Christ in 1 Corinthians 1:17-18, he could reaffirm about his life as an apostle in 2 Corinthians 2:14-16.

Thus, just as Jesus was put on the Cross in order to be raised from the dead, so too Paul is "carrying around in [his] body the death of Jesus," i.e., he is "always being given over to death for Jesus' sake," *in order that* the "life of Jesus" might be "revealed in [his mortal body]" (2 Cor. 4:10-11). Note how Paul uses the categories of Jesus' death and resurrection to interpret his own experience of suffering and sustenance, thereby indicating that Paul's life is mediating the same knowledge of God to the world that was embodied in Christ.

Paul's experiences of suffering and being sustained by God as outlined in 2 Corinthians 4:8-9 can therefore be categorized in terms of Jesus' death and resurrection life:

the dying of Jesus	*the life of Jesus*
Paul is afflicted	but not crushed
Paul is perplexed	but not in despair
Paul is persecuted	but not forsaken
Paul is struck down	but not destroyed

The verb translated "[not] driven to despair" in 2 Corinthians 4:8 is the same word found in 2 Corinthians 1:8, where Paul recounted that in the past he *had* despaired of his life. The move from 2 Corinthians 1:8 to 4:8 shows that Paul had learned his lesson. God's rescuing of Paul in the *past* gave him confidence that God would rescue him in the *future,* so that, empowered by this hope, Paul could endure in the *present.*

Furthermore, the contrasts of 2 Corinthians 4:8-9 underscore the reality that, during this evil age, endurance *in the midst of* adversity, not immediate miraculous deliverance *from* adversity, most profoundly reveals God's power. In his life as an apostle, Paul carries around "the dying of Jesus" (2 Cor. 4:10) as he is given over to "death" (2 Cor. 4:11), and the emphasis on "always" in 2 Corinthians 4:10 stresses that this process of "dying" is for Paul a continual one, since it is an essential part of his calling as an apostle.

Also, Paul's use of the "divine passive" in 2 Corinthians 4:11 gives the theological basis for his conviction that his suffering, like the "death of Jesus," mediates the resurrection power of God, the "life of Jesus," to others. By using the divine passive, "we are always being given over to death [by God]," Paul asserts that his sufferings, like those of Jesus, are not merely coincidental but are part of the divine plan for preaching the Gospel (2 Cor. 2:14; and for Jesus, see Mark 10:33; Rom. 4:25; 8:32). In 2 Corinthians 4:10, Paul "carries" the death of Jesus in his own body; in verse 11, Paul *himself* is the living one whom God gives over to death. This parallel between Paul and Jesus, however, does not lead Paul to conclude that the life he mediates is his own; it remains the "life of Jesus" (2 Cor. 4:11b). Paul is no savior, but merely one whose life reveals the reality of God.

The same holds true of God's people whenever we, like Paul, are led into situations of suffering. Though Paul was "always" being led to death as an essential part of his apostolic calling, all Christians share to varying degrees a call to reveal Jesus through the adversity of their lives. When Christians suffer, they, like Paul, can consequently take courage from the fact that their lives will mediate to others the power of the Resurrection, either through God's act of deliverance or, even more profoundly, through the testimony of their endurance. In either case we are summoned, like Paul, to trust God in the midst of our afflictions (2 Cor. 4:8-15) in the confidence that God will ultimately deliver us (2 Cor. 4:16-18). By so doing, God's power will be manifest in our weakness (2 Cor. 4:7; compare 12:7-10). Paul therefore commands his readers to do *all* things without grumbling or questioning (Phil. 2:14), to rejoice in the Lord *always* (see Phil. 3:1; 4:4), and to have no anxiety about *anything* (Phil. 4:6). A tall order. It almost seems ridiculous, until we realize that to do otherwise would be to call into question God's great promises (remember Rom. 8:28).

When everything is said and done, the Christian's experience of suffering therefore leads to an unexpected place: joy. This should really not surprise us, however, for we know that God, in himself, is our "exceeding joy" (Ps. 43:4). And suffering brings us to God. More specifically, suffering brings us to God *alone*. Suffering, superintended by the Spirit, strips away our self-sufficiency. For as Donald Nicholl observed,

> So long as our lives are in our own hands we will never really give up the very things we need above all to give up if we are to be changed, whether that thing is our money, our house, our good opinion of ourselves, our good name, our health or our very life. What we do not want to give up is precisely the thing that is necessary for us to give up if we are to grow. And we would never do so unless we were thrust into it of necessity by some Other.[20]

Thus, when Paul implored God three times to take away his "thorn in the flesh" (2 Cor. 12:8), God said no. Instead, like he did for Job, God gave Paul what he really needed, namely, *himself*, saying, "My grace is sufficient for you, for my power is perfected in weakness" (2 Cor. 12:9). In response, rather than boasting in his visions (2 Cor. 12:1-4), Paul declared,

> I will all the more gladly boast of my weaknesses, that the power of Christ may rest upon me. For the sake of Christ, then, I am content with weaknesses, insults, hardships, persecutions, and calamities, for when I am weak, then I am strong (2 Cor. 12:9-10).

8

WHY DO GOD'S PEOPLE OBEY HIM?

Holiness and Hope

*For whatever was written in former days was
written for our instruction,
that by steadfastness and by the encouragement
of the scriptures we might have hope.*

ROMANS 15:4

Our study so far has brought us to several basic but far-reaching conclusions. We have seen that faith and hope can exist only where God makes himself known, since God's presence is the catalyst that brings faith and hope to life. Faith is a response to the character of God, while hope springs from the promises God has made. We have also seen that, as a response to his presence and promises, God calls his people to trust and hope in him alone even in the midst of circumstances that call his power and word into question. Under God's sovereignty, the suffering of his people thus becomes part of God's gracious will, through which their faith is purified, their hope is strengthened, and the glory of God is made known in the world. We therefore concluded that endurance in the midst of suffering, not success, health, or wealth, is the mark of a genuine Christian life. Furthermore, this side of Christ's return, it is faith and hope in the midst of suffering, not miraculous deliverance from it, that display most clearly the all-sufficiency of God to a despairing world. In a word, believers are saved in hope, to the glory of God.

Finally, we have seen that the life of faith-fueled hope in God's promises "goes public" in obedience to God's commands, since God's commandments are divine provisions and promises in disguise. Within the context of our covenant relationship with God, he demands what he demands because of what he has provided and promised. Obedience *to* God is always based on a corresponding provision and promise *from* God. God's actions of provision in the *past* lead to trust and hope in him for the *future*, which in turn brings about obedience in the *present*. We must now ask *why* this is the case, in order to understand how hope saves us from a life of disobedience and produces in us the "good works" that glorify our Father in heaven (Matt. 5:16).

HOPE AND DESIRE

Whatever we hope for inevitably determines how we live. The object of our hope determines the contours of our conduct. This is a universal principle of human nature. Even at a trivial level, hope is what motivates us. My sons used to meet me every day when I came home from work with the question, "Did we get any mail?" because they had banked their hope on their grandparents' promise to send them something, and their grandparents had a great track record of package sending! So my sons ran to the door day after day in hope that the promise would be fulfilled. What we hope for invariably determines how we act.

Biblically speaking, hope is a confident expectation for the future, based on what God has done and has promised in the past. But this is only half of the story. If someone promises to do something for us but we have no interest in it, hope remains stillborn. Promises produce hope only when they correspond to the object of our desires. This is true whether the promise comes from our grandparents or from God. Hope becomes the power of our lives only if it is *our* hope. Thus, the promise that "the free gift of God is eternal life in Christ Jesus our Lord" (Rom. 6:23) remains powerless in the lives of those for whom life in Christ means nothing. The promise of an eternity with God remains empty to someone who has no desire to be in his presence, since desire is the other essential aspect of hope. To trust and hope in God, one must *want* to do so.

For this reason, given humanity's sinful desires, hope in God's promises depends on a change in our "wants." This is why Jesus warned his followers not to lay up for themselves "treasures on earth" (Matt. 6:19). For "where our treasure is, there will our heart be also" (Matt. 6:21). In other words, what we desire or value most (our treasure) determines what we long for (the object of our heart's affections). Jesus wants to spare us the pain and disillusionment that result from placing our hopes in false sources of contentment that cannot last:

> "Do not lay up for yourselves treasures on earth, where moth and rust consume and where thieves break in and steal, but lay up for yourselves treasures in heaven, where neither moth nor rust consumes and where thieves do not break in and steal. For where your treasure is, there will your heart be also" (Matt. 6:19-21).

Jesus warns us that in spending our lives we should be wise shoppers, guarding our hearts against the false advertisements of this world. For whatever we value most in life becomes our "treasure." And our treasure becomes our *hope*. In turn, our hope determines how we act, since we always spend our lives on whatever we think will make us happy. As a result, life is one long "treasure hunt" in search of the things we hope will meet our needs.[1] What we really want most in any given circumstance determines what we do in that circumstance. Consequently, Jesus calls us to desire the "treasures of heaven," that is, to love God, rather than the world, with all our heart, soul, mind, and strength (Mark 12:30; see Deut. 6:5), so that our actions will no longer be determined by a desire for what the world has to offer but by a desire for what God has promised. The battle to be Christian is a battle *of* the heart *for* the heart. In the midst of the competing claims of our culture on the one hand and the wisdom of God's word on the other hand, we are in a war over what we really think will satisfy the longings of our heart. Our weapon is the simple question, "What do I think will ultimately make me profoundly happy or content, God's presence and promises or the world's prestige and power—and why?" Or, to put the battle cry of spiritual warfare in other words, "What do I hope will happen in my life?"

So, at a mundane level, even the label on my box of tea can quote Thomas Aquinas, who, knowing human nature, declared, "One loves a thing insofar as it is one's own good." Of course, the tea company desires that, seeing how good their tea is for me, I will "love" it above all others, so that I keep buying it! Life is always a matter of "comparison shopping," in which we decide what we want most and whether it is worth the price. Just as we have to decide between breakfast teas, so too we must decide between Christ and the world.

The problem, of course, is our sinfulness. We want to be the ones to decide what's good for us in accordance with our own desires, quite apart from God's wisdom. In the garden, when the woman saw that the tree was good, delightful, and desirous, she "bought it," having concluded that it was of more value than what God had provided. Thus, the fall into sin took place *before* Eve actually ate from the tree, since she had already fallen to Satan's temptation in her heart. Ever since, mankind has been sold into slavery to sin (John 8:34; Rom. 6:16, 20), having been given over by God to their own lusts (Rom. 1:24, 26, 28). Blinded by the "god of this world" to the "light of the gospel of the glory of Christ, who is the likeness of God" (2 Cor. 4:4), unbelievers remain dead in their trespasses and sin, oblivious to their imprisonment to Satan and to their own passions (Eph. 2:1-3).

On the other hand, having had their eyes opened to God's glory, believers have had the desires of their hearts changed. As a result, we are now engaged in a spiritual battle, a "fight of faith," in which we must battle the temptation to yield to the second-rate treasures of this world (Rom. 6:12-13, 19; Col. 3:5; 2 Tim. 2:22; 4:7). For at its root the struggle between righteousness and unrighteousness is a struggle between our conflicting desires and clashing hopes. As Jesus taught us, "out of the heart come evil thoughts, murder, adultery, fornication, theft, false witness, slander" (Matt. 15:19). So in the words of James 1:8, we must fight against becoming "double-minded." We want to follow Christ, seek first his kingdom and righteousness, and take the gospel to the world, but we also want to be popular, enjoy financial security, and have a risk-free and healthy future.

Jesus understands this conflict, and how enticing the world's power and prestige are. He understands that the drive for security can lead to worshiping a golden calf in the wilderness or a credit card in our wallets. He knows that our hopes become the masters of our lives, dictating how we will spend our time, thoughts, and talents, not to mention eternity. He also harbors no illusions that we can somehow maintain for long two rival sets of desires. One will always win out over the other. In Jesus' words,

> "No one can serve two masters; for either he will hate the one and love the other, or he will be devoted to the one and despise the other. You cannot serve God and [money]" (Matt. 6:24).

As the apostle John put it, seeing in Eve's sin (Gen. 3:5) a model for all sin:

> Do not love the world, or the things in the world. If anyone loves the world, love for the Father is not in him. For all that is in the world, the lust of the flesh ["the tree was good for food"], and the lust of the eyes ["it was a delight to the eyes"], and the pride of life ["the tree was to be desired to make one wise"], is not of the Father but is of the world. And the world passes away, and the lust of it; but he who does the will of God abides for ever (1 John 2:15-17).

Jesus and John are not trying to make us miserable, though self-denial certainly can be painful in the moment. Instead, they are preventing us from the lasting pain that comes from banking our lives on that which does not last into eternity.

At its most fundamental level, therefore, serving or loving God means transforming *where* we place our hopes. Notice that Jesus does not say that we should give up *wanting* a treasure. The issue is what that treasure is—God or the world. Simply put, God wants us to find our happiness in him rather than in what the world promises. Daniel Fuller has put the matter well:

> It has often been observed that what people hope in for a happy future, that they worship; and what they worship, that they inevitably serve. Thus Jesus, when tempted by the Devil in the wilderness, fought back by saying, "Begone, Satan! for it is written, 'You shall worship the Lord your God, and him only shall you serve'" (Matt. 4:10). We worship God when we bank our hope for an eternally happy future both on the prospect of always being able to share with him his joy and on his integrity to keep his great and priceless promises. . . . So when our hearts are full of joy as we believe God, we will not engage in any thinking or conduct that is inconsistent with our hope being in him.

And then the worship of God will inevitably lead to serving him in the sense of obeying his commandments as laws of faith. This obedience that stems from faith in God's promises is the way we serve God.[2]

To serve God we must be convinced that God is worth serving. "For whoever would draw near to God *must* believe that he exists and that he rewards those who seek him" (Heb. 11:6, emphasis added). Looking to God to meet our needs, and living in accordance with that hope, is not simply a matter of willpower but of hoping in his promises more than in what the world advertises. To quote Fuller again: "So believing in God has to involve a 180° turn away (that is, repentance) from the love of money to find contentment and confidence for the future simply in knowing God and depending on his promises."[3]

By repenting of our hope in the promises of this world—the greatest of which become merely rusted metal and short-lived pleasures—and trusting in *God's* promises, we develop a new lifestyle of growing obedience to God, rather than of following the cadence of our culture. And as our hope in God increases, our obedience to his commands becomes more consistent.

Our obedience is not something we do for God, as if he needed us to obey him, but the redeemed way of life God grants to us "for our good" (see Deut. 10:13). God's commands are the pathway to life (read Psalm 119 in its entirety!).

Actions never lie. What we do is a window into what we long for. If we are disobeying God's commands, we are not hoping in his promises, because we do not trust his word. It should not be surprising, therefore, that a God-centered hope, based on faith, is the mainspring of obedience to God's will.

FUTURE GRACE

Among modern students of God's Word, nobody has presented this biblical truth more forcefully than John Piper.[4] He has helped us to see that the goal of the Christian life is that "God be *prized* above all things." In his *Future Grace,* Piper explains that life's

> ultimate purpose is the *praise* of the glory of God's grace. The reason both are aims, and both are ultimate, is that *prizing* is the authenti-

cating essence of *praising*. You can't praise what you don't prize. Or, to put it another way, *God is most glorified in us when we are most satisfied in him.* . . . . Sin is what you do when your heart is not satisfied with God. No one sins out of duty. We sin because it holds out some promise of happiness. That promise enslaves us until we believe that God is more to be desired than life itself (Psalm 63:3). Which means that the power of sin's promise is broken by the power of God's. All that God promises to be for us in Jesus stands over against what sin promises to be for us without him. The great prospect of the glory of God is what I call *future grace*. Being satisfied with that is what I call faith. And therefore the life I write about in this book is called *Future Grace: The Purifying Power of Living by Faith in Future Grace* . . . the promises of future grace are the keys to Christ-like Christian living. By *future* I do not merely mean the grace of heaven and the age to come. I mean the grace that begins now, this very second, and sustains your life to the end of this paragraph. By *grace* I do not merely mean the pardon of God in passing over your sins, but also the power and beauty of God to keep you from sinning. By *faith* I do not merely mean the confidence that Jesus died for your sins, but also the confidence that God will "also with him freely give us all things" (Romans 8:32). Faith is primarily a future-orientated "assurance of things hoped for" (Hebrews 11:1). Its essence is the deep satisfaction with all that God promises to be for us in Jesus—beginning now![5]

Second Corinthians 4:16-18 makes clear that this expectation of what Piper calls future grace was at the center of how Paul coped with his own "wasting away" in this life:

So we do not lose heart. Though our outer nature is wasting away, our inner nature is being renewed every day. For this slight momentary affliction is preparing for us an eternal weight of glory beyond all comparison, because we look not to the things that are seen but to the things that are unseen; for the things that are seen are transient, but the things that are unseen are eternal.

As Piper comments,

The renewing of [Paul's] heart comes from something very strange: it comes from looking at what he can't see. . . . This is Paul's way of not losing heart: looking at what you can't see. What did he see? A few verses later in 2 Corinthians 5:7, he says, "We walk by faith, not by sight." This doesn't mean that he leaps into the dark without evidence of what's there. It means that the most precious and important realities in the world are beyond our physical senses. We "look" at these unseen things through the Gospel. By the grace of God we see what Paul called "the light of the gospel of the glory of Christ who is the image of God" (2 Corinthians 4:4). We strengthen our hearts—we renew our courage—by fixing our gaze on the invisible, objective truth that we see in the testimony of those who saw Christ face to face.[6]

The unseen reality that sustained Paul's faith was the glory of God he saw imaged in the risen Christ (2 Cor. 4:5-6). That was the object of his hope. Paul's confidence in God's promise, that he too would one day share in this eternal glory, kept him persevering in faith. God had opened Paul's eyes to the glory of God himself in Christ, so that Paul had come to see that knowing God was of more value than anything the world has to offer. Piper writes,

> This means that the decaying of his body was not meaningless. The pain and pressure and frustration and affliction were not happening in vain. They were not vanishing into a black hole of pointless suffering. Instead, this affliction was "producing for [him] an eternal weight of glory far beyond all comparison." The unseen thing that Paul looked at to renew his inner man was the immense weight of glory that was being prepared for him not just *after,* but *through* and *by,* the wasting away of his body. . . . When he is hurting, he fixes his eyes not on how heavy the hurt is, but on how heavy the glory will be because of the hurt.[7]

The structure of Paul's thought, like the structure of our covenant relationship as a whole, makes clear yet again that whatever we hope for in the future inevitably determines how we live in the present. The pursuit of a greater good in the future is the only motive strong enough to bring about self-denial in the present. Only the "eternal weight of glory" can outweigh the burdens of this world. If our "greater good" remains what this world has to offer, perhaps even rationalized as the "blessing of God," our lives will inevitably become worldly. Our hopes determine our habits. As Paul put it, if all we look forward to is life on earth, then "Let us eat and drink, for tomorrow we die" (1 Cor. 15:32).

Modern and postmodern culture revolves around a this-world ori-entation; the only long-term "future" our culture hopes for is retirement. This pervasive preoccupation with living as long as possible, as healthy as possible, and as wealthy as possible has dramatically influenced the church in the West. Our knowledge of God is so weak, and our desire for the pleasures of the present is so strong, that it is difficult for us to imagine that life with God in the world to come could be incomparably better than life in this world. We honor heaven with our lips, but our hearts are far from it.

However, we cannot will ourselves away from hoping in this world. Changed desires come about through altered appetites. What is needed in every generation is an acquired taste for God in all his majesty, granted by God himself, so that God's people can value anew living and reigning with Christ. Only a desire for God's kingdom that is greater than a desire for this world can break the stranglehold of materialism. To this end, as Richard Sturch has observed, when the Bible uses images to speak about heaven,

> they are images of a strong reality. Heaven is like the literal heaven, the sky; it is like a garden; like a city, a *garden* city, even; like music; like a solemn liturgy of praise; like a great feast; like the goal of a pilgrimage; like kingship, priesthood, and a victory celebration. To try to reduce such images to a literal and prosaic level is folly not only artistically but theologically. . . . And at the centre of each image is he who is the heart and source of all reality, God himself. . . . God's presence with his people is the heart of their reward. . . . And since God is the supreme good-ness, surely to see and know him is our supreme bliss.[8]

HOPE AND HISTORY

To secure our hope in him and to awaken our desires for his kingdom, God has revealed his glory and proven his trustworthiness in his mighty acts of redemption and judgment throughout history (2 Pet. 2:4-10). The two most central of these acts are the Exodus from Egypt and the Cross and Resurrection of Jesus. The Exodus was the foundation of hope for the faithful throughout the Old Testament, for if God delivered his peo-ple from Egypt, he will certainly save them one day from the oppression of their enemies and from their hard-heartedness as a nation, both of which had climaxed in the Exile.[9] In the same way, having taken upon himself our penalty of death,[10] Jesus' resurrection is a prelude and promise of the resurrection from the dead that awaits all those who trust in God (Rom. 8:11, 29; 1 Cor. 6:14; 15:20; 2 Cor. 4:14; Col. 1:18). If God sent Jesus to the Cross and then raised him from the dead, he will certainly raise those who likewise trust in God (1 Pet. 1:18-21). In Peter's words, "By his great mercy we have been born anew to a living hope through the resurrection of Jesus Christ from the dead" (1 Pet. 1:3).

The life of faith thus takes place between God's initial, past acts of redemption and their consummation in the future. We live today between the Exodus and Israel's final restoration and between the first and second comings of the Christ, between the salvation God has already inaugurated in the midst of history and that day, at the end of history as we know it, when Christ will consummate God's kingdom with the resurrection of those who belong to him (Matt. 24:27-51; Rom. 6:5; 1 Cor. 6:14; 15:23; 2 Cor. 3:18; 4:14-18; 2 Pet. 3:10-12). The future, then, the kingdom of God, has already broken into this "present evil age" (Gal. 1:4; see also Mark 1:14-15), but because it is not yet here in all its fullness (Rev. 20–22), our complete enjoyment of God's perfections must wait until the future. Our experience of the Spirit today is just a "down payment" of the glories to come (2 Cor. 1:22; Eph. 1:13).

Only with such an "already-but-not-yet" view of the kingdom and salvation will we be able to resist the world's temptations. This future focus within the history of redemption should lead us to reject all forms of an over-realized hope, in which God's ultimate promises are transported into the present. When this happens, history takes the place of eternity, the present becomes more important than the future, and the glories of heaven pale before earthly pleasures and rewards. As a result, the gospel of God's presence, made possible by the cross of Christ, is perverted into a means of acquiring health and wealth. Such a health-and-wealth "gospel" is an affront to God's glory.

This side of Christ's return, the reality of the Resurrection is not being inaugurated in material "blessings" but in the "new creation" of those who were formerly "dead through the trespasses and sins" in which they lived (2 Cor. 5:17; Eph. 2:1). Christ's reign as the Son of God is already being established in the lives of his people, not through their success in the world but in their war against the flesh as the sons of God and temple of the Holy Spirit (1 Cor. 15:25; 2 Cor. 6:14–7:1; see Rom. 8:14 in the context of Rom. 8:9-16; Gal. 5:17).

HOPE AND OBEDIENCE TO THE LAW

This link between hope, history, and obedience is clearly illustrated in Psalm 78:5-8:

> (5) He established a testimony in Jacob,
>   and appointed a law in Israel,
> which he commanded our fathers
>   to teach to their children;
> (6) that the next generation might know them,
>   the children yet unborn,
> and arise and tell them to their own children,
> (7) so that they should set their hope in God,
> and not forget the works of God,
>   but keep his commandments;
> (8) and that they should not be like their fathers,
> a stubborn and rebellious generation,
> a generation whose heart was not steadfast,
>   whose spirit was not faithful to God.

According to verse 7, God's mighty deeds have been recorded in the Law of Moses to provide a testimony to what God has done in the past *so that* coming generations might hope in God. Thus, "not forgetting the works of God" is inextricably tied to setting one's hope in God. Focusing on what God has done in the past leads to confidence in what God will do in the future. The psalmist then draws out what this means for the present: instead of "forgetting his works," God's people, having consequently "set their hope in God," should "keep his commandments" (v. 7b).

At first glance, to contrast not forgetting God's works with "keeping his commandments" seems strange. The opposite of not forgetting is usually remembering, not obedience. But for the psalmist, the opposite of obeying God is not disobedience per se, but forgetfulness! His logic is clear: remembering God's past miracles gives hope for the future, which leads to obedience in the present, so that forgetting God's works leads to disobedience. For this reason, the psalmist declares concerning God's past acts:

> We will not hide them from [the] children,
>> but tell to the coming generation
> the glorious deeds of the LORD, and his might,
>> and the wonders which he has wrought (Ps. 78:4).

Conversely, Psalm 78 lists a series of negative examples of those who disobeyed God because they forgot his past wonders (see vv. 9-11, 17-19, 21-29). The reason for Israel's disobedience is therefore clear:

> They did not keep in mind his power,
>> or the day when he redeemed them from the foe;
> when he wrought signs in Egypt,
>> and his miracles in the fields of Zoan (Ps. 78:42-43).

Accordingly, the person who seeks to "keep his way pure" and not "wander from God's commandments" remains fixed on God's word:

> I have laid up thy word in my heart,
>> that I might not sin against thee. . . .
> I will meditate on thy precepts,
>> and fix my eyes on thy ways.
> I will delight in thy statutes;
>> I will not forget thy word (Ps. 119:11, 15-16).

God's people, like the psalmists in Psalms 78 and 119, delight in God's Law, since it is the expression of his character, the account of his mighty acts of deliverance, the deposit of his promises, and the declaration of his corresponding decrees (read all of Psalm 119 again, and note especially the link between hope in God's promises and obedience to his commands in verses 41-48). Moreover, all of these elements are woven into one unified fabric, which forms the whole cloth of our relationship with God. No one thread can be removed without unraveling the entire enterprise: God's character is revealed through what he has done, what he has done becomes the basis for the promises he has made, his promises determine his demands, and his demands flow from his character, which in turn reveals itself through what he does. And so the circle repeats itself throughout history and eternity.

The Law of God is therefore not a list of "do's and don'ts," but the expression of who God is, what he has done, and what he will do for us as we trust in him. As such, God's commands are expressions of what faith looks like in concrete situations, in the daily application of what it means to love God with everything we are, and to love our neighbors as ourselves. God's commands are not the "job description" of an employer that we must do to earn our wage, but the "health regimen" of a doctor (indeed, the "Great Physician" himself—Mark 2:17) which we must obey "that we might overcome our spiritual sickness."[11] As such, the Law's commands are good news! In the words of Psalm 119:93: "I will never forget thy precepts; for *by them* thou hast given me life."

It is this bond between God's character, activity, promises, and commands that explains why the Law evokes such joy and praise throughout Psalm 119. The psalmist rejoices in the Law because his hope for the future and his happiness in the present are both wrapped up in who God is and what he promises, as expressed in his commands. It is only natural, then, that the psalmist would get excited about God's Law.

HOPE, FUTURE GRACE, AND OBEDIENCE

And so Peter not only describes followers of Jesus Christ as those who, "by [God's] great mercy . . . have been born anew to a living hope through the resurrection of Jesus Christ from the dead" (1 Pet. 1:3); he also calls believers to "set your hope fully upon the grace that is coming to you at the revelation of Jesus Christ" so that, "as obedient children," they will not be "conformed to the passions of your former ignorance" (1 Pet. 1:13-14). This *obedience* as God's children, born of their hope in God's coming *grace,* grows out of and prepares them for the fact that the One whom they invoke as Father "judges each one impartially according to his *deeds"* (1 Pet. 1:17a). As a result, they "conduct [themselves] with fear through the time of [their] exile" here on earth (1 Pet. 1:17b).

Unfortunately, most Christians no longer associate their hope in receiving God's grace on judgment day with the necessity of obedience. Nor do we connect knowing God as "Father" with being judged by our deeds. Even less common today is the association between grace and the fear of the Lord.

The key to these relationships, once again, is the link between the past, present, and future in our covenant relationship with God. As Peter points out, the ultimate act of God's grace will take place on that day when Christ is revealed in all his glory. At that time, having been forgiven by his death and made his obedient children by the Spirit, we will take our final steps into his presence, thereby being perfected as a result of seeing him as he is (1 John 3:2). This experience of God's *coming* grace is not merely a future reality, however, but is already being manifest toward us *in advance of* the day of judgment. For believers, the grace at judgment day merely consummates the transformation already begun by God in the present.

Furthermore, to know God personally as Father is to know him also as "Judge," since within a covenant relationship experiencing the grace of God leads to corresponding covenant stipulations (commands), our response to which brings either blessing or curse (see chapter 2). Thus, precisely because the gift we receive by God's grace is nothing less than God's transforming presence, he will judge us by our deeds.

This, then, brings us to the counterpart of hope: fear of the Lord, that is, a confident expectation of a *negative* future. In this sense, the fear of God is focused on God's promise to judge his world in righteousness. As such, it stands as one of God's greatest gifts, since the fear of God, like hope focused on God's other promises, also keeps us from sinning. Hope and fear are thus the guideposts that light up the path of obedience. As the psalmist points out, they are therefore the qualities of our lives in which God delights:

> The LORD takes pleasure in those who *fear* him,
>   in those who *hope* in his steadfast love (Ps. 147:11, emphasis added).[12]

Those who hope in God's grace in the future, that is, "in his steadfast love," flee sin because they fear being separated from his presence. Obeying in order to inherit God's future grace (his covenant blessings) means obeying in order not to inherit his future wrath (his covenant curses). God prepares his children for the day of judgment not only by giving them hope but also by granting them fear, both of which lead to obedience (compare Abraham's faith in Gen. 15:6 with his fear in Gen. 22:12). In Colossians 3:5-6, Paul therefore supports his command to "put to death . . . what is earthly" in our lives by declaring that "on account of these the wrath of God is coming." This helps explain Paul's words in Romans 2:6-11, 13 (which many argue are simply intended to show us our need for forgiveness by highlighting the unreachable standards of the Law; but in so doing they miss the very promise of the Gospel itself):

> For he will render to every man according to his works: to those who by patience in well-doing seek for glory and honor and immortality, he will give eternal life; but for those who are factious and do not obey the truth, but obey wickedness, there will be wrath and fury. There will be tribulation and distress for every human being who does evil, the Jew first and also the Greek, but glory and honor and peace for every one who does good, the Jew first and also the Greek. For God shows no partiality. . . . For it is not the hearers of the law who are righteous before God, but the doers of the law who will be justified.

Hence, in Galatians 5:21 Paul responds to a listing of the "works of the flesh" by again warning the Galatians "that those who do such things shall not inherit the kingdom of God" (see also 1 Cor. 6:9-10). Conversely, those whose lives are characterized by the "fruit of the Spirit" are no longer under the curse of God's Law (Gal. 5:18, 23). For those who are "zealous to confirm [their] call and election" by growing in virtue, there will be "richly provided . . . an entrance into the eternal kingdom of our Lord and Savior Jesus Christ" (2 Pet. 1:3, 5-7, 11).

Once again, this is not a call to earn our salvation through our own efforts (a "works-righteousness"). The "fruit" called for in Galatians 5:16-24 is the fruit "of the *Spirit.*" So too, the "works" that seek for glory in Romans 2:7 are the works that come from a "circumcised heart" brought about by the Spirit (see Rom. 2:29). And the virtues listed in 2 Peter 1:5-7 are all based on the fact that God's power "has granted to us all things that pertain to life and godliness" through revealing and calling us to his own "glory and excellence" (2 Pet. 1:3). For by revealing to us a knowledge of himself, God "has granted to us his precious and very great promises, that through these you may escape from the corruption that is in the world because of passion, and become partakers of the divine nature" (2 Pet. 1:4).[13] In our covenant relationship with God, he gives what he demands, so that even our good works might praise him (Eph. 2:4-10).

The Bible therefore warns us about those who teach "cheap grace," which downplays our need for faithful obedience, turns God's forgiveness into a license to sin, and pits the life of the Spirit against God's Law. Instead of calling for moral transformation (2 Cor. 3:18), cheap grace says, "Don't be so hard on yourself; after all, you're only human! Relax! The Cross and Spirit mean that judgment is over for you!" Cheap grace despises God's authority to judge, winks at sin among God's people, and offers false comfort to those living in sin, rather than summoning them to repentance in the fear of God (Jer. 6:14; 23:9-22; Ezek. 13:1-23; Mic. 3:9-12; 2 Tim. 3:1-9; 2 Pet. 2:1-2, 13-15, 17-22; 3:3-4; Jude 8-18).

Those who hope in future grace, however, know that judgment begins with the household of God (1 Pet. 4:17). As Paul reminds us, "we shall all stand before the judgment seat of God. . . . So each of us shall give account of himself to God" (Rom. 14:10, 12; see also 2 Cor. 5:10). Far from winking at sin, Jesus himself declared to his *disciples,*

> "I tell you, my friends, do not fear those who kill the body, and after that have no more that they can do. But I will warn you whom to fear: fear him who, after he has killed, has power to cast into hell; yes, I tell you, fear him!" (Luke 12:4-5).

The Cross and the Spirit do not free us from judgment, but provide for us the ground (i.e., God's forgiveness) and means (i.e., God's power) to live lives pleasing to God *in preparation for* judgment (2 Cor. 5:9-10; Phil. 1:10-11; 2 Pet. 1:3-11).

THE PATHWAYS TO HOLINESS

The way to escape sin's stranglehold, therefore, is not to try to pull ourselves up by our own bootstraps of determination, or to conjure up more willpower, or to pump up our power of positive thinking. Godliness is not the religious version of a self-help program. Rather, we must maintain our hope in God's glorious future as those who have been born anew because of Christ. We do this by turning to God that he might enlarge our view of his "glory and virtue," show us the value of his "precious and very great promises," and assure us of the power of his Spirit (2 Pet. 1:3-4; Gal. 5:16; Rom. 8:1-39). Hope is the only power strong enough to break the grip of sin in our lives.

There are at least five important pathways to building hope in God.

1) We must read, hear, study, and be taught the Bible. Scripture is the account of God's promises to his people, as well as the record of the ways in which God has proven himself to be committed and dependable, so that we might know *what* to hope for and *why.*

Nothing sustains hope like a serious and sustained study of the Scriptures. From the Bible we learn the history of creation and redemption and the nature of our covenant relationship with God, in which we image forth his glory as our Maker, Sustainer, King, Redeemer, and Judge. "For whatever was written in former days was written for our instruction, that by steadfastness and by the encouragement of the Scriptures we might have hope" (Rom. 15:4). The Bible alone is the Word of God, the sole authority and foundation for our faith. Thus the psalmist declares, "I have laid up thy word in my heart, that I might not sin against thee" (Ps. 119:11).

2) We build hope from our own histories, by recounting the ways in which, as an extension of his past acts of redemption, God has worked in our own lives to prove himself faithful to his promises. The history of redemption continues on in our lives. The Bible stands over our experience as its interpreter, but it does not stand apart from our experience. All of God's people have their own personal track record of God's power and provision.

We do well to remember regularly how God has worked to save us from our rebellion against him and to meet our needs in the months and years since he invaded our lives with his presence. Our lives declare God's faithfulness. In fact, part of our private worship should be devoted to reflecting on the ways in which God has been gracious to us throughout our lives, so that we might continue to hope in him no matter what.

3) Hope is built by remembering our spiritual heritage. We must keep in mind that we are not isolated, autonomous individuals, but part of a long history of redemption that begins in the Garden, runs through the history of Israel, finds its center point in the coming of Jesus, moves out through the church, extends into the specific circumstances surrounding our own coming to faith, and will climax when Christ returns. As believers, we are part of God's *people.* Our lives find their ultimate meaning in being part of God's cosmic plan for his creation.

On the eve of the Exodus, Moses instructed the people that in *generations to come* they were to "remember this day, in which you came out of Egypt, out of the house of bondage, for by strength of hand the LORD brought you out from this place" (Ex. 13:3). Passover was the celebration inaugurated to embody this memory. It would rekindle the memory of how God had delivered *Israel* as his people, and in so doing give them hope for the future. Their personal relationship with God was based on God's long-standing history with the people of which they were a part (see Deut. 26:1-11; Judg. 6:8-9; 1 Sam. 10:17-19; 1 Kings 8:51-53; etc.). In the words of Hosea 13:4: "I am the LORD your God from the land of Egypt; you know no God but me, and besides me there is no savior."

So, too, with the "Lord's Supper." In remembering Christ's death, we look back in order to look forward, knowing that Jesus will not join his people again in this covenant meal "until the kingdom of God comes" in all its fullness (Luke 22:18).

4) Hope is built by learning from the testimony of God's faithfulness in the lives of others. The more we see God's work in the lives of others, the more convinced we become that he will do the same for us. Conversely, we should "always be prepared to make a defense" ourselves "to anyone who calls you to account for the hope that is in you, yet do it with gentleness and reverence" (1 Pet. 3:15). Building up hope within God's people is a mutual enterprise.

5) The most important pathway to hope, and the one to which all others lead, is prayer. To conclude with prayer is not merely a pious "add-on" to the "practical" advice given above. No matter what else we do, we *must* pray, for we are *wholly* dependent upon God himself to enable us to come to grips with the magnitude of his promises and the reality of the One who stands behind them. Hope is not the automatic outcome of "three steps to spiritual growth," but the result of God's invading our lives. And God is not a prisoner of our "spiritual disciplines." The pathway to a life of obedience born of hope is ultimately not something we follow but someone we encounter. Only knowing God himself as he has revealed himself in his Word can create the kind of hope in his promises that brings about obedience to his will. Reading the Bible, remembering our spiritual heritage, personal and corporate, and listening to others are not ends in themselves but the instruments God uses to make himself known. They remain useless unless we come face to face with the living God. Only God can make himself known,

and he does so when and where he desires. As Jesus reminded us, the Spirit, like the wind, "blows where it wills, and you hear the sound of it, but you do not know whence it comes or whither it goes; so it is with every one who is born of the Spirit" (John 3:8). Thus, when all is said and done, the apostle Paul prays that "the God of hope" will "fill us with all joy and peace in believing, so that by the power of the Holy Spirit we may abound in hope" (Rom. 15:13).

The good news of the Gospel is that when we express our dependence on God in prayer, Jesus promises us that the Father withholds no good gift from his children, but delights in giving them his Spirit (Luke 11:13). So, just as Paul prayed in Ephesians 1:17-19, we too can ask "the God of our Lord Jesus Christ, the Father of glory" to open our eyes by his Spirit so that we "may know what is the hope to which he has called [us], what are the riches of his glorious inheritance in the saints, and what is the immeasurable greatness of his power in us who believe."

9

WHAT DIFFERENCE DOES JESUS MAKE?

Faith, Forgiveness, and the Freedom to Obey

*"Blessed is the man who trusts in the LORD,
whose trust is in the LORD."*
JEREMIAH 17:7

*[Jesus] became the source of eternal salvation
to all who obey him.*
HEBREWS 5:9

In the midst of an ever-changing world, the good news is that the life of faith is anchored by the power, provisions, and promises of God. Circumstances may change, but the future is as sure as the character of God himself. No matter what happens, those who trust in God hope in his word.

The Bible also makes clear that hope in God's promises reveals itself in obedience to his commands, since "every one who . . . hopes in him purifies himself as he is pure" (1 John 3:3). Those who are "heavenly minded" therefore depart from evil, defend the defenseless, work for justice, pursue peace, give generously, and even love their enemies (Ps. 34:14; 37:3; Isa. 1:17; Luke 6:27-35; Gal. 6:10; 1 Thess. 5:15; 1 Tim. 6:18; Heb. 13:16).

Many Christians, however, view God's commands simply to be his way of showing us our need for forgiveness. In this view, the Law's chief job is to drive us to despair over our inability to keep it, so that we con-

tinually turn from the Law to the Gospel, from the demand for obedience to the gift of grace. For those who hold this view, Christ brings the
Law to an end in the life of the believer. To them, the life of faith is exclusively a life of accepting God's forgiveness in Christ, since even my
strongest efforts toward obedience are tainted with sin. Hence, faith
replaces the demand for obedience.

Others believe that once a person comes to faith, the Bible's commands are sound "advice" for Christian living and the way we serve
God, the doing of which will lead to rewards from God in addition to
the gift of salvation itself. In this view, Christ makes obedience possible and desirable, but not necessary to be saved. Holiness is therefore
a pursuit of God's "best," in which we show God our sincerity, gratitude, and desire to serve him through our obedience. Thus, obedience
is added to faith.

Still others consider obedience to God's laws to be the necessary
"evidence" of faith. For them, if one truly believes, then obedience
becomes the mandatory sign of something else, namely, faith, which is
the human response to God's grace that actually saves us. The call to
obey thus becomes a call to show the genuine nature of our faith by our
obedience. As a result, faith must lead to obedience as the sign that it is
real. There are therefore *two* things that must be done to be happy as a
Christian: one must trust *and* obey.

In all of these views, obedience may be possible, desirable, or
maybe even necessary as the *by-product* of trusting Christ, but it is not
an essential expression of what it means to trust Christ in and of itself.
For most Christians, faith and hope must be kept distinct from obedience, lest the gospel of grace be compromised. As a result, being saved
"by grace . . . through faith" as a "gift of God—not because of works"
(Eph. 2:8-9) comes to mean that faith in God exists apart from and in
contrast to all human activity, even the "good works" brought about
by Christ (Eph. 2:10).[1]

So even though they may be inextricably tied to each other, faith and
obedience are considered two *different* ways of relating to God. From
this perspective, faith is viewed as a passive acceptance or emotional
embracing of God's gifts, or as merely a mental assent to the truth of the
Gospel, while obedience is an act of the will in response to God's commands. As such, obedience is usually encouraged or even required as a

response to or *outgrowth of* faith, since it is the way of earning rewards from God beyond salvation, or of showing that faith is real. Nevertheless, obedience must not be considered the organic expression of faith itself, lest salvation become a matter of "works."

Moreover, many within this perspective would argue even more radically that since God demands perfection, any attempt to unite faith and works is doomed from the start. As sinners, our obedience is never complete, and even our best attempts to obey God are tainted with impure motives. Any attempt to incorporate obedience into the life of faith is therefore in and of itself a denial of our need for grace.

But whether obedience is viewed as the *recommended response* to faith or as its *compulsory complement,* not to mention rejected altogether as credible, these perspectives do not do justice to the inextricable union of faith, hope, and obedience that is at the heart of our covenant relationship with God or to the nature of God's transforming grace (see chapter 2). Scripture is insistent that obedience is not simply good advice for those who have faith—a desirable but not required outcome of faith in our lives. Nor is it to be added along the way as evidence of a prior faith, or as the next step toward a "deeper Christian life." And the purpose of God's commands is not merely to show us that we are sinners. Simply put, faith and hope do not exist without obedience, since obedience to God's commands is the flowering of faith *itself!*

JESUS' INESCAPABLE DEMANDS

In fulfillment of the Old Testament, the essential link between God's power, provisions, promises, and commands was at the heart of Jesus' preaching. The main point of Jesus' message was the twofold declaration that: 1) *since* the kingdom of God was now being established in and through his life and ministry, 2) *therefore* people should repent and trust in this good news (Matt. 4:17; Mark 1:14-15; see Isa. 52:7; 61:1, from which we get the name "Gospel" and its content as God's rule and reign in the world, that is, the "kingdom" of God). The *provision* of God's powerful, saving reign (the "kingdom of God") supports Jesus' *command* to repent from our self-dependence and to trust in God's promises for our lives. It does so because the dawning of God's kingdom brings with it the *promise* that God's sovereign will is now being inaugurated in the world for the good of his people and for the judgment of the wicked. Jesus' miracles and exorcisms were all aimed at demonstrating the truth of this claim ("The kingdom of God is here!") in order to undergird this command ("Repent and trust in the Gospel!"). As Jesus put it to those who questioned his ministry, "If it is by the finger of God that I cast out demons, then the kingdom of God has come upon you" (Luke 11:20).

In other words, Jesus' miracles and exorcisms were "living parables" designed to make the coming of God's kingdom clear and credible. They testify that the kingdom of God is here and is open to all who repent and trust in Jesus, regardless of their ethnic identity, race, gender, social class, or sin. Indeed, Jesus' Gospel of the kingdom brings with it the promise of forgiveness to *all* those who trust him. The only hindrance to entering the kingdom is being blind to one's need to do so (Mark 2:1-17; 5:21-34; 7:24-30; Luke 24:47; Acts 2:38; 10:43; 13:38; Eph. 1:7; Col. 1:14).

Jesus could make this astonishing promise because, as he himself put it, it was just as "easy" for him, as the messianic King, to forgive sins as it was for him to heal paralyzed legs (Mark 2:9). To the Jewish leaders of Jesus' day, the latter was possible to some who had faith but the former was solely God's business. Jesus' claim, in their view, was blasphemy, since, as they exclaimed, "Who can forgive sins but God alone?" (Mark 2:7). So Jesus healed the paralytic in order to demonstrate that, as the divine Son of Man, the Messiah, he had the "authority on earth" not only to judge sin but also to forgive sins (Mark 2:10; see Dan. 7:13-27 for the background to Jesus as the "Son of Man," whose role is to restore and represent God's people as they together, having been granted authority in the kingdom of God, judge and rule over the nations).

But that was not all that Jesus preached. He also called for obedience as the *characteristic consequence* of having been accepted into the kingdom through the gateway of God's mercy. This is so much the case that in John 15:14 Jesus says to his disciples, "You are my friends *if* you do what I command you" (emphasis added). In Luke 6:46 Jesus asks, "Why do you call me 'Lord, Lord,' and not do what I tell you?" And when the rich young man asks Jesus, "What must I do to inherit eternal life?" Jesus does not hesitate to point him back to the commandments (Matt. 19:16-22; Mark 10:17-22; Luke 18:18-23). Furthermore, Jesus demands that his disciples teach their followers "to observe all that I have commanded you," as an essential aspect of the "Great Commission" (Matt. 28:20). On judgment day, therefore, Jesus will respond to many who say to him, "Lord, Lord," with the surprising declaration, "I never knew you; depart from me, you *evildoers*" (Matt. 7:23), for, "Not every one who says to me, 'Lord, Lord,' shall enter the kingdom of heaven, but he who does the will of my Father who is in heaven" (Matt. 7:21).

These statements from Jesus should be given their full force: our *obedience* to God's commands is the expression of trusting Christ. It is not our words but our deeds that stand the test of Christ's gaze. Love of Jesus is measured by obedience to what he commands (John 14:15 and 15:14). "He who has my commandments *and keeps them,* he it is who loves me" (John 14:21, emphasis added). Not even miracles can substitute for doing what God commands (Matt. 7:22).

Jesus' gospel of forgiveness is not unrelated to the Bible's demand for holiness. Obedience is not a "second step" added to our faith, so that "accepting Jesus as Savior" must be supplemented by "accepting Jesus as Lord." We are not saved by grace and then sanctified (made holy) by our own works. Being a Christian is not a matter of adding our will to God's, our efforts to his. Rather, according to Hebrews 12:1-2, we are to

> lay aside every weight, and sin which clings so closely, and let us run with perseverance the race that is set before us, looking to Jesus the pioneer and perfecter of our faith.

But even this text may be misunderstood, as if it taught that there are two distinct things that must be done to run the race with perseverance (live the life of faith)—that on the one hand we must *put away our sin* and on the other hand we must *look to Jesus,* the author and finisher of our faith. But the two are not unrelated. If Jesus is the One who makes it possible for us to run the race of faith from start to finish, and if running the race entails putting away sin, then Jesus is also the One who makes it possible for us to put away sin, without which faith will not persevere.

Thus, "putting away sin," which is faith in action, is the means to persevering, which we do by depending on Jesus from beginning to end. In other words, repenting from the disobedience of disbelief, and the life of persevering faith that this brings about, which entails *obeying* God, are all one expression of "looking to Jesus." One cannot exist without the other. Repentance from sin, faith in Christ, and obedience are so closely related as organic reflexes of each other that the writer to the Hebrews can say that Jesus, "the pioneer and perfecter of our *faith*" . . . "became the source of eternal salvation to all who *obey* him" (Heb. 12:2; 5:9, emphasis added).

There is only *one* thing, not two, that we must do to be saved: trust God with the needs of our lives. This one thing, trust in God's provision (now supremely manifested in Christ) will show itself, from beginning to end, in our *many* acts of repentance and obedience ("laying aside every weight, and sin which clings so closely") as we learn to trust God more and more in more and more circumstances.

THE FULFILLMENT OF THE LAW

In Matthew 5:17, Jesus therefore cautions his disciples not to think that he has come to "abolish the law and the prophets" but rather to understand that he has come to fulfill them.[2] This statement applies to every aspect of life under the old covenant law, including the ritual purity regulations, dietary restrictions, and sacrificial system. The need for such a fulfillment is immediately apparent from Israel's history under the old covenant. Since under the old covenant the majority of Israel remained hard-hearted, having received the Law but not the Spirit, God's Law encountered a people who could not keep its original intention (Ex. 32:9; 33:3-5; 34:9; Deut. 29:2-4; Isa. 6:9-13; 29:13; Ezek. 20:5-29). As a result, "the letter" (the Law without the Spirit) "kills" by bringing Israel under God's covenant curses (2 Cor. 3:6; see Ex. 32:15-29; Deut. 27:15-26; 28:15-68; 29:16-28; Gal. 3:10).

Nevertheless, God chose Israel as the place of his presence, which made her distinct from all other nations (Ex. 33:16; 1 Kings 8:14-53). But because Israel could not fulfill her mandate to mediate God's glory through her faithfulness to the covenant (Ex. 19:1-6), God instituted a "symbolic holiness" to represent the fact that his presence was still located in her midst. As a consequence, rather than being separate from the nations ("holy") in terms of a transformed character, the Law sepa-rated Israel from the nations by virtue of a series of symbolic actions, such as circumcision, food laws, and acts of ritual purity. In the hands of a hardened nation, even the Ten Commandments could only be kept externally as a matter of compulsion rather than being concrete expres-sions of what love looks like in everyday life. Under the old covenant, the Law therefore functioned to separate Israel from the nations *sym-bolically*, inasmuch as the people as a whole remained no different from the nations *spiritually*.

For example, circumcision separated Israel from the nations ethni-cally, but its real purpose was to point to the reality of a Spirit-trans-formed, "circumcised" heart (Deut. 10:16; Jer. 4:4; 9:26; Rom. 2:25-29). In the same way, ritual purity was required in order to enter the temple, but its intent was to signal the need for a clean heart in order to be in God's presence (Lev. 10:8–15:33; Ps. 24:3-6; 51:10-17; Jer. 13:27; Heb. 10:22). So, too, the sacrificial system under the old covenant pointed for-ward to the death of the Christ as the one true sacrifice. Passover com-memorated the exodus from Egypt as a precursor of the "second exodus" after the Exile, when God's people would be delivered not only circum-stantially but also spiritually (Isa. 4:2-6; 40:3-5; 43:1-3, 14-21; 64:1-4). The civil laws, such as what to do with an ox that gores (Ex. 21:28-36), or how to deal with breaches of contracts (Ex. 22:9-10), or how to pro-vide for the poor from one's harvest (Lev. 19:9; 23:22), though intended to be models of what love would look like in economic affairs, at least maintained societal order for an ungodly nation. The theocratic laws and the institution of kingship in Israel's history pointed forward to that day when God himself would rule and reign over his people through his Son, the Davidic Messiah (2 Sam. 7:12-16). Finally, even the Promised Land was not an end in itself; it was to be a launching pad for the spread of God's dominion to the ends of the earth in fulfillment of Genesis 1:28.

Once we see that the Law as a whole embodied God's character and promises, and pointed forward to a reality yet to come, it becomes evi-dent that Jesus did not reject the Law itself as inferior or inadequate. Nor did he set the Law aside because it demanded too much, as if the Gospel somehow makes God's holiness less a reality. Rather, Jesus *fulfilled* the Law perfectly in his life in order to be the perfect sacrifice for sins in his death, thereby creating a people who, being increasingly conformed to his image, will be separate from the nations not by outward observances but by virtue of changed lives resulting from transformed hearts (2 Cor. 3:18; 4:4-6; 5:15-17; 1 Pet. 2:9-12). Indeed, because Jesus' death for our sins makes it possible for God's transforming presence to dwell in our midst, the coming of God's kingdom (his reign over our lives as his people) brings with it an uncompromising demand for a life of obedience to God's Law, which Jesus stressed will never "pass away" as long as the world exists (Matt. 5:18; Luke 16:17).

The Sermon on the Mount, therefore, does not present Jesus as a new Moses with a new law. The inescapable demand of the Gospel is nothing other than obedience to God's commands as reaffirmed and taught by Jesus himself (Matt. 7:24-27; 11:29; 28:20). In pointing past one's external obedience to the character of the heart, Jesus is simply emphasizing what the Law and the prophets demanded from the beginning, thereby declaring that his followers are to "fulfill" the *original intention* of the Law.[3]

This is why Jesus can link adultery under the old covenant with lust under the new, or murder with anger, or can contrast retaliation with self-giving, or loving one's neighbor with loving one's enemy, and so on. It is why Paul can equate idolatry with covetousness and summarize the entire Law in the command to love one's neighbor as oneself, just as Jesus did (Matt. 5:21-48; 22:34-40; Mark 12:28-34; Rom. 13:8-10; Gal. 5:14). This is also why the letter to the Hebrews understands the Sabbath in terms of living by faith (Heb. 4:1-10). The principle at work in all these texts is illustrated in Mark 7:14-23, where Jesus explained that his disciples no longer maintained ritual purity because it is not what goes into a person that defiles him but "what comes out of a man is what defiles a man" (Mark 7:20). Jesus' disciples no longer keep the laws of ritual purity not because these laws were wrongheaded but because their hearts have been made pure. Rather than merely being clean outwardly, they are clean inwardly. Rather than being different from the world only in terms of external symbols and the constraint of civil law, those who follow Jesus manifest a different way of life from the heart (Mark 7:21-22). And when the reality comes, the symbols that pointed to it under the old covenant become a matter of personal preference. Under the new covenant, clean hearts, expressed in pure lives, replace washed hands. The same goes for the so-called "moral laws," though the Law itself makes no distinction between "ceremonial" and "moral laws," since all function equally as stipulations of the old covenant.

Thus, under the old covenant, Israel was commanded not to murder; under the new covenant, followers of Jesus are prohibited from even losing their temper, since their hearts have been transformed! And those who do not lose their temper need not worry about committing murder. Likewise, since Jesus' death fulfilled the old covenant sacrificial system, the ceremonial regulations surrounding it have been fulfilled by stipulations corresponding to the changed heart of God's people (see 1 Cor. 11:23-34; etc.). Being the temple of God's presence brings with it a call to reflect the holiness of God himself (see, for example, 1 Cor. 6:12-20; 2 Cor. 6:14–7:1).

This is not a move toward lawlessness, as if the Gospel restructures the nature of our covenant relationship with God. Just the opposite! God's saving act in Christ—by which we are forgiven, granted his Spirit, set free from the power of sin, and declared righteous in advance of the final judgment (the historical prologue)—calls for a faith in God's promises that obeys his commands (the covenant stipulations) in order that we might be judged righteous when Christ returns, rather than be condemned for our rebellion (the covenant blessing and curse). Christians do not reject or replace the Law; they express in their lives the very reality to which it pointed! They love God with everything they are, and their neighbor as themselves.

Given their symbolic function of pointing to the realities of the new covenant, Christians may keep the religious practices of the old covenant as testimonies to their faith, especially for the sake of their mission to the Jews and when worshiping with Jewish believers (Acts 21:17-26; Rom. 14:1-12; 1 Cor. 9:19-23). Now that Christ has come, however, it is forbidden to make the old covenant *binding* on members of the new, as if one had to become a Jew in order to be a full-fledged member of God's people. To do so would be to deny the efficacy and sufficiency of the cross of Christ as the act of God's grace by which the new covenant was established and to which the old covenant pointed all along (Gal. 2:21). This was clearly understood by Paul, who could circumcise Timothy for the sake of their mission to the Jews (Acts 16:1-5) and yet castigate the "Judaizers" who demanded that Christians be circumcised in order to enjoy the fullness of the Spirit (Gal. 2:4-5; 5:2-12; 6:12; Phil. 3:2).

The reason for this apparent inconsistency between denying the need to keep the Law (after all, the Law itself commands circumcision, ritual purity, not murdering or committing adultery, keeping kosher, and the celebration of the festivals, etc.!), and at the same time demanding that we keep the commandments of God, is that the symbolic function of the old covenant is no longer in force now that Christ has established the realities to which it pointed. The contrasts and parallels established in the following texts make this distinction between the Law's functions under the old and new covenants explicit:

1 Corinthians 7:19a	For neither circumcision nor uncircumcision counts for anything,
Galatians 5:6a	For . . . neither circumcision nor uncircumcision is of any avail,
Galatians 6:15a	For neither circumcision counts for anything, nor uncircumcision

1 Corinthians 7:19b	but keeping the commandments of God.
Galatians 5:6b	but faith working through love.
Galatians 6:15b:	but a new creation.

Being a member of Israel as an ethnic people and living like a Jew under the old covenant is no longer essential now that the new covenant has arrived. "Neither circumcision nor uncircumcision counts for anything." Now what counts is whether one fulfills the Law's call to love others as the outworking of our faith, which is the expression of what it means to be a "new creation" in Christ (2 Cor. 5:17). Moreover, these parallels indicate that to be a "new creation" (Gal. 6:15b) is to live a life of faith characterized by "keeping the commandments of God" (1 Cor. 7:19b), which can be interpreted in terms of "faith working through love" (Gal. 5:6b). This is what counts, now that the new covenant has dawned.

THE NEW COVENANT

Since Jesus *is* Israel's long-awaited Messiah, his demand for obedience should not surprise us. It is simply the implication of the fact that he has inaugurated the "new covenant" promised by the prophets (Luke 22:20;

1 Cor. 11:25; 2 Cor. 3:6; Heb. 8:1-13; 10:16). The most important description of the contours of the new covenant is found in Jeremiah 31:31-34, whose argument, summarized and separated into its individual assertions, runs as follows (the bracketed phrases represent my understanding of the logic of the passage):[4]

(31)   "Behold, the days are coming, says the LORD, when I will make a new covenant with the house of Israel and the house of Judah.

(32a)   [Specifically,] I will not make it like the covenant which I made with their fathers . . .

(32b)   [since] they broke this covenant of mine

(32c)   [even though] I was their husband, says the LORD.

(33a)   [The reason the new covenant will be different in this regard is that] this is the covenant which I will make with the house of Israel after those days, says the LORD: I will put my Law within them, and I will write it upon their hearts;

(33b)   [The result of this new covenant will be that] I will be their God, and they shall be my people.

(34a)   [The ultimate consequence of this new covenant relationship in which I am their God and they are my people is that] no longer shall each man teach his neighbor and each his brother saying, 'Know the LORD,'

(34b)   [because] they shall all know me, from the least of them to the greatest, says the LORD;

(34c)   [The basis for all of this is that] I will forgive their iniquity, and I will remember their sin no more."

The first thing to note is that the new covenant is the divinely promised answer to the perennial problem of Israel's hard-hearted rebellion against the Lord. Given Israel's history of being unfaithful to the covenant, God declared that not even the intercession of a Moses, not to mention Jeremiah himself, could avert God's coming anger in the judgment of the Exile (Jer. 15:1; compare 9:12-16; 11:14; 14:11). As the Lord proclaimed through Jeremiah,

"From the day that your fathers came out of the land of Egypt to this day, I have persistently sent all my servants the prophets to them, day after day; yet they did not listen to me, or incline their ear, but stiffened their neck. They did worse than their fathers" (Jer. 7:25-26).[5]

What is needed, therefore, is nothing less than a new beginning, one in which God's people will be decisively and radically changed in their relationship to God. Jeremiah thus looked to a *future* in which Israel's stubbornness would no longer characterize her response to God. The adjective "new," used to describe this coming covenant in Jeremiah 31:31, points to a reality yet to be fulfilled, which Jeremiah holds forth as Israel's only hope after the destruction of the Exile (compare Jer. 31:1-30, 35-40).

Second, the nature of this new covenant is described in Jeremiah 31:32-33 by contrasting it to the Sinai covenant made with the fathers at the Exodus (see Jer. 11:1-6). The grim news is that the fathers, "when I brought them up from the land of Egypt" (Jer. 11:7), as well as the Israel and Judah of Jeremiah's day (Jer. 11:9-10; compare 22:9-10),[6] have broken the old covenant "in the stubbornness of [their] evil heart" (Jer. 11:8). They thus stand under the wrath of God (Jer. 11:11). In stark contrast, the essential difference between the new and old covenants is not that a new *type* of covenant will be established or that a new *content* will be given to the old, but that, unlike the Sinai covenant, the new covenant will not be *broken*. Unlike the Sinai covenant, the new covenant will be an "everlasting covenant which will never be forgotten" (Jer. 50:5).

Jeremiah 31:33 states the reason for this confidence. The new covenant will not be broken because in it God will place his law "within them" or "write it upon their hearts."[7] Such a writing of the Law on their hearts is the reversal of the situation in Jeremiah's day, in which the *sin* of Judah was "written with a pen of iron; with a point of diamond it is engraved on the tablet of their heart" (Jer. 17:1). In other words, her hardened disobedience will be replaced with an obedience to God's covenant stipulations as intended in his Law. Against the backdrop of Israel's stubborn rebellion from the Exodus onward, this "writing the Law on the heart" can only mean that in the new covenant Israel's rebellious nature will be fundamentally *transformed*. In contrast to the conflict under the old covenant between God's commandments and the desires of Israel's "heart" (compare, for example, Num. 15:39), under the new covenant there will be harmony between God's Law and the inward desires and decisions of his people.

The image of the Law being placed "within" and "written on the heart" thus evokes a people who accept God's Law and keep it willingly. In the "new covenant," the Law will not be cast off, or obeyed only grudgingly. Nor will it be used as a self-justifying badge of honor. Instead, the Law will encounter a transformed people who will fulfill the covenant stipulations (including the call for a humble repentance and contrite heart that looks to God for mercy and forgiveness—Ps. 51:1-17; Mic. 6:8; Matt. 23:23), so that their relationship of faithfulness to God will be maintained, and God's covenant promise will be realized: "I will be their God, and they will be my people" (Jer. 31:33c).

Third, verse 33 establishes that keeping the Law, in *response* to God's act of redemption (compare Jer. 31:1-30), is that which maintains the new covenant relationship between God and his people. Rather than declaring that the Law will be negated in the new covenant, Jeremiah 31:31-33 emphasizes just the opposite. Far from dismissing the Law, Jeremiah stresses that it is the ability to keep the Law as a result of having a transformed nature that distinguishes the new covenant from the covenant at Sinai. The contrast between the two covenants is not a contrast between two different conditions for keeping the covenants (i.e., obedience vs. faith), but a contrast between two different responses to the same Law.

Finally, verse 34 states the consequence of this promised transformation of God's people and its ultimate foundation. Having God's Law written on their hearts, the people of the new covenant will no longer be a mixed multitude in which a small remnant who knew the Lord had to call the nation *itself* to repentance. Under the old covenant, one belonged to the covenant community by birth, so that it was possible to be part of Israel ethnically but not spiritually. One could be circumcised in the flesh as an Israelite without being circumcised in heart. Only a small subset of the nation, the "remnant" (Rom. 11:5), were spiritually circumcised, that is, they were not only part of Israel physically but also had their hearts changed by God so that they were able to keep the covenant. Under the new covenant, however, all those who are members of God's people will know the Lord personally, having been "born again" by the Spirit (John 3:3-8). In other words, what was true of the faithful remnant under the old covenant, like Elijah and the seven thousand who did not bow their knees to Baal (1 Kings 19:18), will be true of *all* God's people under the new covenant (Rom. 11:1-24). The people of the new covenant, *by definition*, will have changed, "circumcised hearts," signified by baptism as the sign of faith (Col. 2:11-12; see also Acts 2:38; 8:12; 18:8; 19:4; Rom. 2:28-29; 4:11). As a result, the witness of the people of God will no longer be to one's "neighbor" within the covenant community but from the covenant community to the world (Matt. 28:18-20).

Jeremiah 31:34 therefore points to a time when the role of the priests as mediators of the will, knowledge, and presence of God will no longer be necessary. Having transformed their hearts, God will renew his people's ability to know him *directly*, whereas under the Sinai covenant the presence of God had to be veiled from the people due to their sinful, "stiff-necked" state, in order to protect them from being destroyed by God's glory (compare Jer. 7:26; 19:15 with Ex. 33:3, 5 and Deut. 9:6, 13; and compare Ex. 34:29-35 with 2 Cor. 3:7-14). Verse 34 therefore concludes by stressing that the foundation of the new covenant is the fact that God will "remember their sin no more." The changed condition of God's people as a whole, their divinely granted ability to keep the Law, their renewed access to the presence of God, and their consequent witness to the world around them are all based entirely on God's act of forgiveness as the foundational provision of the new covenant.

Today we know that this forgiveness was brought about by the life, death, and resurrection of the Christ, whose coming consequently inaugurated the new covenant. This is the point made in Hebrews 10:11-18, which explicitly quotes the promise from Jeremiah 31:34:

> And every priest stands daily at his service, offering repeatedly the same sacrifices, which can never take away sins. But when Christ had offered for all time a single sacrifice for sins, he sat down at the right hand of God, then to wait until his enemies should be made a stool for his feet. For by a single offering he has perfected for all time those who are sanctified. And the Holy Spirit also bears witness to us; for after saying,

> "This is the covenant that I will make with them
> after those days, says the Lord:
> I will put my laws on their hearts, and write them on their minds,"

> then he adds,

> "I will remember their sins and their misdeeds no more."

Where there is forgiveness of these, there is no longer any offering for sin.

When Christ died for our sins as the one true sacrifice (to which the sacrifices of the old covenant had pointed), the veil in the temple that separated God's glory from his people split in two; when Christ rose from the dead, the power of sin over our lives broke; when Christ ascended to the Father, the Spirit was poured out in our hearts that we might be raised to new life with him. Thus, in and through Christ, God's people have been "perfected for all time" as those God already considers holy in his sight and is now making holy in their lives. In response, the Gospel is the declaration that the long-awaited "end times" or "last days" when God would gather his people to himself under a "new covenant," as part of a "new creation" submitted to his reign in the "kingdom of God," began with Christ's first coming (Mark 1:14-15; Luke 22:20; Acts 2:14-36; 2 Cor. 3:6; 5:17; Gal. 6:15; Heb. 1:2; 8:1-13; 9:26).

Although the Bible nowhere teaches that God's people will live perfect lives this side of Christ's return (1 John 1:8), it does assume that by the power of the Spirit those who trust in God and hope in his promises, having been forgiven of their sins, will live in growing obedience to his commands as they learn to depend upon his word. This is what it means to be in a new covenant relationship with God. For as God declares in another key Old Testament passage about the new covenant, Ezekiel 36:27, "I will put my spirit within you, and cause you to walk in my statutes and be careful to observe my ordinances."

This passage makes clear that Spirit-caused obedience, based on the cleansing of our sins, is a key characteristic of the new covenant (Ezek. 36:22-28). As a description of this forgiveness, we read in Ezekiel 36:25 that God promises one day to "sprinkle clean water" upon his people and to cleanse them "from all [their] uncleannesses, and from all [their] idols." Like Jeremiah, Ezekiel then announces that God will give his people a "new heart" and a "new spirit," having taken out their "heart of stone" and having replaced it with a "heart of flesh" responsive to his will (Ezek. 36:26). What Jeremiah describes using the language of the new covenant, forgiveness, and the Law written on the heart, against the backdrop of the Sinai covenant, Ezekiel pictures in terms of ritual cleansing and the pouring out of the Spirit, using his experience as a priest as the point of comparison. Like the priests in the temple, all of God's people will one day be purified in order to enter into his presence and mediate his glory to the world (see Ex. 19:6; 1 Pet. 2:9).

It was precisely this experience of being cleansed from sin and empowered for obedience (as depicted by Ezekiel) that Jesus alluded to in his conversation with Nicodemus, when he declared, "Truly, truly, I say to you, unless one is born from above, he cannot see the kingdom of God" (John 3:3, mg.). For as Jesus says in John 3:5, "unless one is born of *water* [forgiven for one's sins] and the *Spirit* [empowered to keep the Law], he cannot enter the kingdom of God." In other words, only those who experience the reality of the new covenant will enter into God's kingdom. Being accepted into the kingdom is like being "born again," this time "from above," i.e., from God (John 1:12-13; 3:4), since it is a completely new beginning in life, with a new power for living it.

THE LAW OF THE GOSPEL AND THE GOSPEL IN THIS LAW

The fact that under the new covenant God writes the Law on his people's (transformed) hearts, having granted them forgiveness and the Spirit, is why Jesus insisted in the Sermon on the Mount that the ultimate intention of God's Law must now be kept! Indeed, Jesus' followers must even love their enemies and pray for those who persecute them (Ex. 23:4-5; Prov. 25:21; see Matt. 5:21-48). Looking at it from the outside, Jesus' demands seem impossible to the point of being ridiculous. But Jesus is serious. In fact, he warns us that "whoever . . . relaxes one of the least of these commandments and teaches men so, shall be called least in the kingdom of heaven; but he who does them and teaches them shall be called great in the kingdom of heaven" (Matt. 5:19). Why does Jesus insist that teaching and obeying his commands is the pathway to greatness?

The answer to this question resides in the fact that Jesus ties his commands to the kingdom. Obedience is the pathway to greatness because Jesus has established the reign of God over his people, which entails God's Spirit being poured out in our lives. The command to live under God's dominion, first given to Adam and Eve at creation, can therefore be restored with the inauguration of the kingdom, since the power of God's presence in our midst is the dawning of the new creation. Jesus' demands flow from his gifts. Jesus therefore commands what he commands because of the reality of the Cross (forgiveness) and the Spirit (God's power), not to mention his defending us before God so that nothing can separate us from his love (Rom. 8:33-39). Anyone who diminishes Jesus' commands is, in reality, downsizing the significance of Jesus' life, death, resurrection, and ascension. To deny the *need* to obey is to deny the *power* to obey that comes with Christ's establishment of God's rule over his people.

The difficulty of the commands is merely a reflection of the greatness of the Gospel. Jesus' *expectation* is built on his *anticipation* of what God will do in the lives of his people! Jesus demands the *humanly* impossible precisely because his provisions are *supernatural*. The magnitude of Jesus' commands must mean, therefore, that they are tied to the grandest promise of all, namely, the promise that God himself will work in every circumstance to conform us to the image of Christ (Rom. 8:28-29).

This is why Jesus teaches the seemingly impossible requirements of the Law in the Sermon on the Mount, warning that "unless your righteousness exceeds that of the scribes and Pharisees, you will never enter the kingdom of heaven" (Matt. 5:20), while also declaring that he will give rest to "all who labor and are heavy laden" because "my yoke is *easy*, and my burden is *light*" (Matt. 11:28-30, emphasis added). The "yoke" in this text is Jesus' own interpretation of the Law's intention and significance, in contrast to the interpretation of the Law given by the Pharisees![8] The "burden" too heavy to carry is not emotional distress or personal problems but trying to keep the Law without the Spirit. In contrast, Jesus' demands, though more *difficult* than the Pharisee's interpretation of the Law, are nevertheless a yoke that is *easy* to bear and a burden that is *light* to carry because of the coming of the kingdom and inauguration of the new covenant.

On the one hand, Jesus shows that God's commandments are harder than what the Pharisees taught because the original intent of the Law speaks to the moral condition of the heart, rather than merely regulating external and symbolic behaviors. In this sense, our righteousness must "exceed" what the Pharisees required. Ritual purity is not enough; we must be pure of heart. Adultery is really a matter of lust, and murder of anger. Jesus makes clear that the Law prohibits the former as an expression of the latter. Adultery is the outcome of lust, and murder is the result of anger. Thus, in putting this yoke of the Law on his follow-ers, Jesus is not giving them a new set of commandments. He is simply demonstrating that outward observance to the Law's commands is not what it means to do the will of God, since the Law is an expression of God's character and promises, not merely a list of external duties. "Right" actions often remain merely a smoke screen covering up our most sinful attitudes of pride and self-reliance.

On the other hand, Jesus' yoke is easy and his burden is light in com-parison to the teaching of the Pharisees because he is not calling for a superhuman display of willpower, or setting up a utopian ideal that we should never expect to attain. Rather, Jesus' teaching on the Law is "easy" because, in bringing the kingdom, *Jesus is providing what he demands!* Based on human resources alone, Jesus' demands remain ide-alistic dreams. But with God *all things* are possible, even the transfor-mation of the human heart from the love of money to the love of God (Mark 10:27). Jesus' demands are "light" because God himself will enable us to keep them. Jesus' burden is "easy" because it is the "bur-den" of trusting in God's promises and relying on his Spirit, a "burden" made possible by Christ himself.

THE HEART OF THE GOOD NEWS

Jesus' call for true obedience to God's commands was an essential part of his message because it reflected the central purpose of his ministry. This purpose was crystallized in the statement of Mark 10:45, where Jesus declared that, as the "Son of Man," he "came not to be served but to serve, and to give his life as a ransom for many." In fulfillment of Isaiah 52:13–53:12 (see especially Isa. 53:12, to which Jesus alludes in Mark 10:45), Jesus' death was the means by which God's people may be forgiven and cleansed of their sins. Jesus accomplished this by offer-ing his own life to God in ransom for the lives of his followers. In a shocking turn of events, the "Son of Man" from Daniel 7:13-27, who is to incorporate God's people into his own destiny of judging the world and being served by all nations, first comes as the "suffering Servant" of Isaiah 53, who gives his life as a sacrifice for the sins of his people and calls his followers to join him in being a slave to all (Mark 10:35-45).

The death of Christ was the necessary foundation for God's work of establishing his reign on earth under the new covenant, for, in view of the world's rebellion (Rom. 1:18-32; 3:9-18, 23), the kingdom can only be built on the forgiveness of sins (Jer. 31:34; Ezek. 36:25). But God's mercy cannot compromise his holiness or contradict his covenant promise to curse sin. If it did, he would be going against his own character, thereby denying his commitment to glorify himself in all things (see chapter 4). If God were simply to wink at sin, or to forgive it without upholding his justice and judgment, then God's faithfulness and the truth of his character would be called into question. God's commitment to maintain his own glory *demands* that he punish those who disregard his word and thereby dishonor his reputation.

If God is to forgive us, the penalty for our sin must therefore be paid. In the technical language of theology, the death/blood of Christ is therefore the means by which God fulfills the need for *atonement* prefigured in the sacrifices of the old covenant (compare, for example, Rom. 3:25-26, 4:25, 5:8, 8:3; 1 Cor. 6:11; 11:23-26; 15:3-5; 2 Cor. 5:21; and Col. 1:19-20 against the backdrop of Lev. 4:13-24; 10:17; 16; 17:11, and the extended arguments of Heb. 7:7-28 and 9:1–10:18). Thus, in Christ, "we have *redemption* through his blood, the forgiveness of our trespasses" (Eph. 1:7, emphasis added). As our great high priest, Christ not only mediates the offering before God but also is *himself* that offering (Heb. 7:27; 9:26-28).

This is where God's indescribable mercy breaks into our lives: instead of requiring *us* to pay the price, God pays it *himself* with the perfect life of his only Son. Not having sinned himself, Jesus is able to give his life as a ransom for ours. Thus, Christ "died for sins once for all, the righteous for the unrighteous, that he might bring us to God" (1 Pet. 3:18). For in his sinlessness as a man, and in his identity as the divine Son of God, Jesus was able to pay the penalty for the sins not just of one man but of all humanity. In the words of Hebrews 9:26, Jesus "has appeared once for all at the end of the ages to put away sin by the sacrifice of himself" (compare Heb. 10:12). The result of Jesus' atoning death in our place is the *reconciliation* we enjoy with God as new creatures in Christ, since "in Christ God was reconciling the world to himself, not counting their trespasses against them" (2 Cor. 5:17-21). Though we were formerly his enemies, the Gospel declares that our warfare with God can be ended and our rebellion against him forgiven.

Jesus' death therefore *substitutes* for the punishment that would otherwise be ours. Hence, we are "saved" from the consequences of our sin the moment we begin to trust God's promise of forgiveness made possible by the perfect life and atoning death of Christ (Isa. 53:11-13; Acts 10:43). In Paul's words, "we are now justified [declared "not guilty" before God's judgment] by his blood," and can therefore be fully confident of being "saved by [Christ] from the wrath of God" to come (Rom. 5:9; compare 1 Thess. 1:10).

As an act of complete grace ("while we were yet sinners Christ died for us"—Rom. 5:8), the final verdict to be handed down at the last judgment concerning our eternal destiny has already been declared in advance (Rom. 5:1; 8:30; 10:9-13; compare Acts 13:38-39)! In this sense too, the rule of God's kingdom, which is established with his judgment, has been inaugurated in anticipation of its final consummation (John 5:24, 29; 12:31; 1 John 4:17). With our first "mustard seed" of faith, God grants to us his forgiveness and engages all of his saving power on our behalf in accordance with his promises, because Jesus is now ruling over us as our sovereign King. Because of Christ's death and by virtue of our faith, we enter into a covenant relationship with God in which he becomes our God and we become his people (2 Cor. 6:16-18). Our penalty is paid; our future is secure: "So Christ, having been offered once to bear the sins of many, will appear a second time, not to deal with sin but to save those who are eagerly waiting for him" (Heb. 9:28). As John Piper has put it,

> The good news is that God himself has decreed a way to satisfy the demands of his justice without condemning the whole human race. Hell is one way to settle accounts with sinners and uphold his justice. But there is another way. The wisdom of God has ordained a way for the love of God to deliver us from the wrath of God without compromising the justice of God. And what is this wisdom? The death of the Son of God for sinners![9]

THE SCANDAL OF THE CROSS

The center point of the Bible's message, therefore, is Jesus of Nazareth.[10] The heart of Jesus' message was that the long-awaited kingdom of God was now being established through his life and ministry, which he demonstrated through his miracles, exorcisms, and gathering of disciples. This could only mean that Jesus is Israel's "Messiah" ("Christ"), that is, the one "anointed" to be her final King and deliverer (Matt. 16:13-20; 23:10; 26:63-64; Luke 23:2; John 20:31; Acts 5:31; 13:23; etc.). As such, Jesus is also Lord of lords and King of kings, the Savior and judge of the world, the incarnation of God himself (Ps. 17:7; Isa. 43:3, 11; Hos. 13:4; John 4:42; 2 Tim. 1:10; 2 Pet. 1:1, 11; 1 John 4:14). People are therefore called to repent and to trust in the good news that God's rule is breaking into the world (Mark 1:14-15; Matt. 4:12-17; Luke 4:14-21, 43; compare Isa. 52:7; 61:1).

But Jesus' means for inaugurating the kingdom was scandalous. The kingdom did not come in the way people expected. Rather than wiping out the Romans and liberating Israel politically to be the new rulers of the world under Christ's authority, the kingdom of God was established through the suffering and death of the Messiah himself. Those whom the people expected the Messiah to condemn ended up condemning the Messiah! The judgment of God that should have fallen on the wicked (Matt. 3:1-12; Luke 3:1-18) fell on Jesus! Instead of judging the pagans, Jesus' pathway to the glory of God's reign over the world was his own death on a Roman cross as a matter of political expediency (Matt. 27:11, 37; Mark 10:32-34; Luke 9:51; 23:2-3).

In accordance with Deuteronomy 21:23, the Jews therefore interpreted Jesus' death on the "tree" as a sign that he had been cursed by God for his presumption, blasphemy, and attempt to lead the people astray. He was, in their eyes, a false messiah. This was also Paul's conclusion before his encounter with the living Christ, so that out of zeal for God's Law he initially persecuted Christians as dangerous heretics (Acts 5:27-33; 8:3; Gal. 1:13; 3:13; 1 Cor. 15:9; 1 Tim. 1:13). Even John the Baptist had wondered if Jesus could really be the Messiah, since John's own stand for the kingdom was costing him his life (Matt. 11:3). If the kingdom was here, why was its king, God's Son, and those who stood with him, still suffering under the sin and unrighteousness of this world? Christ's suffering and death on the Cross, together with the continued suffering of his followers, therefore became a "stumbling block" to Jews and "folly to Gentiles," who could not accept the thought of a crucified Messiah or a suffering deity (1 Cor. 1:23).

Nevertheless, God certified Jesus as Israel's Messiah and God's Son by raising him from the dead and seating him at his right hand in glory, from where he will return to judge the living and the dead and to establish the kingdom in all its fullness (Mark 8:34-38; 14:62; Acts 2:22-36; 10:42; 17:31; Rom. 1:3-4; 1 Cor. 15:23-26; 2 Cor. 5:10; 1 Thess. 4:13–5:11; 2 Tim. 4:1, 8; Titus 2:13; 1 Pet. 4:5; see chapter 8). As we stressed earlier, Jesus' resurrection is God's stamp of approval on his life and death, thereby demonstrating that on the Cross Jesus was not being cursed by God for his own transgressions but for those of his people (Gal. 3:13-14; 1 John 2:2; 4:10). In view of the Resurrection, Peter declared, "Therefore let all Israel be assured of this: God has made this Jesus, whom you crucified, both Lord and Christ" (Acts 2:36). The earliest written formulation we have of the Gospel, quoted by Paul in 1 Corinthians 15:3-5, can consequently summarize the good news in five brief statements:

> that Christ died for our sins according to the Scriptures,
> that he was buried,
> that he was raised on the third day according to the Scriptures,
> and that he appeared to Peter,
> and then to the Twelve.

SAVED BY GRACE

This side of the Cross, we now know what the Old Testament prophets and even the angels longed to learn, namely, how cowards like Abraham and adulterers and murderers like David could be forgiven and treated as just without compromising God's justice (1 Pet. 1:10-12). Under the old covenant, with its symbolic sacrificial system, it appeared as if God was simply ignoring the sins of those who trusted in him for forgiveness (Rom. 3:25). After all, "it is impossible that the blood of bulls and goats should take away sins" (Heb. 10:4). The life of an animal can hardly pay the penalty for the sin of those made in the image of God. In the shadow of the Cross, however, it is possible to see that Jesus is the reason God can justify the ungodly without compromising his own integrity (compare Rom. 4:1-8).

Thus, when God forgave his people during Israel's history under the old covenant, he did so looking forward to the cross of Christ. When God forgives us today under the new covenant, he looks back at that same cross. The cross of Christ in the midst of history was the center-piece of God's plan before the foundation of the world (1 Pet. 1:20). As such, Christ's death is the ground of God's forgiveness both retroactively and proactively. "Christ . . . died for sins once for all" (1 Pet. 3:18). Nobody, from Adam and Eve to the person sitting in church next to you, was ever forgiven apart from the mercy of God made possible by the death of Christ.

This is why the Bible teaches that we are saved by God's "grace." Being forgiven, declared justified, receiving the Spirit, and living the life of faith, not to mention our resurrection from the dead and inheriting the glory of Christ at end of history, are all a gift from God. As Brian Vickers has said, the coming of the kingdom is thus "a wonderful, Trinitarian act."[11]

There are therefore no "entrance requirements" that must first be fulfilled before God will break into our lives. Nor is our resultant life of faith one of "cooperating with God," in which we add our efforts to his. Christ is both the author and the perfecter of our faith. We are not and will not be justified by our own "works," as if we could earn our salvation through our efforts or deserve it because of some distinctive in us (Rom. 4:5). We are justified solely by Jesus' blood (Rom. 5:9), which unleashes all of God's power and promises on our behalf, both now and throughout eternity. Our salvation is totally a matter of God's mercy in extending forgiveness to people who do not deserve it and cannot earn it. God makes us "alive, when [we] were dead through the trespasses and sins in which [we] once walked" (Eph. 2:1-2). So, "by grace we have been saved through faith; and this is not your own doing, it is the gift of God" (Eph. 2:8).

The best news we will ever hear is that forgiveness and the eternal life it brings are the "free gift of God . . . in Christ Jesus" (Rom. 6:23). The magnitude of this merciful gift can be seen in the fact that this "free gift," even though it "follows many trespasses," nevertheless still "justifies" us before God (Rom. 5:16). Jesus paid the penalty for our sins as our ransom, so that God might bring us back to himself and treat us as if we had never sinned in the first place! The work of the Spirit is to open our blind eyes to the truth and wonder of what Christ has done on our behalf, so that we might be reconciled with God and delivered from our slavery to sin. For, as Jesus said to his disciples, "If you continue in my word, you are truly my disciples, and you will know the truth, and the truth will make you free" (John 8:31-32). But inasmuch as the Jews of Jesus' day did not understand the kind of freedom that Jesus was offering them, he declared:

> "Truly, truly I say to you, every one who commits sin is a slave to sin. The slave does not continue in the house for ever; the son continues for ever. So if the Son makes you free, you will be free indeed" (John 8:34-36).

This "freedom" from sin and the promise to join Jesus in God's "house" forever is the difference Jesus makes. Such freedom to obey and its promise of eternal life is the full measure of what it means to be saved by grace through faith.

CONCLUSION

Who Are We?

The Marks of a Christian

And it is my prayer
that your love may abound more and more,
with knowledge and all discernment,
so that you may approve what is excellent,
and may be pure and blameless
for the day of Christ,
filled with the fruits of righteousness
which come through Jesus Christ,
to the glory and praise of God.
PHILIPPIANS 1:9-11

The mark of a Christian, like that of the faithful remnant throughout Israel's history, is the presence of God in one's life. We cannot confess that Jesus is Lord apart from the Holy Spirit invading our lives (1 Cor. 12:3). To "see the kingdom of God," one must therefore be "born from above" (John 3:3, mg.); conversely, "Any one who does not have the Spirit of Christ does not belong to him" (Rom. 8:9).

The good news of the Gospel is the forgiveness bestowed on God's people as a result of Christ's death, which makes it possible for God to dwell in their midst without destroying them, but instead transforming them into his own likeness (2 Cor. 3:18). So, when Peter saw that Cornelius, a pagan Gentile, had received the Spirit, he was forced to conclude that God had called Cornelius to be a member of his chosen people, a descendant of Abraham by faith—the case was open and shut (see Acts 10:44-48; 11:17).

As a result of the history of redemption, even pagan Gentiles who entrust their lives to God because of Christ are incorporated into his chosen people as sons and daughters of Abraham, since they too, like Abraham, have received the provision of God's presence. In fulfillment of Genesis 12:1-3, Gentile believers are thus "blessed with Abraham who had faith" (Gal. 3:8-9), since the death of Christ has made it possible for "the blessing of Abraham," namely, the Spirit's presence in their lives, to come upon them (Gal. 3:14). In fact, after hearing what had happened to Cornelius, even those within the Jerusalem church who had earlier resisted accepting Gentile believers as full-fledged members of God's covenant people had to agree that "to the Gentiles also God has granted repentance unto life" (Acts 11:18). Through the cross of Christ and pouring out of his Spirit, God had now made one people out of both Jews and Gentiles by grafting Gentiles into the line of the faithful remnant from throughout Israel's history (Luke 2:32; Acts 10:45; 11:18; 13:47; 15:3, 12-19; Rom. 3:29-30; 11:24; Eph. 2:11-22; Col. 1:27). "Once [Gentiles] were no people but now [they] are God's people; once [they] had not received mercy but now [they] have received mercy" (1 Pet. 2:10).

"Godly Grief"

It is important to note that Cornelius's experience of the Spirit was clear evidence that God had given him the gift of repentance. One of the first signs that God's Spirit has invaded our lives is that we begin to recognize just how wrongheaded our former way of life really was. In response, we feel remorse as it becomes clear that we were living as if God did not exist. We regret our former independence and self-reliance. By encountering God, we see that sin is not simply a series of misguided decisions but an affront to God's very character and glory. And so, aware of our guilt, we turn from our past way of life and throw ourselves on the mercy of God, knowing that our only hope is the forgiveness and freedom available in Christ. If we are going to be delivered from ourselves and from the God-denying culture around us, we know that God himself must do it (2 Cor. 4:4-6).

Such Spirit-instigated remorse over our sin, whether for the first, seventh, or the 490th time (Matt. 18:21-22), though painful to be sure, is a great gift. Paul even calls it a "godly grief," since it "produces a repentance that leads to salvation and brings no regret" (2 Cor. 7:10).[1] Thus, the sorrow is not an end in itself. Its offspring, repentance, is the essential, Spirit-enabled, life-changing resolve to reverse our behavior, a resolve expressing itself in taking our first steps in a new direction. Though its impact is lifelong, repentance involves an initial change in both attitude and action.

"Godly" grief, therefore, is not merely "feeling bad." People feel guilty for all kinds of reasons other than realizing that they have offended God. Such "worldly grief produces death" (2 Cor. 7:10). For rather than driving us back to God, "worldly sorrow" causes us to focus even more on how inadequate and hurt we are, thereby furthering the death that comes from living for self (compare 2 Cor. 5:15).

"Worldly grief" is the anguish that comes from missing out on what the world has to offer. "Godly grief" is the remorse that arises when we realize we have missed out on the approval and blessing of God. "Worldly grief," with its focus on the values and promises of this world, produces the same death from which it comes. "Godly grief" brings the repentance that leads to salvation because it has God as its source and thereby leads to the life from which it comes. "Worldly grief" cares about what the world thinks of us; "godly grief" cares about grieving the Spirit.[2] "Worldly grief" can be overcome with time, with some plea-sure in other areas of life, or with a good dose of denial, escape, or willpower. The only remedy for the pain of "godly grief" is repentance.

Those who realize that their lives are an inescapable distortion of what God intends them to be no longer downsize the gravity of their sins by comparing themselves to others or by offering God excuses for their actions. Nor do they attempt to escape their guilt by vowing to "try harder next time" or by offering God some other apparent achievement to make up for their idolatry. Instead, they respond like King David did when he was confronted with his adultery and murder:

> Have mercy on me, O God,
>   according to thy steadfast love;
> according to thy abundant mercy
>   blot out my transgressions.
> Wash me thoroughly from my iniquity
>   and cleanse me from my sin!
>
> For I know my transgressions,
>   and my sin is ever before me.

> Against thee, thee only, have I sinned
>   and done that which is evil in thy sight,
> so that thou art justified in thy sentence
>   and blameless in thy judgment.
> Behold, I was brought forth in iniquity,
>   and in sin did my mother conceive me. . . .
>
> Hide thy face from my sins,
>   and blot out all my iniquities.
>
> Create in me a clean heart, O God,
>   and put a new and right spirit within me (Ps. 51:1-5, 9-10).

All of us have a sinful heart like David's, regardless of how well we keep it under wraps. To encounter the holiness of God therefore is to see our own sin, and to understand that our sins against others are, in reality, sins against God (Ps. 51:44). And to know that we have sinned against God is to recognize that we deserve God's righteous judgment, so that we cry out for mercy and restoration (Ps. 51:1, 10).

This is why the Bible is often so hard to read, and why we avoid reading it so often, for it exposes us for who we are. Like a scalpel in the hands of a skilled surgeon, it cuts away to the cancer of our disbelief. On the way to enjoying the pleasures of God's healing presence (see Ps. 16:11!), reading the Bible can therefore cause great pain. As the book of Hebrews puts it,

> the word of God is living and active, sharper than any two-edged sword, piercing to the division of soul and spirit, of joints and marrow, and discerning the thoughts and intentions of the heart. And before him no creature is hidden, but all are open and laid bare to the eyes of him with whom we have to do (Heb. 4:12-13).

Again, the purpose of this spiritual surgery is not simply to make us feel bad but to produce repentance, that we may enter the sabbath rest of trusting God with our lives (Heb. 4:11).

To sum up, "godly grief" and the repentance it brings about is a Spirit-produced remorse concerning our ungodliness, and the resulting determination to forsake our sin and to obey God, based on the conviction that God's promise of forgiveness and the power of the Spirit in our lives (both made possible by Christ) are our only hope for this new beginning. Together with "faith toward God," this "repentance from dead works" is the "foundation" of the Christian life (Heb. 6:1).

THE GIFT OF THE GOSPEL

This call to repent makes it all the more necessary to remember that faith-obedience is the work of *God*. Otherwise we pervert the Gospel into yet another attempt to justify ourselves (Eph. 2:8-10). The Bible nowhere teaches that we must first "get our act together" before God can forgive us. "Dead" people cannot make themselves alive (Eph. 2:1). "Children of wrath" cannot be born again on their own (Eph. 2:2-3; see John 3:3-5). "Slaves" to sin cannot liberate themselves (Rom. 6:17-22; 1 Cor. 7:23).

Repentance, like salvation as a whole, is a gift of God's sovereign grace in accordance with his unconditional election, not an act of human initiative or a self-generated decision (Acts 5:31; 11:18; 13:48; 2 Tim. 2:25). This does not mean that our responsibility to repent is somehow lessened. As we see from Peter's declaration in Acts 2:38, repentance, though a gift from God, can also be *commanded* as a *condition* for forgiveness. God's kindness and mercy do not destroy the need to repent. Nor do they blot out God's coming judgment. Instead, God's mercy and patience with his people, in anticipation of his coming judgment, are meant to "lead [us] to repentance" (Rom. 2:4; see also Acts 17:30; 2 Pet. 3:9). And as the expression of this mercy, God's command to repent is the very instrument he uses to bring us to repent. As Thomas Schreiner and Ardel Caneday have argued so forcefully, the Bible's warnings of God's judgment, admonitions to repent, and call to a persevering faith in the midst of adversity are the very means God uses to deliver his people from the wrath to come.[3]

Thus, we must resist downsizing repentance and faith into a change of mind and mental assent concerning the truth of data from the past. [4] Repentance and faith are not "decisions" we make once and for all. The Holy Spirit's invasion of our lives is the *beginning* of our transformation into the character of God, not its end (2 Cor. 3:18). By God's grace and power, all believers are therefore "in process." The life of faith is not per-fection overnight, but progression over a lifetime (2 Pet. 1:5-7). It is inconceivable to think that the same Spirit who raised Jesus from the dead would come into our lives and then do nothing. Where the Spirit is at work, our love and its "fruits of righteousness" abound "more and more" as we mature in our dependence upon Christ (Phil. 1:9-11). A growing, persevering faith in God's promises, expressed in obedience to his commands, is both the gift and call of God. As we read in 1 Peter 1:2, we have been "chosen and destined by God the Father and sanctified by the Spirit *for obedience to Jesus Christ*" (emphasis added).

"THE OBEDIENCE OF FAITH"

For many people, however, coming face to face with the Bible's call to obedience seems to put them right back on the treadmill of trying to live up to other people's expectations. Only now it is worse! Now *God* is the One who is expecting them to live up to *his* standards!

In view of this common response, and since God's glory is at stake in his commands, it is crucial that we once again get our facts straight. The call to obedience is not about earning points with God in order to show him how sincere we are. Nor is God commanding us to obey a standard that is beyond us. We are *not* being set up for failure. God is not trying to drive us to despair by his demands, in order to take us from the "Law" to the "Gospel," as if they were two different messages.

The structure of the covenant makes clear that in calling us to obedience God is simply and yet profoundly calling us to trust *his* promises and rely on *his* power in our lives (see chapter 2). The decrees of God are a description of what the presence of God means for our daily lives (1 John 3:9); every command of God is a promise of God in disguise. The call to obedience is a source of joy and wonder over God's great gift of salvation. In fact, the Gospel seems too good to be true! God demands what he does because he promises that "no temptation has overtaken us that is not common to man," for "God is faithful," so that "he will not let [us] be tempted beyond [our] strength, but with the temptation will also provide the way of escape, that [we] might be able to endure it" (1 Cor. 10:13). God will never require more from us than he gives to us! The good news, therefore, is that there is no excuse for sin.

In other words, both the *means* and the *result* of being saved by God's grace is what Paul called "the obedience of faith," that is to say, faith's obedience, the obedience that inextricably and organically belongs to faith as its expression (Rom. 1:5).[5] It is not surprising then that the central purpose of Paul's ministry was to bring about obedience to God as the expression of trusting in God's promises (compare Rom. 1:5 with Rom. 15:18). This is what mattered most to Paul, since the goal of God is to display the glory of his grace through the transformed lives of his people (Eph. 1:3-14). In describing his life as an apostle, Paul therefore writes,

> I will not venture to speak of anything except what Christ has wrought through me to win *obedience* from the Gentiles, by word and deed, by the power of signs and wonders, by the power of the Holy Spirit, so that from Jerusalem and as far round as Illyricum I have fully preached the *gospel of* Christ (Rom. 15:18-19, emphasis added).

We are not accustomed to identifying the Gospel of grace with obedience. But notice once again that Paul "wins *obedience*" when he preaches the *Gospel,* since obedience is the expression of genuine faith "in public." For this reason, when Paul confronted the Corinthians concerning their ungodly way of life, he told them to "examine yourselves, to see whether you are holding to your *faith*" (2 Cor. 13:5, emphasis added). In other words, they were to "test themselves" to see if they were in fact temples of God's Spirit (compare 2 Cor. 13:5 with 2 Cor. 6:14–7:1). And the test was a simple one: would they repent of their sins or not (2 Cor. 12:21). Right conduct is the outward expression of right faith. Faith without works is "dead" or "barren" because faith cannot exist or "live" without them (James 2:14-26).

THE MARKS OF GOD'S PRESENCE

Paul and James do not mince words in these passages. Life and death are at stake! The issue is whether their readers really know Christ, since Christians and non-Christians alike will "appear before the judgment seat of Christ, so that each one may receive good or evil, according to what he has done in the body" (2 Cor. 5:10; see Rom. 2:6-11).

When God examines the lives of his people on judgment day, he will see not only the *death* of Christ on their behalf, but also the *life* of Christ having been reproduced in their obedience (Rom. 6:2, 4), not perfectly overnight, but progressively over a lifetime, until that day when they stand perfected in his presence (Phil. 1:11). Having been justified by his grace, our Lord will say to us, in accordance with the resources that he has granted us, "Well done, good and faithful servant; you have been faithful over a little, I will set you over much; enter into the joy of your master" (Matt. 25:23). Having kept what the covenant requires, repentance and the obedience of faith, we will not suffer God's judgment.[6]

But our salvation redounds to God's praise, not our own, since *God* is the One who makes us "worthy of his call" by bringing about our repentance and enabling our "work of faith" (2 Thess. 1:11-12). Hence, the manner of our lives glorifies the mercy and saving character of our Lord Jesus. When all is said and done, God, not us, receives the honor for our lives, inasmuch as they are his work of grace. As Jesus assured his people,

> "My sheep hear my voice, and I know them, and they follow me; and
> I give them eternal life, and they shall never perish, and no one shall
> snatch them out of my hand. My Father, who has given them to me,
> is greater than all, and no one is able to snatch them out of the Father's
> hand. I and the Father are one" (John 10:27-29).

Hence, the declaration "not guilty" at the judgment seat of Christ will not be based on anything we have ever done for God (as if such a thing were even possible!), but on what God has done, is doing, and will do for us right up to the end.[7] Of course, no required "minimum standard" or quantitative amount of obedience is ever stated in the Scriptures. To suggest such a thing is to miss the point completely. The Spirit works powerfully within us not to meet some minimum requirement but to cause us to *delight* in God's will in *all* that we do. The desire of those who have the Spirit is not to see how *little* they can trust God but how much!

Finally, then, if our salvation, from our forgiveness in Christ, through our obedience by the Spirit, to our glorification in God's presence, is all the work of God on our behalf, it follows that our lives as Christians will be marked by praise and thanksgiving to God for what he has done, is doing, and will do in our lives. In short, the goal of theology (encountering God) is doxology (praising God) in word and deed.

Creating this desire to give God all the credit for our lives is the central purpose of the Spirit's presence in and among God's people (Matt. 5:16; John 16:14). Since we know that our "good works" are, in reality, the product of God's good work within us, he is the One who should be thanked and praised for all things everywhere at all times by all people. "What have you that you did not receive? If then you received it, why do you boast as if it were not a gift?" (see 1 Cor. 4:7).

Of course, those who do not know the Creator, Sustainer, Redeemer, and Judge attribute their fortunes and achievements to luck, fate, biology, societal forces, their own abilities, or their will to survive, all of which are subtle forms of idolatry. There is only "one God, the Father, from whom are all things and for whom we exist, and one Lord, Jesus Christ, through whom are all things and through whom we exist" (1 Cor. 8:6). Those who love God give thanks to him alone for the circumstances of their lives, knowing that God is working all things together (even suffering!) for the good of making them like Christ (Rom. 8:28). "For from him and through him and to him are all things. To him be glory for ever" (Rom. 11:36). In the words of Psalm 100,

> Make a joyful noise to the LORD, all the lands!
> Serve the LORD with gladness!
> Come into his presence with singing!
>
> Know that the LORD is God!
>   It is he that made us, and we are his;
> we are his people, and the sheep of his pasture.
>
> Enter his gates with thanksgiving,
>   and his courts with praise!
>   Give thanks to him, bless his name!
>
> For the LORD is good;
>   his steadfast love endures for ever,
>   and his faithfulness to all generations.

In creating anew a people who praise God with their mouths (Ps. 34:1; 118:28-29) and honor God in their bodies (1 Cor. 6:20), the dominion of God is revealed as the dominance of sin is broken. As new creatures in Christ, those who once suppressed the truth about God and refused to honor him or give thanks (Rom. 1:18-23) become a people whose God is the Lord and whose purpose for living is to glorify him (Rom. 15:6). Thus, to quote from the Psalms again:

> Thou art my God, and I will give thanks to thee;
>   thou art my God, I will extol thee.
> O give thanks to the LORD, for he is good;
>   for his steadfast love endures for ever! (Ps. 118:28-29).

Inasmuch as God is the sovereign Creator and Sustainer of all things, who rules all things for the good of his people, this call to thanksgiving extends to every circumstance and situation in life. It is the "will of God in Christ Jesus" that we "give thanks in *all* circumstances" (1 Thess. 5:18). It follows, then, because God is at work in us, that the *way* we "work out our own salvation with fear and trembling" is by doing "all things without grumbling or questioning, that we may be blameless and innocent, children of God without blemish in the midst of a crooked and perverse generation" (Phil. 2:12-15a).

In many ways, therefore, the "fight of faith" comes down to a fight for contentment, expressed in thankfulness (Eph. 5:20). Contentment is the fruit of trust in God's sovereignty and hope in his promises. Thus, there is "great gain in godliness" only when it is accompanied "with contentment," since "godliness" without contentment is a worthless self-contradiction (1 Tim. 6:6-8). Discontent and worry are votes of "no confidence" in God's ability to run our small corner of the universe! Even when we pray for our *needs* we must do so "without anxiety about anything," but "with thanksgiving" make our requests known to God (Phil. 4:6). Thanksgiving in the midst of need is the expression of faith in the sovereign love of God! And God's command to give thanks is comprehensive because his grace is all-encompassing: "whatever you do, in word or deed, do everything in the name of the Lord Jesus, giving thanks to God the Father through him" (Col. 3:17).

THE SUM OF THE MATTER: A NEW CREATION FOR GOD'S GLORY

So we end where we began, with the recreation through Christ, as our "second Adam," of men and women who, through their dependence on

God for all things, spread the glory of his sovereignty to the ends of the earth (see chapters 1 and 2). Hence, in bringing us back to God's original intention in the Garden of Eden, Jesus declares that as "the Son of man" he is "lord even of the sabbath" (Mark 2:28). In other words, as the Son of God, Jesus is the One who employs his sovereignty to meet our needs, demonstrated in his willingness to feed his hungry disciples and heal the man with a withered hand on the Sabbath (Mark 2:23–3:6). Under the new covenant, with the "Law written on our hearts" (Jer. 31:31-34), we therefore no longer "keep the Sabbath" by ceasing to work one day a week but by resting in Christ's commitment to lead, guide, and provide for us every day of our lives in every circumstance.

And trust him we can! Jesus, as Lord of the Sabbath, knows our needs and "works" to meet them in accordance with his wisdom, will, and love. As the Lord of the Sabbath, Jesus died for our sins, was raised for our justification, and ascended to the Father so that he might pour out the Spirit in our lives (Acts 2:29-36). Moreover, Jesus intercedes for us at the right hand of God to thwart all of Satan's designs and accusations against us (Rom. 8:34; Heb. 7:25; 9:24; 1 John 2:1). And one day Christ will return in all his glory to gather us into the presence of the Father for all eternity (Mark 13:24-27; 14:62; 1 Thess. 1:10; Heb. 9:28; Rev. 22:20).

Certainly, then, since "we seek the city [of God] which is to come" when Christ returns, let us "through him . . . continually offer up a sacrifice of praise to God, that is, the fruit of lips that acknowledge his name" (Heb. 13:15). As trophies of his grace, God gets *all* the credit for *every* aspect of our lives of faith, "for we are his workmanship, created in Christ Jesus for good works, which God prepared beforehand, that we should walk in them" (Eph. 2:10). All of our "fruits of righteousness" come "through Jesus Christ, to the glory and praise of God" (Phil. 1:11). For the Great *Commission* (Matt. 28:18-20a), as an expansion of the Great *Commandment* (Matt. 22:34-40), is made possible by the Great *Provision and Promise* (Matt. 28:20b): "Lo, I am with you always, to the close of the age."

Notes

Chapter One
Why Do We Exist?

1. Anthony A. Hoekema, *Created in God's Image* (Grand Rapids, Mich.: Eerdmans, 1986), 14. Hoekema's study is the best full-length work currently available on the biblical meaning and significance of the term "image of God."

2. Ibid., 4. It is worth quoting Hoekema's summary in full: "The image of God in man must therefore be seen as involving both the structure of man (his gifts, capacities, and endowments) and the functioning of man (his action, his relationships to God and to others, and the way he uses his gifts). To stress either of these at the expense of the other is to be one-sided. We must see both, but we need to see the structure of man as secondary and his functioning as primary. God has created us in his image so that we may carry out a task, fulfill a mission, pursue a calling. . . . To see man as the image of God is to see both the task and the gifts. But the task is primary; the gifts are secondary. The gifts are the means for fulfilling the task" (73).

3. In Genesis 1:26-28 there are two Hebrew words used to describe mankind's identity, which are also represented in the English translation: mankind is created "in our *image*, after our *likeness*" (Gen. 1:26). A careful study shows that these two words do not refer to two different aspects of humanity, but are simply synonyms. Thus, Genesis 1:27 uses the same word twice to describe humanity ("image"), while Genesis 5:1, where we encounter the same motif again, simply uses the word "likeness" without using the word "image" at all, only to speak of being in one's "likeness" and "image" in 5:3. So, as synonyms, both terms can be used parallel to each other, one or the other can be used by itself, or, as in Genesis 5:3, both can be used in reverse order. Hence, we must not conclude from Genesis 1:26 that humanity has two different aspects, i.e., a spiritual nature (one's "image") and a physical nature ("one's likeness"), or a spiritual and psychological nature, or a rational and emotional nature, etc. To be created in God's "image" or after his "likeness" expresses the same reality and refers to a person in his or her totality.

4. Daniel P. Fuller, *The Unity of the Bible*, unpublished syllabus, revised edition, 1974, vii-4. The same point has now been made in Fuller's *The Unity of the Bible: Unfolding God's Plan for Humanity* (Grand Rapids, Mich.: Zondervan, 1992), 109. Much of what follows in this chapter and throughout this book is indebted to the work of Daniel Fuller and his student John Piper, who, as God's instruments of grace, taught me how to do biblical theology and modeled how to live in light of it (see footnotes below).

5. Meredith Kline *Images of the Spirit* (South Hamilton, Mass.: Gordon-Conwell Theological Seminary, 1986 [1980]), 28.

6. Jean Danielou, *In the Beginning . . . Genesis I-III* (Baltimore: Helicon, 1965), 38.

7. For an analysis of this movement, see Peter Jones, *The Gnostic Empire Strikes Back: An Old Heresy for the New Age* (Phillipsburg, N.J.: Presbyterian and Reformed, 1992).

8. Paul R. House, *Old Testament Theology* (Downers Grove, Ill.: InterVarsity, 1998), 59. House's very helpful theology traces the theme of theology proper, i.e., the identity, nature, and purpose of God, throughout the Old Testament.

9. John Piper, *Desiring God: Meditations of a Christian Hedonist* (Sisters, Ore.: Multnomah; expanded edition, 1996), 44-45; the quote is from Jonathan Edwards, "Dissertation Concerning the End for Which God Created the World," *The Works of Jonathan Edwards, vol. 1* (Edinburgh: Banner of Truth Trust, 1974), 102. For Edwards's essay and an insightful introduction to it, see John Piper, *God's Passion for His Glory: Living the Vision of Jonathan Edwards* (Wheaton, Ill.: Crossway, 1998). The idea that God "went public" in creation is taken from Daniel Fuller's *Unity*, chs. 8 and 9.

10. For a development of this important point, see John Piper, *The Pleasures of God: Meditations on God's Delight in Being God* (Sisters, Ore.: Multnomah, revised and expanded version, 2000).

11. Fuller, *Unity*, 136.

12. Piper, *Desiring God*, 32.

13. Joy Davidman, *Smoke on the Mountain: An Interpretation of the Ten Commandments* (Philadelphia: Westminster, 1974 [1954]), 23.

14. For the development of the link between worship and obedience, see Fuller, *Unity*, 150-151.

15. Blaise Pascal, *Pascal's Pensees*, trans. W. F. Trotter (New York: E. P. Dutton, 1958), 113; as quoted by Piper, *Desiring God*, 18.

Chapter Two:
What Does It Mean to Know God?

1. Mark R. Talbot, "Does God Reveal Who He Actually Is," in Douglas S. Huffman and Eric L. Johnson, eds., *God Under Fire: Modern Scholarship Reinvents God* (Grand Rapids, Mich.: Zondervan, forthcoming, 2001). Talbot also points out that "God's *faithfulness* depends on his power (see 2 Sam. 7:8-16; Ps. 91:1-3; Isa. 31:4-5; Jer. 35:18-19; Hag. 2:23; Zech. 1;17; Rev. 19:11-16), as does the *trustworthiness* and *certainty* of his word (see Jer. 7:3-7; 19:1-3, 15; 32:14-15; 38:17-23; Zech. 8:2-3; Rev. 19:11-16), as does his *power to save* (see Ps. 80:7; Isa. 47:4; 51:12-16; Jer. 11:20; 50:33-34; Mic. 4:1-4; Zech. 3:8-10; 12:5; Mal. 3:1; 4:1-3; Rev. 11:15-18; 19:1-8) as well as his *goodness* and his *love* . . ."

2. C. S. Lewis, "The Weight of Glory," in Lewis, *The Weight of Glory and Other Essays* (Grand Rapids, Mich.: Eerdmans, 1965), 1-15, 2.

3. The missing element in this introductory work is a sustained development of the history of redemption into which these themes must be integrated. Such a framework would stretch from creation, Sabbath, and first exodus under the old covenant, to the "second exodus" in Christ, the new creation, and the reconstituted Sabbath under the new covenant. For an introduction to this framework, see Graeme Goldsworthy, *Gospel and Kingdom: A Christian Interpretation of the Old Testament* (Carlisle, England: Paternoster, 1994). For more detailed pre-

sentations, see Geerhardus Vos, *Biblical Theology: Old and New Testaments* (Grand Rapids, Mich.: Eerdmans, 1948); John Bright, *The Kingdom of God* (Nashville: Abingdon, 1953); David E. Holwerda, *Jesus and Israel: One Covenant or Two?* (Grand Rapids, Mich.: Eerdmans, 1995); and especially the works of William J. Dumbrell: *Covenant and Creation* (Nashville: Thomas Nelson, 1984); *The End of the Beginning: Revelation 21–22 and the Old Testament* (Homebush West, NSW, Australia: Lancer; distributed by Baker, Grand Rapids, Mich., 1985); and *The Search for Order: Biblical Eschatology in Focus* (Grand Rapids, Mich.: Baker, 1994).

4. Though we will develop this point later, to avoid confusion I should point out that I am not a "Sabbatarian," even if the day of rest is moved to Sunday. I do not believe that the command given to Israel to keep a literal Sabbath must be kept by Christians, though of course a regular pattern of corporate worship is essential. Keeping the Sabbath under the old covenant was a symbolic reminder of the fundamental truths of creation and covenant, which are fulfilled under the *new* covenant in a life of faith-producing obedience seven days of week (Heb. 3:16–4:13). In Christ, every day is the Sabbath! With transformed hearts, we now keep the Sabbath by trusting in God to meet our needs in every circumstance, manifesting this faith by a life of growing contentment expressed in righteousness (1 Tim. 6:6-16). Thus, since the Sabbath was a symbol, the issue of whether under the new covenant we honor one day of the week above another as a remembrance of God's love and commitment to his people is a matter of personal preference and conscience before the Lord (Rom. 14:5-6).

5. For this point and its implications, see the important work of John H. Sailhamer, *The Pentateuch as Narrative: A Biblical-Theological Commentary* (Grand Rapids, Mich.: Zondervan, 1992), 84-86. Sailhamer argues convincingly that the phrase translated "without form and void" in Genesis 1:2 pictures the world not as a formless mass of cooling gases in space, but as an "uninhabitable stretch of wasteland, a wilderness not yet inhabitable by human beings," that is to say, "the condition of the land before God made it 'good'" (84, n.8, 85). The key to seeing this is the parallel between the use of this image in Genesis 1:2 and its uses in Deuteronomy 32:10 and Isaiah 45:18. Thus, "Deuteronomy 32 draws on the same imagery (v. 10) to depict Israel's time of waiting in the wilderness before their entry into the good land" (86). The prophets too used this same imagery from Genesis 1:2 to describe Israel's time of exile, during which the land again became "uninhabitable" and a "desert," and the light of the heavens was gone (86, pointing to Jer. 4:23-26). "The description of the land in Genesis 1:2, then, fits well into the prophet's vision of the future. The land lies empty, dark, and barren, awaiting God's call to light and life. Just as the light of the sun broke in upon the primeval darkness heralding the dawn of God's first blessing (Gen. 1:3), so also the prophets and the apostles mark the beginning of the new age of salvation with the light that shatters the darkness (Isa. 8:22–9:2; Matt. 4:13-17; John 1:5, 8-9)" (86).

6. Unfortunately, we know from the history of Israel in the Old Testament that the nation as a whole did not "keep the Sabbath." See, for example: Ex. 16:27; Neh. 13:15-18; Jer. 17:14-23; Ezek. 20:13-16; Amos 8:4-6; and Hos. 2:11. For this reason, the question of what it means to keep the Sabbath became extremely important in post-biblical Judaism and in the ministry of Jesus (see, for example, Matt. 12:1-14; Mark 2:18–3:6; Luke 6:1-11; 13:10-16; 14:1-6; John 5:9-

18; 7:21-24; 9:13-17). The Gospel accounts argue that if the Sabbath signifies God's commitment to meet his people's needs, then Jesus was not breaking the Sabbath when he worked to heal and forgive, since his actions embodied the very heart of what the Sabbath meant. As Jesus put it, "The Sabbath was made for man, not man for the Sabbath" (Mark 2:27). Hence, as the authoritative Son of Man, Jesus is "lord even of the Sabbath," which is to say that he is the one who has the sovereign right to use it as he sees fit for his people's good.

7. Paul R. House, *Old Testament Theology* (Downers Grove, Ill.: InterVarsity, 1998), 61, 63.

8. Bernhard W. Anderson, *From Creation to New Creation: Old Testament Perspectives* (Minneapolis: Fortress, 1994), 129; the quote is from H. Wildberger.

9. See Lev. 26:12; Jer. 7:23; 11:4; 24:7; 30:22; 31:33; 32:38; Ezek. 11:20; 14:11; 36:28; 37:23, 27; Zech. 8:8; 2 Cor. 6:16.

10. John Piper, *Desiring God: Meditations of a Christian Hedonist* (Sisters, Ore.: Multnomah; expanded edition, 1996), 50. For a profound exposition of the relationship between God's promises for the future and the life of faith in the present, see Piper's companion volume, *Future Grace* (Sisters, Ore.: Multnomah, 1995), with its restatement of this fundamental point on page 9.

11. This insightful summary of one of the main themes of biblical theology is a central pillar in Piper's work.

12. Jon D. Levenson, *Sinai and Zion: An Entry into the Jewish Bible* (San Francisco: Harper and Row, 1985), 37.

13. Ibid., 43.

14. The impetus for the conviction that there is a uniform covenant structure providing the essential framework for understanding all of the covenants in the Bible comes from the pivotal work of G. E. Mendenhall, "Covenant Forms in Israelite Traditions," *The Biblical Archaeologist* 1 (1954), 50-76, which demonstrated that the basic covenant form in Israelite tradition was based on the form of the suzerain treaty that existed throughout the ancient Near East. For a detailed survey of the modern study of the covenant, see Ernest W. Nicholson, *God and His People: Covenant and Theology in the Old Testament* (Oxford: Clarendon, 1986), 3-117.

There were two basic kinds of covenants in the ancient Near East. The first was a *partnership* treaty established between equals, which was based on mutual demands and commitments. In this partnership, both parties agree as peers to fulfill obligations and to keep promises toward each other. This is not the kind of treaty formula that provides the foundation for the Old Testament covenant structure. Instead, as Mendenhall argued, the covenant structure in the Old Testament is based on the ancient Near Eastern practice of establishing *unilateral* or "suzerainty" treaties between a great king and a lesser king or between a sovereign and a helpless people, i.e., his vassals, whom the great king has redeemed or rescued from some danger. These unilateral covenants are not based on mutual obligations but on what the king has already done to protect, deliver, or rescue his vassals. These acts of deliverance are codified in historical prologues that summarize what has already taken place in the past, on the basis of which a relationship has now been established (for example, Ex. 20:1-2). Having rescued them in the past, the king makes covenant stipulations with his people that must be met if they desire to *continue* as his people and enjoy his ongoing protection. Thus, the covenant blessings for the *future* are based on keeping the covenant stipulations in the *present* that flow from the great act of redemption and provision in the *past*.

In other words, God used the historical experience of the ancient Near East as a vehicle for revealing what his relationship with his people was to be like. God is the great king and we are his vassals. Out of his benevolence he has rescued us from our plight. Having made us his people, he informs us of the covenant stipulations that flow out of and maintain the relationship he has inaugurated. The keeping of these covenant stipulations (which God himself enables!) makes it possible not only for God to maintain his rule over us in the present but also for him to commit himself to doing that in the future, since our lives of obedience to the covenant glorify him.

15. I am aware that this is a controversial approach to the Bible, since a Law/Gospel contrast has dominated the interpretation of the Bible ever since the Protestant Reformation. Indeed, this Law/Gospel contrast became the centerpiece of the two predominant biblical-theological systems of the twentieth century, dispensationalism and modified covenant theology, despite their differences in many other areas.

Both of these systems inherited from the Lutheran Reformation a theological framework in which the Bible is interpreted from the perspective of two fundamentally different messages: a "Law" message and a "Gospel" message. This contrast divides the Bible into three major periods of history: a "Gospel" message to Abraham (justification by grace through faith); a "Law" message to Adam, Moses, and Christ (works righteousness); and a repetition of the Abrahamic "Gospel" message to the church on the basis of Jesus' own perfect keeping of the Law (justification by grace through faith).

Moreover, in and of themselves, the Law/Gospel messages are seen to be in fundamental *conflict,* so that two diametrically opposed ways of relating to God run through the heart of the Bible. In this view, the "Gospel" is the message of what God has done, is doing, and *promises* to do for us, while the "Law" is what God *demands* from us. While the Gospel is "good news," the Law becomes "bad news" because it brings us into a place of failure so that, as Law-breakers, we become bankrupt in our attempt to earn righteousness through our works. As a result, when Adam and Eve break the commandment in the garden they find themselves under the condemnation of God, because the Law demands sinless perfection. *In the same way,* the purpose of the holy and just and good Law later given under Moses (Rom. 7:12), *which once again demanded sinless obedience just as God did before the Fall,* was to show us our sin and to make our sin even more sinful by bringing about repeated acts of disobedience (compare Rom. 3:20; 5:13, 20; 7:7-8).

So the Law, with its demand for sinless perfection, drives me to despair (like Luther's experience in the monastery). Positively, the Law does this by declaring to me the holy righteousness of God and proclaiming his judgment on all those who break his commands. Negatively, the Law does this by showing me all the ways that I fail to live up to God's expectations. Thus, in this reading of the Bible, everybody begins by being condemned under the Law of God, which is viewed as distinct from the gracious provisions of God. God always comes to us first with a word of Law, a word of demand. In this way, God shows us our need for himself by showing us our own sin. Furthermore, the consequence of being under the Law is a downward spiral of despair: the more we try to keep the Law, the more we realize that we are law-breakers. The more we respond to our plight by making vows of religious will, the more depressed we become because of our inability to keep them. The Law consequently brings us to our knees, depressed by our inability to keep it.

The good news is that, once we have been brought under condemnation by the Law, God himself responds by giving us the Gospel. The Gospel replaces the Law by replacing a system of demand with a message of promise. Instead of having to keep the Law's demand for sinless perfection in order to be righteous in God's sight (which in our fallen state nobody can do), all we have to do is to trust the Gospel. As a result, the Law/Gospel contrast becomes a contrast between "works" and "faith."

In the Law/Gospel contrast model, the unity of the Bible comes out of this diversity, since from the beginning of the Bible to the end the Law drives us to the Gospel so that we might be saved by grace. The Bible's unity derives from the unification of two conflicting messages in an overarching and unified divine purpose.

In this reading of the Bible, it is therefore important to see that the Law of Moses and its system of "works-righteousness," by which we are summoned to try to earn our righteous standing before God by virtue of our own obedience to God's Law, is a parenthetical act of God that was never intended to save us but rather was intended to drive us to the Gospel. In other words, the Law of Moses drives us back to the Gospel of Abraham and forward to the Gospel of Jesus. Under the Gospel, we cease our attempt to earn our righteousness through our obedience and instead simply accept God's provision for our salvation through Jesus.

Finally, then, in the Law/Gospel model, God gives commandments to Adam and Eve before the Fall as a test, in order to see whether they will be entitled, by virtue of their own obedience, to a further blessing of God that is *not yet* theirs. This blessing is usually associated with the right to eat of the tree of life in order to live forever. Hence, God's commandment places Adam and Eve in a probationary period during which, through their obedience to God's commands, they will inherit God's ultimate blessing. However, when Adam and Eve fail to inherit God's blessings through their obedience (because of their sin), God turns from this Law principle or "covenant of works" to the Gospel or "covenant of grace," by which God's people are granted his blessings *unconditionally*. Nevertheless, God has not abandoned his righteous character: God's blessings can only be given in response to perfect obedience to his commands; salvation is always merited as a matter of "works righteousness." In blessing his people in spite of their sin, God is therefore granting to them what Christ has merited through *his* perfect obedience in their place as their "second Adam." In other words, Christ keeps the Law or "covenant of works" perfectly and then gives to us the blessings he has earned.

For further representative examples of dispensationalism and covenant theology, see John S. Feinberg, ed., *Continuity and Discontinuity: Perspectives on the Relationship between the Old and New Testaments* (Wheaton, Ill.:

Crossway, 1988); Geerhardus Vos, *Biblical Theology: Old and New Testaments* (Grand Rapids, Mich.: Eerdmans, 1985 [1948]); Meredith G. Kline, *Kingdom Prologue: Genesis Foundations for a Covenantal Worldview* (Overland Park, Kan.: Two Age, 2000); and Mark W. Karlberg, *Covenant Theology in Reformed Perspective* (Eugene, Ore.: Wipf and Stock, 2000). For an analysis of these respective systems, see Daniel P. Fuller, *Gospel and Law, Contrast or Continuum: The Hermeneutics of Dispensationalism and Covenant Theology* (Grand Rapids, Mich.: Eerdmans, 1980).

Chapter Three:
What Went Wrong and What Has God Done About It?

1. For Genesis 2:15, I prefer the translation, "The LORD God took the man and put him in the garden of Eden *to worship and obey,*" not the more traditional translation, "to till it and to keep it." The question posed by this passage is the nature of the purpose for which God placed the man into the garden in Eden *before* the Fall. The problem with the more common translation is that the narrative as a whole seems to indicate that the first "work" done in the garden takes place *after* the Fall as part of the curse (Gen. 3:23). For the translation suggested here, see the linguistic arguments put forth by U. Cassuto, *A Commentary on the Book of Genesis,* vol. 1 (Jerusalem: Magnes, ET 1972 [1961]), 122-123; and John Sailhamer, *Genesis,* Expositor's Bible Commentary, vol. 2, (Grand Rapids, Mich.: Zondervan, 1990), 44-45, 47-48. In addition to his linguistic arguments, Cassuto points out (122) that later rabbinical teaching read the text to refer to worship and obedience, arguing that the command in Genesis 2:15 referred to the offering of sacrifices in the garden. The rabbis argued that the reference in Genesis 2:15 to the fact that man was "to serve God" parallels Exodus 3:12, while the command "to keep" in Genesis 2:15 parallels Numbers 28:2, both of which refer to worshiping God, the latter by offering a sacrifice (compare Genesis Rabbah 16:5). Regardless of the strength of these parallels, this line of argument shows that the rabbis read the text as referring to worshiping God and keeping his commands. If taken this way, the appropriate contrast between mankind's task in the world pre- and post-Fall is maintained. Prior to the Fall, mankind is to worship and obey God by exercising dependence upon his provision and obedience to the commandment to eat of all the trees except one. Hence, in Sailhamer's words (48), "The importance of these two infinitives can be seen in the fact that the narrative returns to precisely them in its summary conclusion of the state of mankind after the Fall. The man and the woman were created 'for worship' (le'obdah, 2:15), but after the Fall they were thrown out of the garden 'to work the ground' (la'abod 'et ha'adamah, 3:23). In the same way they were created 'for obedience' (lesomrah, 2:15), but after the Fall they were 'kept' (lismor, 3:24) from the tree of life." This play on words is crucial, not just poetic!

2. Paul R. House, *Old Testament Theology* (Downers Grove, Ill.: InterVarsity, 1998), 62.

3. I am indebted for this reading to Gordon Hugenberger, who has argued in his unpublished lectures at Gordon-Conwell Theological Seminary that the garments provided for Adam and Eve in Genesis 3:21 convey the same significance as the covering of Noah's nakedness in Genesis 9:23, the forgiveness represented

by the use of such a covering in Psalm 32:1, and the legal significance of garments in the ancient Near East as representing one's inheritance rights (see Gen.
37:23; Ex. 22:26; Judg. 14:13, 19; Ezek. 16:8-16). Against this backdrop, we
can understand why the father clothes the prodigal son upon his return home in
Luke 15:22, and why Paul says in Galatians 3:27 that we are "clothed" with
Jesus as our garment (our inheritance), since our inheritance as God's people is
found in Christ. For the use of this same imagery to describe our final redemption, see Revelation 16:15.

4. John H. Sailhamer, *The Pentateuch as Narrative: A Biblical-Theological
   Commentary* (Grand Rapids, Mich.: Zondervan, 1992), 157.

5. Ibid., 158.

6. Ibid., 160.

7. I owe this insight to Jon D. Levenson, *Sinai and Zion: An Entry into the Jewish
   Bible* (San Francisco: Harper and Row, 1985), 128-129.

Chapter Four:
Why Can We Trust God, No Matter What Happens?

1. Although the focus of my attention is different, I am indebted for the main point
   of this section and for most of the examples that follow to John Piper, *The
   Justification of God: An Exegetical and Theological Study of Romans 9:1-23*
   (Grand Rapids, Mich.: Baker, 1983), 84-97.

2. Ibid., 90.

3. See ibid., 82-89, for these examples and a development of this idea, as well as
   his chapter, "The Righteousness of God in Romans 3:1-8," 103-113 in the same
   work.

4. Though it is beyond our present purposes to pursue this in detail, and though
   the issues are complex, I would submit for your thinking that Psalm 143 is also
   a key to understanding Paul's argument against "works of the law" in Galatians
   2:15-21. Paul's statement that "by works of the law shall no one be justified"
   (Gal. 2:16) is a reference to Psalm 143:2. And as Psalm 143 makes clear, what
   justifies the psalmist is God's righteousness. This is what the psalmist trusted
   in and what all the "just" trust in (Hab. 2:4)—the latter text is also in view in
   Galatians 2:15-21, as alluded to by Paul's reference to living by faith to God.
   Thus, doing the "works of the law," which is Paul's description of what Psalm
   143 means when it speaks of being God's servant, was the old covenant
   response to God's saving righteousness, not the basis or source of salvation.
   Though faith and its obedience is absolutely essential, it is God's work of grace
   on our behalf which enables that response, not our response itself, that saves
   us. Paul is simply reaffirming what Psalm 143 taught. For the arguments in
   favor of seeing Psalm 143; Genesis 15:6; and Habakkuk 2:4 as behind Paul's
   argument in Galatians 2:15-21, see Roy E. Ciampa, *The Presence and Function
   of Scripture in Galatians 1 and 2* (Tübingen: J. C. B. Mohr [Paul Siebeck],
   1998), 178-220.

   The problem Paul faced in Galatia was that some Jewish Christians (the
   "Judaizers") were arguing that faith in Christ necessitated also becoming a Jew
   in order to be a full-fledged member of God's people. From their perspective, to
   live like a Gentile, even as a follower of Christ, was to be outside of God's

covenant people, and hence, by definition, to be a "sinner" separated from God (Gal. 2:15, 17). Hence, they wanted those Gentiles who believed in Jesus to become Jews and to live under the old covenant (become circumcised, keep the Jewish food laws, calendar, religious festivals, and ritual purity laws).

However, now that the messiah had come, what justifies believers is their trust in *Jesus'* faithfulness, the new covenant manifestation of God's grace, which was expressed in his commitment to glorify the Father by saving his people through going to the Cross (Gal. 2:16, 20). God's saving acts under the old covenant all point forward to and are fulfilled by the coming of the Christ. Hence, now that Christ has come, we must trust in God's saving work under the new covenant, to which the old covenant pointed all along. Not to do so is to deny that Jesus is the Messiah; not to do so exclusively is to deny that Christ's saving work is sufficient.

Moreover, trusting in Christ will evidence itself not in "works of the law" (i.e., the life of faith and its obedience as this was expressed under the old covenant), but in being crucified with Christ (putting to death our sinful passions as cursed by God) and in Christ's living in us (trusting in Christ's resurrection power by which we will manifest the fruit of the Spirit in fulfillment of the Law, thus no longer falling under the curse of the Law itself—Gal. 2:20; 5:18, 23-24). In other words, the promise to Abraham that makes us members of God's people is not circumcision or ethnic identity under the old covenant, but the Spirit who enables us to keep the Law from the heart, which God has now poured out on all those who trust in Christ (Gal. 3:14).

Since the "works of the law" were the appropriate response to God's saving righteousness under the old covenant, there is nothing wrong with them per se. Correctly understood, they point forward to and symbolize God's saving work in Christ, which is the basis upon which even the believers under the old covenant were saved (Rom. 3:21-26). Accordingly, if someone now has faith in Christ, he may still "live like a Jew," as long as he does not make living like a Jew mandatory for others. This is because it is the death of Jesus, not keeping the old covenant, that saved those who believed under the old covenant (though obscured in our English translations, this is the point of Galatians 2:16a, which literally says, "knowing that a man is not being justified from works of the law if he is not [or, unless he is] being justified through the faith of Jesus Christ").

Since the reality to which the old covenant was pointing has arrived, the symbols of the old covenant become a matter of personal preference. In Paul's day, one could go to the temple if one so desired, but it was no longer necessary, since Jesus was the real sacrifice and believers were now the temple of God's presence. This is also why Paul can say that it does not matter whether a person is circumcised (that is up to him); what matters is "keeping the commandments of God," "faith working through love," and being a "new creation" (1 Cor. 7:19; Gal. 5:6; 6:15), since this is the expression of being a "real Jew" with a "circumcised heart" (Rom. 2:25-29; Phil. 3:3; Col. 2:11-15). That Paul can contrast the command to be circumcised with keeping the commandments of God indicates that under the old covenant the Law functioned as a symbol of a changed heart. As Jesus taught, the prohibition of murder was intended to point to a changed heart that does not even lose its temper; not committing adultery points to not lusting; loving one's neighbor points to loving one's enemy; and so on (Matt. 5:17-48).

Unfortunately, with a hard heart, one could keep the Law externally and feel self-justified in doing so, all the while being under God's judgment. In other words, it was possible to be circumcised, go to the temple, not murder, pay alms, keep ritual purity laws, and honor God with one's lips, while the heart was still "far from" him (Isa. 29:13; Mark 7:1-8). In fact, this was Israel's experience as a whole (2 Cor. 3:12-14). To insist on the continuing validity of the old covenant, therefore, was to place God's people back in a situation in which the majority of Israel remained hard-hearted and under God's curse for breaking the covenant.

In the end, then, it was not *Christ* who made it evident to Paul that believers no longer needed to live under the old covenant (as if Christ brought a radically new message not found in the Old Testament; see also Luke 24:25-27); it was the Law itself and Israel's history of rebellion under the Sinai covenant that led Paul to "die to the Law" (Gal. 2:19). Paul's reading of the Law (for example, passages such as Ps. 143; Gen. 15:6; Hab. 2:4) in light of his encounter with Christ on the road to Damascus made him realize that Christ had fulfilled the Law and had enabled Christians to fulfill it in their new lives of obedience to God's law under the new covenant (Jer. 31:31-34; Ezek. 36:25-28). To insist on the continuing validity and necessity of the old covenant, now that Christ has come, is to "nullify the grace of God" made possible by the cross of Christ and expressed in the new life of faith (Gal. 2:21a summarizes 2:20). For if justification could have come under the old covenant, then Christ would not have needed to die (Gal. 2:21b).

For the implications of this perspective, see chapters 8 and 9.

5. For Israel's ten major acts of unbelief, see Ex. 5:21; 14:11; 15:24; 16:2; 17:2f.; 32:1-6; Num. 11:1, 4-9; 12:1; 14:2.

6. This is the point made by the understanding of Israel's history set forth in the Old Testament. As Hans Walter Wolff, *Anthropology of the Old Testament* (Philadelphia: Fortress, 1974), 152, puts it,

> Israel understands its beginnings and its continuing history largely as being the fulfillment of Yahweh's *promises*: the rise of the nation, the gift of the promised land, Israel's mission among the nations, the kingdom and the continuance of the house of David, the catastrophes of the period of the judges and the kings, and then especially the Babylonian exile, the return home from exile, the new beginning in Jerusalem and, above all, the fulfillment of the promises in Israel's new covenant, in the incorporation of the world of the nations and in complete world-wide renewal. The hopes of the individual too only have their basis, continuance and power in as much as they are included in these *promises* to Israel and the nations. The expectations of all these transformations, however, are founded solely on Yahweh's word, which became known to Israel as *promise* to the patriarchs and then primarily as the proclamation of judgment and the pledge of salvation through the prophets (emphasis added).

7. John Calvin, *Institutes of the Christian Religion,* 3.11.29, ed. John T. McNeill, trans. Ford Lewis Battles, Library of Christian Classics, vol. 20 (Philadelphia: Westminster, 1977 [1960]), 575.

Chapter Five:
Why Does God Wait So Long to Make Things Right?

1. Paul's statement that "We walk by faith, not by sight" (2 Cor. 5:7) is one of the most misinterpreted statements concerning the meaning of faith. The point of this text is that Paul trusts in God's promises as the ultimate reality and lives accordingly; he does not live as if his present suffering were the sum of life. Thus, as Timothy B. Savage points out (*Power through Weakness: Paul's Understanding of the Christian Ministry in 2 Corinthians,* Society for New Testament Studies Monograph Series 86 [Cambridge: Cambridge University Press, 1996], 184), Paul "fixes his gaze on what cannot be seen (4:18), his inner glory, not his outer affliction (4:17), his inward renewal, not his external decay (4:16), the new age, not the old (4:18), resurrection life, not present dying (4:10, 11), the weighty, not the trifling (4:17), the eternal, not the temporal (4:18), the heavenly, not the earthly (5:1-2). In short, he adopts a perspective of faith . . . of trusting that, for the present eschatological moment, glory really does come to expression through affliction." Paul's emphasis in this passage on his confident knowledge of the future makes clear, therefore, that "faith" is not an irrational leap into the dark that calls for accepting the truth of something that makes no sense or has no foundation in reality. Just the opposite! "Faith" is trusting in the promises of God for the future, not in spite of what one knows but *because of* what one knows. The lack of "sight" in this passage does not refer to the uncertain *basis* of faith but to the fact that the consummation of God's promises has not yet been realized. Paul's point in 5:7 is not epistemological (i.e., that we can only know things "by faith," since we have no certain reasons for believing, i.e., no "sight"), but eschatological (i.e., that we live in the present by trusting God's promises for the future, the down payment of which we are already experiencing in the Spirit). For these points, see my *2 Corinthians,* NIV Application Commentary (Grand Rapids, Mich.: Zondervan, 2000), 214-215, 223.

2. John Calvin, *Institutes of the Christian Religion,* 2.42, ed. John T. McNeill, trans. Ford Lewis Battles, Library of Christian Classics, vol. 20 (Philadelphia: Westminster, 1977 [1960]), 590.

3. Israel's hard-heartedness or "stubbornness" toward God, ever since her beginning as a people, is a central theme in Jeremiah. Israel's stiff-necked nature explains why Israel's history as a nation was one of perpetual disobedience and why there was a need for a new covenant that would bring about a changed heart, forgiveness for her sins, and empowerment for obedience (Jer. 31:31-34; Ezek. 36:22-28). For Jeremiah's emphasis on Israel's sinful state, see Jer. 3:17; 7:24; 9:13; 13:10; 16:12; 17:23; 18:12; 19:15; 23:17. For the theme of Israel's faithlessness to God, and her eventual restoration under the new covenant, see Raymond C. Ortlund, Jr., *Whoredom: God's Unfaithful Wife in Biblical Theology* (Grand Rapids, Mich.: Eerdmans, 1996).

4. John Bright, *A History of Israel* (Philadelphia: Westminster, second edition, 1976), 356.

5. See, for example, Isa. 2:3-4; 7:15-17, 29; 11:6-8, 40; 45:23; 55:12-13; 60:18-22; 65:25; Jer. 31:10-14; Ezek. 34:25-31; 36:8-15; Hos. 2:20-24; Joel 3:18; Amos 9:13-14; Mic. 5:9-10.

6. See Isa. 9:2-7; 11:1-9; 45:14-25; 51:9-11; 60:1-22; 61:5-7; Jer. 33:19-26; Ezek. 37:15-28; Amos 9:11-12. For a good summary of this material, see Ronald E. Clements, *Old Testament Theology: A Fresh Approach* (Atlanta: John Knox, 1978), 144-148.

7. Walter Eichrodt, *Theology of the Old Testament*, vol. 1, trans. J. A. Baker (Philadelphia: Westminster, 1961), 480.

8. Bright, *History of Israel*, 364.

9. Jurgen Moltmann, *Theology of Hope: On the Ground and the Implications of a Christian Eschatology*, trans. James W. Leitch (New York: Harper and Row, 1967), 91.

10. Dietrich Bonhoeffer, *Letters and Papers from Prison: The Enlarged Edition*, ed. Eberhard Bethge (New York: Macmillan, third edition, 1971), 372-373.

11. For this important theme, see Ex. 13:3-16; 15:1-18; Deut. 1:30; 4:31-34; 7:17-18; Josh. 24:1-28; Judg. 2:1; 6:8-9; 1 Sam. 10:17-18; 1 Kings 8:53; 1 Chron. 17:21; Ps. 44:1-8; 81:10; 106:21; Jer. 11:14; 34:13.

12. I am indebted for this insight to Daniel P. Fuller's unpublished lectures on Romans 1–8, given at Fuller Theological Seminary in 1976.

13. See Rom. 11:32-36; 1 Cor. 10:31; 2 Cor. 4:15; 8:19, 23; Eph. 1:3-12; 3:8-11; Phil. 1:9-11; 2:9-11; Col. 1:25-27; 1 Pet. 1:6-7.

Chapter Six:
Why Is There So Much Pain and Evil in the World?

1. John Hick, "The Problem of Evil," in *A Modern Introduction to Philosophy: Readings from Classical and Contemporary Sources*, revised edition, ed. Paul Edwards and Arthur Pap (New York: Free Press, 1965), 453-459, 453.

2. Bertrand Russell, *Why I Am Not a Christian and Other Essays on Religion and Related Subjects*, ed. Paul Edwards (New York: Simon and Schuster, 1957), vi.

3. Gregory A. Boyd, *God of the Possible: A Biblical Introduction to the Open View of God* (Grand Rapids, Mich.: Baker, 2000), 99. As this quote intimates, Boyd takes the Arminian conviction concerning the existence of free will to its logical but unorthodox outcome. In view of the existence of human free will, Boyd concludes, self-consistently but in denial of one of God's essential attributes, that God's sovereignty and hence his *foreknowledge* are limited. He believes this since our not-yet-determined free choices are creating a future that is not fixed, and hence not yet known, even by God (94).

Hence, except in those extreme cases where someone's character is so settled that he or she becomes entirely predictable, "Scripture teaches us that God literally finds out *how* people will choose *when* they choose. He made us self-determining agents, and prior to our determining ourselves in one direction or another, the only reality that exists for God to know concerning our future is the *possible* directions we may take" (66, final emphasis added). Therefore, for Boyd, the Bible teaches that some things are determined by God's sovereignty and can consequently be known by God in advance, while all of our decisions as free agents are left open, to be determined by our own free-will choices. Hence, the future we create by our choices is still unsettled and cannot be known by God (compare 14, 19, 21, 54, 86). When it comes to our free-will choices, God knows only the possibilities and probabilities of our actions. In Boyd's words, "To whatever degree the future is yet open to be decided by free agents, it is unsettled. To this extent, God knows it as a realm of possibilities, not certainties" (15). Hence, "the picture of God as the 'God of the possible' creates a people who do not wait for an eternally settled future to happen. Through God's grace and power, they help *create* the future" (94; compare 69).

This "open view of God" posits that God decided not to "micromanage" all things, but to leave the most significant aspects of the future to be "resolved by the decisions of free agents" (31). The aspects determined by our free choices are indeed the "most significant," since they include our love for God, our eternal destiny, and the unfathomable myriad of circumstances and events that come about by virtue of human decisions, including all evil.

In Boyd's view, to speak of God's total sovereign control over all things consequently demeans God's sovereignty, because "it takes a greater God to steer a world populated with free agents than it does to steer a world of preprogrammed automatons" (31). "God determines whatever he sees fit and leaves as much of the future open to possibilities as he sees fit. The God of the possible creates the 'Choose Your Own Adventure' structure of world history and of our lives within which the possibilities of human free choice are actualized" (44). For "in a cosmos populated by free agents, the outcome of things—even divine decisions—is often uncertain" (58).

It is beyond our purpose to enter into a detailed discussion of the interpretations of the Bible that lead to these, in my view, erroneous conclusions. But see the theological responses of Bruce A. Ware, *God's Lesser Glory: The Diminished God of Open Theism* (Wheaton, Ill.: Crossway, 2000).

4. Boyd, *God of the Possible*, 40, referring to Luke 7:30 and 2 Peter 3:9.

5. Ibid., 102.

6. C. S. Lewis, *Mere Christianity* (London: Collins, 1952), 49; quoted in Clark H. Pinnock, "Responsible Freedom and the Flow of Biblical History," in *Grace Unlimited*, ed. Clark H. Pinnock (Minneapolis: Bethany, 1975), 94-109, 99. I recommend this volume of essays for a good overview of the free will, "Arminian" position. In addition, see the essays in Clark H. Pinnock, ed., *A Case for Arminianism: The Grace of God, the Will of Man* (Grand Rapids, Mich.: Zondervan, 1990). Pinnock, Boyd, and other "open" or "free-will" theists argue for the necessity of free will based on the presupposition that love demands independent choice (see *God of the Possible*, 63-64, 96-97). But they go beyond the views of classical Arminianism represented by Lewis in positing that human freedom means, by definition, an open future and a corresponding limitation of God's foreknowledge.

On the one hand, this view reinterprets specific affirmations of the biblical record concerning God's sovereignty and foreknowledge (for example, Gen. 15:13-14; 1 Kings 13:2-3; Ps. 139:16; Isa. 44:28; 46:9-10; 48:3-5; Jer. 1:5; 29:10-11; Ezek. 26:7-21; Matt. 26:34; John 6:64, 70-71; 21:18-19; Acts 2:23; 4:28; Gal. 1:15-16; 1 Pet. 1:20) to refer only to limited events, to general circumstances, to parameters, intentions, or plans that could not be thwarted by human decisions, or to predictable outcomes, probabilities, and percentages, rather than being examples of a universally applicable truth concerning God's sovereign control and foreknowledge of all of reality.

On the other hand, the "openness of God" view takes at face value, without regard for their genre or historical setting, the biblical statements concerning God's feelings of frustration, regret, and surprise, his changes of mind, his testing of his people, his statements of inquiry and discovery, and the use of conditional language when speaking about the future (for example, Gen. 6:6; 22:12; Ex. 4:1-15; 16:4; 32:14; 33:1-3, 14; Num. 14:11-20; Deut. 8:2; 9:13-29; 13:1-3; 1 Sam. 15:10-11, 35; 2 Kings 20:1-6; 1 Chron. 21:15; 2 Chron. 12:5-8; 32:31; Isa. 5:2-5; 63:10; Jer. 3:6-7, 19-20; 7:31; 18:4-11; 19:5; 26:2-3, 19; Ezek. 22:30-31; Hos. 8:5; Joel 2:12-13; Amos 7:1-6; Jonah 3:10; 4:2; Matt. 26:39; Acts 7:51; 2 Pet. 3:9, 12).

As a result, free-will theists posit that God is the Creator of independent, self-determining beings whose choices are beyond his own knowledge, so that the future is partly settled and foreknown by God and partly unsettled and therefore unknown by God. For another presentation of free-will theism, see David Basinger, *The Case for Freewill Theism: A Philosophical Assessment* (Downers Grove, Ill.: InterVarsity, 1996). For the related "openness of God" perspective, see Clark H. Pinnock, et al., *The Openness of God: A Biblical Challenge to the Traditional Understanding of God* (Downers Grove, Ill.: InterVarsity, 1994); and John Sanders, *The God Who Risks: A Theology of Providence* (Downers Grove, Ill.: InterVarsity, 1998). It is beyond our present purpose to respond to their individual interpretations of the biblical texts, which would take a book in itself. For a response in principle to this view of a limited God (if not in nature, at least in his self-determined practice and effect), and a positive portrayal of God's all-encompassing sovereignty, see John Piper, *The Pleasures of God: Meditations on God's Delight in Being God,* revised and expanded edition (Sisters, Ore.: Multnomah, 2000). For a direct response, see R. K. McGregor, *No Place for Sovereignty: What's Wrong with Freewill Theism* (Downers Grove, Ill.: InterVarsity, 1996).

7. Boyd, *God of the Possible,* 31, wants to make it clear that the view he represents is not to be confused with this "process thought." As he emphasizes, "God is not at the mercy of chance or free will. This understanding of divine sovereignty contrasts sharply with a popular liberal theological movement called 'process theology.' Some evangelical authors have wrongly accused open theists of being close to process thought, but in truth the two views have little in common. Process thought holds that God *can't* predetermine or foreknow with certainty *anything* about the distant future. Open theists rather maintain that God can and does predetermine and foreknow *whatever he wants to* about the future" (31). "To confess that God can control whatever he wants to control leaves open the question of *how much* God actually does want to control" (51). Nevertheless, in the view of open theists, since God does not predetermine the decisions of people, he cannot know them.

8. Winfried Corduan, *Handmaid to Theology: An Essay in Philosophical Prolegomena* (Grand Rapids, Mich.: Baker, 1981), 138. Corduan's summary and criticism of process theology provide a helpful introduction to a very complicated philosophical problem. See especially his treatment of the work of John Cobb, 137-141.

9. Alfred North Whitehead, "God and the World," in *Process Theology: Basic Writings,* ed. Ewert H. Cousins (New York: Newman, 1971), 85-99, 93. This volume serves as a good introduction to the main thinkers and perspectives of process theology.

10. Harold Kushner, *When Bad Things Happen to Good People* (New York: Avon, 1981), 113.

11. Ibid., 44.

12. Boyd, *God of the Possible,* 105-106, emphasis added.

13. Boyd, ibid., 101, rightly criticizes the Arminian view of "simple foreknowledge" (that God knows the future but can do nothing about it, due to the free will of humanity) as being inconsistent with the Bible's teaching about foreknowledge itself. As Boyd rightly points out, "whenever the Bible speaks of God's fore-knowledge, it is to emphasize his ability to control what comes to pass, not to declare that he knows a future he can't control." For this reason, Boyd concludes that God must not foreknow all things, since he does not control all things, and vice versa. The only other conclusion to be drawn, which Boyd cannot accept, is that "the horrors of world history and the eternal torment of the damned somehow make a positive contribution to God's creation" (102). This latter con-clusion, as difficult as it is to understand fully, is my own.

14. Kushner, *When Bad Things Happen,* 43.

15. Ibid.

16. Boyd, *God of the Possible,* 99.

17. For helpful historical, theological, and practical expositions of God's sovereignty and its implications for everyday life, see J. I. Packer, *A Quest for Godliness: The Puritan Vision of the Christian Life* (Wheaton, Ill.: Crossway, 1990); Thomas R. Schreiner and Bruce A. Ware, eds., *Still Sovereign: Contemporary Perspectives on Election, Foreknowledge, and Grace* (Grand Rapids, Mich.: Baker, 2000); and Thomas J. Nettles, *By His Grace and for His Glory* (Grand Rapids, Mich.: Baker, 1986). For the classic presentation of this issue as central to the Reformation, see Martin Luther, *The Bondage of the Will* (Grand Rapids, Mich.: Revell, 1998 [1957]).

18. See Gen. 8:22; 15:13; 40:13, 19; 50:20; Ex. 3:19; 4:21; 7:3; Deut. 31:16; 1 Sam. 17:45-47; 1 Kings 13:2; 2 Chron. 20:15-17; Job 38:12; Ps. 89:9; 135:5-7; Prov. 21:1; Isa. 6:9; 44:28; 45:1; Jer. 14:22; Joel 2:21-25; Hag. 1:11; John 6:64; Acts 2:23; 4:26-28; 17:26; Rev. 17:7.

19. This line is my translation. The Hebrew word translated "evil" here can mean in this context "evil," "distress," or "adversity"; see F. Brown, S. R. Driver, D. A. Briggs, *A Hebrew and English Lexicon of the Old Testament,* trans. E. Robinson (Oxford: Clarendon, 1976 [1972]), 948.

20. John Piper, *Desiring God: Meditations of a Christian Hedonist* (Sisters, Ore.: Multnomah; expanded edition, 1996), 38-39. In addition to his full-length work, *The Pleasures of God* (see above, note 6), see Piper's discussion in *Desiring God,* 35-40, for a summary of the biblical basis and implications of God's sovereignty.

21. The next three paragraphs are taken from my commentary, *2 Corinthians,* NIV Application Commentary (Grand Rapids, Mich.: Zondervan, 2000), 74-75.

22. C. H. Spurgeon, "Divine Sovereignty," *The New Park Street Pulpit: Containing Sermons Preached and Revised,* vol. 1 (Edinburgh: Banner of Truth Trust, 1981 [1856]), 185-192, 185.

23. John W. Wenham, *The Enigma of Evil: Can We Believe in the Goodness of God?* (Grand Rapids, Mich.: Zondervan, 1985 [1974]), 44. Because he takes humanity's freedom as his starting point, Wenham's solution to the problem is not always satisfying. For a thoroughgoing application of God's sovereignty to suffering, see Jerry Bridges, *Trusting God, Even when Life Hurts* (Colorado Springs: NavPress, 1988). For an insightful treatment of the relevant biblical passages, see D. A. Carson, *How Long, O Lord? Reflections on Suffering and Evil* (Grand Rapids, Mich.: Baker, 1990).

24. Originally found in Tertullian (*Apologeticus* 50), who was himself converted in 193 A.D. by witnessing the courage of Christians facing torture and death for their faith.

25. From the "Introduction" to Paul Marshall, *Their Blood Cries Out: The Untold Story of Persecution Against Christians in the Modern World* (Dallas: Word, 1997), xxi.

26. Ibid., 254-255.

27. For an analysis of the lack of information and the social factors that have led to this silence, see Marshall. Horowitz sees a historical precedent for the current situation: "The ignorance and silence displayed by Western Christian communities toward the suffering of fellow believers completes the litany of parallels to earlier, sordid chapters of the world's history. This history warns us that evangelical and Catholic communities in the Third World are acutely vulnerable, are profoundly worthy of our actions and prayers, are the people whose present fates can easily become ours if we remain indifferent to their fates" (ibid., xxi).

28. Ibid.

Chapter Seven:
Why Do God's People Suffer?

1. Unfortunately, in many quarters of the church today we have perverted the Gospel into a magical means of gaining physical healing and material comforts through "name it and claim it" faith-formulas and "positive confessions" of healing in spite of one's apparent "symptoms." For an analysis of this movement, see D. R. McConnell, *A Different Gospel: A Historical and Biblical Analysis of the Modern Faith Movement* (Peabody, Mass.: Hendrickson, 1988).

2. Compare, for example, the desire of Ignatius (d. ca. 115 A.D.) to be devoured by wild beasts in Rome so that he might "truly be a disciple of Jesus Christ," quoting 1 Corinthians 15:32 in his *Letter to the Romans,* iv-v.

3. This focus and foundation of comfort finds an enduring expression in the first question of the Heidelberg Catechism (1563):

> Question 1. What is your only comfort, in life and in death?
>
> That I belong—body and soul, in life and in death—not to myself but to my faithful Savior, Jesus Christ, who at the cost of his own blood has fully paid for all my sins and has completely freed me from the dominion of the devil; that he protects me so well that without the will of my Father in heaven not a hair can fall from my head; indeed, that everything must

fit his purpose for my salvation. Therefore, by his Holy Spirit, he also assures me of eternal life, and makes me wholeheartedly willing and ready from now on to live for him.

Quoted from Mark A. Noll, ed., *Confessions and Catechisms of the Reformation* (Grand Rapids, Mich.: Baker, 1991), 137 (following the 1962 translation of Miller and Osterhaven).

4. In the West, this approach has been made popular by Elisabeth Kubler-Ross. See her, *Death: The Final Stage of Growth* (Englewood Cliffs, N.J.: Prentice Hall, 1975).

5. George MacDonald, *Life Essential: The Hope of the Gospel,* ed. Rolland Hein (Wheaton, Ill.: Harold Shaw, 1974 [1892]), 49.

6. Paul R. House, *Old Testament Theology* (Downers Grove, Ill.: InterVarsity, 1998), 428.

7. Ibid., 427. Appropriately, House's chapter title for his treatment of the book of Job is, "The God Who Is Worth Serving."

8. Bernhard W. Anderson, *Understanding the Old Testament,* second edition (Englewood Cliffs, N.J.: Prentice-Hall, 1966), 513.

9. House, *Old Testament Theology,* 431.

10. I owe this portrayal of Job's negative responses to God to Anderson, *Understanding the Old Testament,* 514-515.

11. For a development of this court/trial theme throughout Job, see Norman C. Habel, *The Book of Job: A Commentary,* Old Testament Library (Philadelphia: Westminster, 1985), 30-31, 54-57, 63, 65.

12. Ibid., 65.

13. Anderson, *Understanding the Old Testament,* 517.

14. Ibid., 518.

15. House, *Old Testament Theology,* 430.

16. C. S. Lewis, *The Problem of Pain* (New York: Macmillan, 1972), 53.

17. C. S. Lewis, *Till We Have Faces: A Myth Retold* (San Diego: Harcourt and Brace, 1984), 308. I am indebted to my colleague Gerald Root for helping me understand these texts and for the reference to *Till We Have Faces.*

18. C. S. Lewis, *A Grief Observed,* 61, 76, 44, as quoted in Donald Nicholl, *Holiness* (New York: Seabury, 1983), 133.

19. This is my own translation of 2 Corinthians 2:14a. The Greek word in view, θριαμβεύειν, was used to describe the conducting of the Roman triumphal processions that took place in celebration of Rome's victories in battle. As such, it is often translated "to lead in triumph." But note that Paul is not the one leading the parade; rather, Paul is the one being led by God. For the substantiation of this translation and its implications for understanding the relationship between Paul's suffering and the power of the Spirit in his apostolic ministry, see my *Suffering and Ministry in the Spirit: Paul's Defense of His Ministry in II Corinthians 2:14–3:3* (Grand Rapids, Mich.: Eerdmans, 1990; now available through Paternoster), 7-37.

20. Nicholl, *Holiness,* 134.

Chapter Eight:
Why Do God's People Obey Him?

1. For a profound discussion of this insight and its implications for our relationship to God, see John Piper, *Desiring God: Meditations of a Christian Hedonist* (Sisters, Ore.: Multnomah; expanded edition, 1996). Piper's work provides the foundation for this present chapter, which is merely my own exposition of his insights. I cannot recommend strongly enough that Piper's own work be studied, since it cannot be matched in terms of its clarity and power of presentation. For another development of Piper's thought, see Sam Storms, *Pleasures Evermore: The Life-Changing Power of Enjoying God* (Colorado Springs: NavPress, 2000).

2. Daniel P. Fuller, *The Unity of the Bible: Unfolding God's Plan for Humanity* (Grand Rapids, Mich.: Zondervan, 1992), 150-151.

3. Ibid., 150.

4. In addition to his *Desiring God* (see note 1), see Piper's, *Future Grace: The Purifying Power of Living by Faith in Future Grace* (Sisters, Ore.: Multnomah, 1995) for a depiction of the "practical" implications of the Bible's future orientation.

5. Piper, *Future Grace*, 9-13.

6. Ibid., 359.

7. Ibid., 359-360.

8. Richard Sturch, "On Being Heavenly Minded," in Anthony N. S. Lane, ed., *The Unseen World: Christian Reflections on Angels, Demons and the Heavenly Realm* (Carlisle, England: Paternoster; and Grand Rapids, Mich.: Baker, 1996), 65-74, 65-68. Sturch, 66-70, unpacks the biblical images of "heaven" as indicating God's superior power, omniscience, goodness (the positive associations of light; compare James 1:17), bliss (compare 2 Cor. 12:2), and the final state of the redeemed, including a state of mind attuned to the presence of God in awareness and fulfilled desire (John 17:3; 1 Cor. 13:12; 1 John 3:2; Rev. 21:3-4; etc.).

9. See, for example, Josh. 3:7-17; 4:23-24; Judg. 6:7-10; 1 Kings 8:46-53; Ps. 77:11-20; 80:7-13; 106:6-47; Isa. 11:11-16; 43:14-21; 51:9-11; Jer. 11:1-14; 23:5-8; Ezek. 20:33-38; Hos. 2:14-15; Mic. 7:15-17.

10. See Mark 10:45; Rom. 3:21-26; 4:25; 5:8-10; 2 Cor. 5:15; Gal. 2:20; 3:13; Col. 1:22; Heb. 2:9; 7:23-28; 9:14; 1 Pet. 3:18. For a very helpful presentation of the significance of the cross of Christ as the "penal substitution" for our sins, see J. I. Packer's essay, "What Did the Cross Achieve? The Logic of Penal Substitution," *Tyndale Bulletin* 25 (1974), 3-45, now reprinted in *The J. I. Packer Collection*, selected and introduced by Alister McGrath (Downers Grove, Ill.: InterVarsity, 1999), 94-136. In Packer's words, "The notion which the phrase 'penal substitution' expresses is that Jesus Christ our Lord, moved by a love that was determined to do everything necessary to save us, endured and exhausted the destructive divine judgment for which we were otherwise inescapably destined, and so won us forgiveness, adoption and glory. To affirm penal substitution is to say believers are in debt to Christ specifically for this, and that this is the mainspring of all their joy, peace and praise both now and for eternity" (*J. I. Packer Collection*, 114).

11. Fuller, *Unity of the Bible,* 56.

12. I owe this insight to Hans Walter Wolff, *Anthropology of the Old Testament* (Philadelphia: Fortress, 1974), 153.

13. Second Peter 1:3-11 thus exhibits the covenant structure that runs throughout the Bible: 1) verses 3-4 contain the Historical Prologue recounting God's mighty acts of redemption in the past, which bring with them promises for the future; 2) verses 5-7 set forth the Covenant Stipulations that flow from these acts and promises; 3) verses 8-11 declare the Covenant Blessing and Curse that derive from obedience and disobedience to the covenant respectively.

Chapter Nine:
What Difference Does Jesus Make?

1. This reading takes the "works" in Ephesians 2:8-9 to include any and all human activity, even the "good works" brought about by Christ that are spoken about in Ephesians 2:10, rather than referring only to those self-generated performances or distinctives by which we attempt to earn God's blessings. Over against this view, we have argued that the "faith" contrasted with "works" in Ephesians 2:8-9 actually includes the "good works" spoken of in 2:10, which are also emphasized to be a gift, i.e., the product of God's recreating us in Christ. We must be careful to distinguish between "works" that we bring to God thinking they merit his blessings and those "good works" that are the expression of faith and the result of God's saving grace in our lives. In other words, we must distinguish between works prior to being saved by faith and the works that are the expression of our saving faith.

2. There has been much discussion in recent years concerning the meaning of the so-called "antitheses" in Matthew 5:17-48 (see Matt. 5:21, 27, 31, 33, 38, 43). The basic issue is whether the teaching of Jesus is in antithetical contrast to what had been taught in the Old Testament law, or whether, as I argue here, Jesus' teaching unpacked the significance of the Law itself in view of the new realities of the coming of the kingdom. The key to deciding this issue is understanding what Jesus meant when he said that he had not come to abolish the Law and the Prophets, but to "fulfill them" (Matt. 5:17). One's interpretation of this verse will determine how one understands the contrasts that follow, as well as the larger question of the relationship between Jesus and the Old Testament. For a helpful albeit technical discussion of the various views, see Robert A. Guelich, *The Sermon on the Mount: A Foundation for Understanding* (Waco, Tex.: Word, 1982), 138-142. In what follows, I take the view that in this context "fulfill the Law" means, "to bring to its final conclusion all that the Law stood for" (H. Ljungman, quoted by Guelich, 139-140), because Jesus had now come "as the one who brings [the] new relationship between God and humankind promised in the Scriptures" (Guelich, 142). This new relationship does not mean a new way of relating to God but rather a new power with which to respond to God's will. So the Law and the Prophets retain their continuing validity. Matthew 5:17-20 demands, I believe, that we reject any attempt to pit Jesus' teaching against the Law or the Prophets. Nor does it teach that Jesus fulfilled the Law by keeping it perfectly in our place so that we no longer need to do so, but can rely on his having done it for us.

3. This conclusion is based on my understanding of the structure of Matthew as a whole and its implication for understanding what Matthew is saying about Jesus. It has long been recognized that the phrase "and it happened when Jesus finished" (literal translation) occurs five times in Matthew's Gospel (7:28; 11:1; 13:53; 19:1; 26:1). Taking this phrase as indicative of major divisions between sections of his work, many have argued that Matthew's Gospel falls into five sections, together with an introduction and conclusion. The first of these major sections is the Sermon on the Mount (Matt. 5–7). From this observation many have concluded that Matthew is intending to portray Jesus as a "second" or "greater Moses," with the sections of the Gospel reflecting the five books of the Pentateuch. They then draw different conclusions about what this means for our understanding of Jesus, some stressing continuity with the Law (as the "second Moses," Jesus continues teaching God's Law), others discontinuity (as the "greater Moses," Jesus' "Gospel" replaces Moses' "Law"). For a discussion of this issue and its implications, see Jack Dean Kingsbury, *Matthew: Structure, Christology, Kingdom* (Philadelphia: Fortress, 1973), 1-23. Kingsbury has shown that it is too simplistic to argue that the entire Gospel of Matthew can be subsumed under this fivefold structure. Nevertheless, it cannot be denied that with these phrases Matthew sets off five distinct blocks of discourse material. We must only be careful not to read too much into or out of this observation! Kingsbury correctly stresses that we must take seriously "Matthew's own summary of the contents of his work as being 'the Gospel of the Kingdom' (26:13; 24:14; compare also 4:23; 9:35)" (5). My point here is simply that in view of Matthew 5:17-48 and the fact that this sermon is explicitly said to take place on a mountain, we should read the Sermon on the Mount not as a new law from a new Moses but rather as part of Jesus' response to the Old Testament Law itself. Matthew's structuring of Jesus' teaching into five large discourses is intended to indicate that Jesus' teaching ought to be seen as equal in authority even with the most sacred of Israel's traditions, the Law of Moses. Jesus too is speaking God's word to his people! Thus, Jesus' understanding of the Law is not to be taken as merely one more interpretation in a long line of rabbinic opinions; rather, it represents God's own understanding of Old Testament revelation. In Kingsbury's words, the five-discourse structure "calls attention to Jesus, the Messiah, whose words are of the status of divine revelation" (7).

4. This section is adapted from my earlier work, *Paul, Moses, and the History of Israel: The Letter/Spirit Contrast and the Argument from Scripture in 2 Corinthians 3* (Peabody, Mass.: Hendrickson, 1996), 129-135.

5. For this same motif of the "stubbornness" of Israel's evil heart as the basis of the perpetual disobedience of the people, see Jeremiah 3:17; 7:24; 9:13; 13:10; 16:12; 17:23; 18:12; 19:15; 23:17.

6. For the point that the covenant people and their leaders have continued to break the covenant, see Jeremiah 2:8; 5:31; 6:13, 17; 10:21; 14:18; 23:13f.; 27:16.

7. See Hans Walter Wolff, *Anthropology of the Old Testament* (Philadelphia: Fortress, 1974), 43-46, 51-54, where he shows that the "heart" in the Old Testament represents one's intellectual and rational functions. Wolff defines the "heart" as the inward "place" where the vital decisions of the will are made and as the faculty that represents one's driving desires and longings. As that which describes "the seat and function of reason," the heart therefore "includes everything that we ascribe to the head and the brain—power of perception, reason,

understanding, insight, consciousness, memory, knowledge, reflection, judgment, sense of direction, discernment. These things circumscribe the real core of meaning of the word" (51). In the Old Testament view of humanity, the heart is not only the seat of volition and desire but also the organ most often associated with the function of understanding and intellectual knowledge. In support, Wolff points to passages such as Deuteronomy 29:3-4 to illustrate that the heart is "destined for understanding," and Proverbs 15:14 and Psalm 90:12 to show that the "essential business" of the heart is to seek knowledge and wisdom (46-47). In Wolff's words, "there is an easy transition in the use of the word from the functions of the understanding to the activity of the will. The Israelite finds it difficult to distinguish linguistically between 'perceiving' and 'choosing,' between 'hearing' and 'obeying.' . . . Thus the heart is at once the organ of understanding and of will" (51).

8. The understanding that the "yoke" in Matthew 11:30 refers to Jesus' interpretation of the Law is based on the parallel to this passage in Matthew 23:4, where we read that the burden the Pharisees put on people's shoulders was "heavy." So Jesus' view of the Law, the "yoke" to be carried, is being contrasted with the Pharisaic understanding: Jesus' view was "easy" and "light"; their "yoke" was "heavy." This view is confirmed by the well-known use of the word "yoke" in Jewish literature as a metaphor for obedience to God as required by the Law. For a helpful summary of this material, see Robert H. Gundry, *Matthew: A Commentary on His Literary and Theological Art* (Grand Rapids, Mich.: Eerdmans, 1982), 219.

9. John Piper, *Desiring God: Meditations of a Christian Hedonist* (Sisters, Ore.: Multnomah; expanded edition, 1996), 59.

10. This section is adapted from my essay, "Am I Not Good Enough? Why Jesus Had to Die for My Sins," in *This We Believe: The Good News of Jesus Christ for the World,* ed. John N. Akers, John H. Armstrong, and John D. Woodbridge (Grand Rapids, Mich.: Zondervan, 2000), 79-98.

11. Expressed in his written response to this paragraph.

Conclusion:
Who Are We?

1. The following paragraphs are built on my understanding of Paul's argument in 2 Corinthians 7:2-16 as outlined in my *2 Corinthians,* NIV Application Commentary (Grand Rapids, Mich.: Zondervan, 2000), 306-327.

2. For an insightful summary of these points, see Ralph P. Martin, *2 Corinthians,* Word Biblical Commentary, vol. 40 (Waco, Tex.: Word, 1986), 232-233: "In contrast to godly sorrow is the sorrow that is of the world. . . . This sorrow is a type that includes pain and regret, similar to godly sorrow. However, the result in this case is not repentance, but death. . . . Worldly sorrow comes about because of the unwelcome consequence of sin. The person who exhibits this response of worldly sorrow may indeed seek to avoid similar future actions and their consequences. But in no instance is the person driven to *God,* for that individual feels no deep-seated remorse over actions taken against *God.* Rather it is more a regret that one has acted foolishly or been discovered in a lapse, like king Saul's admission, 'I have played the fool, and erred exceedingly' (1 Sam. 26:21).

Repentance involves the whole person—knowing, feeling, willing . . . and is more than an emotional reaction. . . . 'Recognition of sin by itself is not repentance; it may be defiance. Nor is sorrow for sin repentance, if it be alone in the mind; it may be remorse or despair. Abandonment of sin, by itself, may be no more than prudence'. . . . The criterion in evaluating the worth of an individual's 'sorrow' lies in its *effect*" (emphasis added). Martin points to the contrasts between Esau (Gen. 27:38; Heb. 12:16-17) and David (Ps. 51:12-19) or Judas and Peter (Matt. 27:3; Luke 22:31-34) as illustrations of the two types of sorrow (233).

3. See their important work, *The Race Set Before Us: A Biblical Theology of Perseverance and Assurance* (Downers Grove, Ill.: InterVarsity, 2001).

4. There are some who argue that the idea of repentance in the New Testament refers *only* to a change of mind or an assent to the truth of something. One of the strongest supporters of this view is Zane C. Hodges. See his works *Grace in Eclipse: A Study on Eternal Rewards* (Dallas: Redención Viva, 1985); and *The Gospel Under Siege: A Study on Faith and Works* (Dallas: Redención Viva, 1981). Hodges asserts that, "The primary New Testament words for repentance . . . signify simply a change of mind. They *do not have* the sense of the English word for repentance which almost suggests turning from sin, with overtones of sorrow and contrition. . . . But the notion that one must decide to abandon his sin in order to be saved is actually based on reading the English meaning of 'repentance' into some New Testament texts" (*Grace in Eclipse*, 113, n.5). He goes on to agree with Gordon H. Clark, *Faith and Saving Faith* (Jefferson, Md.: The Trinity Foundation, 1983), 118, when he writes, "Faith, by definition, is assent to understood propositions . . . all saving faith is assent to one or more Biblical propositions."

Though it is beyond our purpose to offer a detailed rebuttal, it is important to see that this view does not take seriously the active, volitional content of both faith and repentance in the New Testament. Moreover, Hodges wrongly attempts to divorce the New Testament concepts of "repentance" and "faith" from their Old Testament backdrop, in which they refer to "turning around" and "trust" respectively. For the Old Testament background to the meaning of "repentance" and "faith" in the New Testament, see E. Würthwein, "μετανοέω," in G. Kittel and G. Friedrich, eds., G. W. Bromiley, trans., *Theological Dictionary of the New Testament*, vol. 4 (Grand Rapids, Mich.: Eerdmans, 1967), 980-989; and A. Weiser, "πιστεύω," *Theological Dictionary of the New Testament*, vol. 6 (1968), 182-196. The concern that motivates Hodges and those of like mind is the unfounded fear that if repentance involves a real change of life, then the Gospel will be perverted into "works righteousness," i.e., the attempt to earn God's favor through our actions or obedience.

This danger is avoided once we see that the repentance and obedience demanded by the Gospel are *both* enabled by the Holy Spirit, so that God is the one who gives what he demands. There is no thought of somehow earning God's forgiveness or justification to begin with, nor is the final judgment by works based on our *own* attainments. From start to finish, salvation is the work of God on our behalf. The attempt to reduce the meaning of "repentance" simply to a "change of mind" does not do justice either to the contexts in which the word is used or to the role of the Holy Spirit in the life of faith. Indeed, it is Hodges' view that actually results in an "eclipse" of grace, since his view does not allow God's act of grace to encompass its full sphere of activity.

5. Many commentators do not understand the phrase "the obedience *of faith*" in Romans 1:5 in this way. Instead, they take the genitive, "of faith," to be explanatory. In this view, Romans 1:5 ought to be translated, "the obedience, which is faith," so that the "obedience" in view is actually faith in Christ or the Gospel, in contrast to obedience to God's Law. In other words, faith is being defined as obedience to the message of the Gospel. For an influential representative of this position, see Ernst Käsemann, *Commentary on Romans,* trans. Geoffrey W. Bromiley (Grand Rapids, Mich.: Eerdmans, 1980), 14-15. Käsemann argues for this position because he wants to avoid the very thing that I believe Paul is saying, namely, "the consequence that sanctification in active obedience is the true point of faith" (15). In contrast, I understand the meaning of the genitive, "of faith," to be "the obedience that faith does," or the "faith that acts in obedience," taking the genitive either to be a genitive of source or a subjective genitive. Both are possible grammatically. Ultimately, only a study of Paul's theology as a whole will enable one to decide this issue. For a helpful listing of the seven ways in which this phrase has been understood by scholars, see C. E. B. Cranfield, *A Critical and Exegetical Commentary on The Epistle to the Romans,* vol. 1, International Critical Commentary (Edinburgh: T and T Clark, 1975), 66.

6. The position I am advocating is based on a reassessment of the traditional Lutheran, Calvinistic, and dispensational view of the relationship between the Law and the Gospel. This traditional view saw a conflict between the two, with the Law viewed narrowly as God's demand for sinless obedience as the ground of our salvation, while the Gospel called for faith in God's offer of grace in Christ, who kept the Law perfectly in our place. Hence, Christ was understood to bring the Law to an "end" (in the sense of "abolishment"), "that every one who has faith may be justified" (Rom. 10:4). The Law/Gospel contrast therefore becomes a contrast between the "works righteousness" taught by the Law and justification by faith alone as taught in the Gospel. In this view, the Law *itself* taught a legalism that Adam and Israel failed to keep but that God himself continues to demand in order to drive us to the Gospel.

In recent times, this view has come under severe attack. Though there is no new consensus yet to replace the old one, three basic approaches (as well as many variations) have risen to the surface. Some scholars argue that the issue in the early churches surrounding the Law was simply a cultural or ethnic one, so that what the New Testament—Paul especially—rejects is the role of the Law in establishing the social and ethnic "boundary markers" that prevented Jews and Gentiles from enjoying fellowship with one another. In this view, only circumcision, food laws, the Jewish feasts, and the laws concerning ceremonial and ritual purity are outdated, because these are the aspects of the Law that divided Jew and Gentile. The "legalism" of the Law, therefore, has to do only with the misuse of this subset of the Law. When Paul says that Christ is the "end" of the Law or speaks against the "works of the law," he thus means merely those laws and/or their application that separated Jews and Gentiles.

Others argue that Paul was not speaking against the Law at all, but against a prevalent *perversion* of the Law into legalism. In this view, the designation "works of the law" does not refer to what the Law itself taught, even in its subsets, but to this perversion of the Law, since there was no word for "legalism" in the Greek of Paul's day. Thus, in opposing "works of the law," Paul is actually out to rescue the Law *itself* as that which also taught faith. Hence, when correctly understood, the Law and the Gospel teach the same thing. When Paul says that Christ is the "end" of the Law, he means "end" in the sense of "goal" or "fulfillment," another common meaning of the word translated "end" ($\tau\acute{\epsilon}\lambda o\varsigma$) in Romans 10:4. This view therefore argues for the theological unity of the Law and the Gospel.

Still others argue that the contrast in Paul's thought between the Law and the Gospel is a contrast between the two eras of God's dealing with his people within redemptive history. The rubrics of "Law" or "works of the law" (as that which the Law itself commanded as a whole) and "Gospel" or "faith" are thus often being used to summarize what is also commonly called the old and new covenants, old and new ages, or creation and new creation. I find this "eschatological view" the most compelling. In this perspective, Paul is not contrasting two different ways of salvation, since the principles of salvation and structure of the covenant are the same in both ages. Nor is he explicitly fighting a perversion of the Law into legalism as the *basis* of one's salvation, since it is doubtful that this theological perversion was as widespread as usually assumed (though there were no doubt legalistic Jews in the first century, who kept the Law only externally and used their "obedience" as a basis for presumption and pride before God and others). And it cannot be demonstrated that Paul's phrase "works of the law" refers to something different than, or a subset of, what the Law as a whole taught. Instead, the eschatological view argues that more is at stake in Paul's polemic against the Law or the "works of the law" than a legalistic perversion of the Law or sociological barriers between Jews and Gentiles, though this was surely the way in which the issue often surfaced in practice. The problem Paul was up against was the temptation to think that even though the Messiah had come, the old covenant was still in force. Such a view would imply that the new age of the new covenant, together with the dawning of the new creation, had not yet decisively arrived with the coming of Christ and that his death was not the sole and sufficient means of God's grace (in the full sense of this word), to which the Law merely pointed as its symbolic embodiment (see chapters 8 and 9).

According to the "eschatological view," the Judaizers were arguing that one had to be both a Jew *and* a follower of Christ to be a full-fledged member of the new covenant. Christ may offer one forgiveness, but unless one also becomes a Jew, he will never experience the fullness of the Spirit. Paul rejects this attempt to bring the old covenant into the new as an affront to the sufficiency of the Cross (Gal. 2:21) and a failure to recognize that the new age had in fact dawned with the Resurrection. To require becoming a Jew (or any other "second step") in order to experience the fullness of the Spirit calls into question whether one has experienced the Spirit at all, since sanctification, like justification, takes place solely by faith in Christ alone. To add anything to Christ is to deny Christ himself.

Moreover, to maintain that the Sinai covenant is still necessary now that the Messiah has arrived fails to recognize that under the Sinai covenant God's presence had remained veiled from the people because the Law had been given to Israel without the Spirit (2 Cor. 3:6-15). In other words, the primary function of the old covenant within redemptive history was to bring Israel as a nation under God's curse for breaking the covenant (Gal. 3:10; 4:1-3). In contrast, because the cross of Christ establishes the new covenant, the Spirit was being poured out in full measure on Jews and Gentiles alike who trust in Jesus, regardless of their ethnic or religious identity (Gal. 3:1-5). To mix the two epochs was therefore like trying to mix oil and water in terms of God's purposes within the history of redemption. Furthermore, the Gentiles' reception of the Spirit *as Gentiles* is a sure sign that, in view of what Christ has accomplished, God no longer requires adherence to the old covenant in order to be part of his people. The new age has arrived! To insist on living under the Law as it functioned under the Sinai covenant can only mean, therefore, that one is not yet relying solely on Christ as Messiah for salvation.

The issue is complex, and by no means settled. Unfortunately, the various views now competing for acceptance have not yet made it out of the technical literature into works more accessible to the non-scholarly world. One important exception is the work of Daniel P. Fuller, *Gospel and Law, Contrast or Continuum: The Hermeneutics of Dispensationalism and Covenant Theology* (Grand Rapids, Mich.: Eerdmans, 1980). Fuller represents the "Law perverted into legalism" view. For the "sociological" or "boundary markers" view, see the representative work of James D. G. Dunn, *Jesus, Paul and the Law: Studies in Mark and Galatians* (Louisville: Westminster/John Knox, 1990). For a helpful survey of the various positions, see still, Douglas Moo, "Paul and the Law in the Last Ten Years," *Scottish Journal of Theology* 40 (1987), 287-307; and now Frank Theilman, *Paul and the Law* (Downers Grove, Ill.: InterVarsity, 1994), 14-47. For a brief survey of the current debate within its historical development, see my own, "Paul and His Interpreters since F. C. Baur," in Gerald F. Hawthorne, Ralph P. Martin, and Daniel G. Reid, eds., *Dictionary of Paul and His Letters* (Downers Grove, Ill.: InterVarsity, 1993), 666-679.

7. In the words of G. B. Caird, *New Testament Theology*, completed and edited by L. D. Hurst (Oxford: Clarendon, 1995) 118, salvation therefore has "three tenses," since "salvation is a threefold act of God: an accomplished fact, an experience continuing in the present, and a consummation still to come." Paul can therefore refer to our justification as an accomplished fact in our lives (Rom. 3:24; 4:5; 5:1, 9); as a present status in which we live as "slaves of righteousness" rather than "slaves of sin," since we were "justified in the name of the Lord Jesus Christ and in the Spirit of our God" (1 Cor. 6:11; see Rom. 5:21; 6:13, 16); and as "the hope of righteousness" for which we wait "through the Spirit, by faith" (Gal. 5:5; see Matt. 12:37; Rom. 2:13; 3:20, 30). Caird, 119-120, shows that this is not unique to Paul but is a common emphasis throughout the New Testament: Christians have been saved once for all, but they are also being saved, working out their salvation, and looking forward to a salvation yet to come (Rom. 13:11; Phil. 3:20; compare Heb. 9:28; 1 Pet. 1:5). They have been set free, but they have to live as free persons, standing fast in their new freedom (Gal. 5:1; 2 Cor. 3:17; compare 1 Pet. 2:16), while they wait for their final liberation. They have been washed clean, but the cleansing process continues (2 Cor. 7:1; compare James 4:8; 1 John 1:7), until perfect unity is attained (Rev. 19:8). The decisive victory over the powers has been won, but the war goes on until no enemies are left to challenge the sovereignty of God.

General Index

Scripture Index